GREENLAND

40°

50°

BAFFIN BAY

DAVIS
STRAIT

Ellesmere Island

Axel
Heiberg
I.

ef Ringes
I.

60°

Devon I.

Bylot I.

Lancaster Sound

Bathurst
I.

Cornwallis I.

lle I.

Resolute

Barrow Str.

BAFFIN ISLAND

Winter
H.

Viscount
Melville
Sound

15

Somerset
I.

Prince of
Wales
I.

5

Gulf of Boothia

FOXE
BASIN

McClintock
Channel

6

Boothia
Peninsula

Melville
Peninsula

CTORIA

ISLAND

7

King
William
I.

8

Cambridge
Bay

10

9 Gjoa Haven

Hudson Strait

60°

Point
Turnagain

11

Queen Maud
G.

70°

onation G.

Kent
Peninsula

WEST

TERRITORIES

Southampton
Island

ARCTIC CIRCLE

KEEWATIN

Back's Great Fish River

ZIE

HUDSON BAY

N A D A

Great
Slave
Lake

Churchill

80°

Port Nelson

MANITOBA

ERTA

SASKATCHEWAN

110°

100°

90°

V·R

Ever since the days of John Cabot and Columbus, men have searched for a practical Northwest Passage from Europe to the Far East. In 1906, Roald Amundsen in the fishing sloop *Gjoa* triumphantly completed the first voyage from east to west. It remained for the nuclear-powered submarines, *Nautilus, Skate,* and *Seadragon,* to prove the possible commercial value of the Atlantic to Pacific water route sought by mariners since the time of the first Elizabeth.

Drawing upon all available sources, including Vilhjalmur Stefansson's private research material, Ernest Dodge has written an up-to-date history of the search by sea for the Northwest Passage. His book is an adventure-filled saga of endurance, courage, and suffering. Quotations from contemporary logs and explorers' reports sharpen these accounts where human villainy menaced the expeditions as much as ice, freezing cold, scurvy, bears, and hostile Eskimos. Inexperienced officers and crews also contributed to the disasters which so often befell the tiny ships.

Here are the early voyages of Luke Foxe, Sebastian Cabot, Martin Frobisher, Henry Hudson, Thomas James and many others, along with descriptions of the later expeditions led by Captain James Cook, William Edward Parry, and the ill-fated Sir John Franklin. Included are tales of mythical explorers and legendary islands, as well as the first complete account of the only American attempt at the Passage and the identification of the mysterious "Clerk of the *California*."

The recent exploits of nuclear submarines have stimulated an increasing interest in the Arctic regions and their potential economic and strategic importance. This book is the first to offer a complete and comprehensive study of the four-century old search for a Northwest Passage through the Arctic Circle.

ABOUT THE AUTHOR

Ernest S. Dodge is the Director of the Peabody Museum of Salem, Massachusetts, and editor of *The American Neptune*. A special student in Anthropology at Harvard University, 1936-38, he was recently awarded a Guggenheim Fellowship for the year 1960-61.

Northwest by Sea

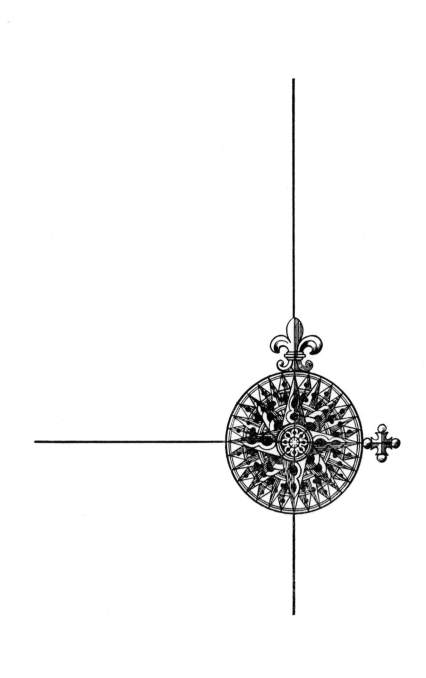

Northwest by Sea

ERNEST S. DODGE

NEW YORK

OXFORD UNIVERSITY PRESS

1961

Acknowledgments

I began this book in one snowstorm and finished it in another. Between the two my work was lightened by patient and gracious people who helped make the writing of this book a rare pleasure. My family, especially my wife Irene, has not only endured but aided and abetted my vague ways and solitary week ends. Several difficult passages were overcome while enjoying the hospitality and the quiet study of Martha and Russell W. Knight in Casco, Maine.

Stephen Phillips has been very generous with his many rare books on Arctic exploration. Vilhjalmur Stefansson has given me good advice and welcomed me to his incomparable library at Dartmouth. His former assistant librarian, Mary S. Fellows, suggested obscure and important references. Members of the staff of the Boston Athenaeum, as cheerful as they are competent, have furnished other literary sources. The Trustees of the Peabody Museum of Salem have been always encouraging, and my colleagues in the museum have given the friendly superior help which is my constant good fortune. Particular acknowledgment is made to Paul O. Blanchette, who has been indefatigable in finding books, M. V. Brewington who has read this entire manuscript and made many excellent suggestions, and to Eugenia N. Ford, whose ingenuity successfully deciphers my erratic penmanship. To Veronica Ruzicka I am grateful for the clear maps. None of these kind people is responsible for any faults that may herein be found—the responsibility is of course mine alone.

In the interests of clarity and consistency I have arbitrarily solved the problem of changes in geographical names by using modern forms except in quotations and, in a few instances, where the obsolete form is important to the context.

Ernest S. Dodge

Danvers, Massachusetts
13 March 1960

Chronological Tables

Voyages Searching for a Northwest or Related Passage

COMMANDER (OR PILOT)	SHIPS	SAILED	RETURNED
John Cabot	Matthew	2 May 1497	6 August 1497
John Cabot	Five ships—names unknown	early May 1498	
Gasper Corte-Real	Two ships	1500	1500
Gasper Corte-Real	Three ships	15 May 1501	8–11 October 1501
Miguel Corte-Real	Three ships	10 May 1502	20 August 1502
Thomas Aubert	Pensée	1508	
Sebastian Cabot	Two ships	March 1508 (1509?)	1509
John Rastell	Barbara Mary Barking and others	1517	
John Rut	Mary of Gilford Samson (not Dominus Vobiscum)	10 June 1527	October 1527
Giovanni da Varrazano	Dauphine	17 January 1524	early July 1524
Estévan Gomez	One ship	February 1525	
Jacques Cartier	Two ships	20 April 1534	1 September 1534
Jacques Cartier	Great Hermina Little Hermina Emerilon	three days after Easter 1535	1 July 1536
Richard Hore	Trinity William (not Minion)	1536	1536
Jacques Cartier	Several ships	23 May 1541	
Sir Hugh Willoughby Richard Chancellor	Bona Esperanza Edward Bonaventure Bona Confidentia	20 May 1553	(Chancellor) 1554

vi

COMMANDER (OR PILOT)	SHIPS	SAILED	RETURNED
Richard Chancellor	*Edward Bonaventure* *Philip and Mary*	early July 1555	November 1556
Stephen Borough	*Searchthrift*	29 April 1556	1557
Martin Frobisher	*Gabriel* *Michael* a pinnace	1576	1576
Martin Frobisher	*Aid* *Gabriel* *Michael*	1577	1577
Martin Frobisher Capt. Yorke Capt. Fenton Capt. Best Capt. Carew Capt. Filpot Capt. Tanfield Capt. Courtney Capt. Moyles Capt. Upcot Capt. Newton Capt. Randal Capt. Kendall Capt. Harvey Capt. Kinnersley	*Aid* *Thomas Allen* *Judith* *Anne Frances* *Hopewell* *Bear* *Thomas* of Ipswich *Emanuel* of Exeter *Frances* of Foy *Moon* *Emanuel* of Bridgewater *Salamander* of Weymouth *Dennis* *Gabriel* *Michael*	31 May 1578	1578
Arthur Pet Charles Jackman	*George* *William*	30 May 1580	26 October 1580
Olivier Brunel	One ship	1584	
John Davis	*Sunshine* *Moonshine*	June 1585	30 September 1585
John Davis	*Mermaid* *Sunshine* *Moonshine* *Northstar*	7 May 1586	6 October 1586
John Davis	*Elizabeth* *Sunshine* *Ellen*	19 May 1587	15 September 1587
Cornelius C. Nay Brant Tetgales Jan H. van Linschoten William Barents	*Swane* *Mercurius* of Enkhuysen *Mercury* of Amsterdam (not *Messenger*) and a fishing boat	5 June 1594	15 September 1594

COMMANDER (OR PILOT)	SHIPS	SAILED	RETURNED
Cornelius C. Nay William Barents	Griffoen Swane Hoope Mercurius Winhont Mercury A yacht of Rotterdam	2 July 1595	26 October to 18 November 1595
Jacob van Heemskerck Jan C. Rüp William Barents	Two ships	10 May 1596	1597
George Waymouth	Godspeed Discovery	2 May 1602	5 August 1602
James Hall John Knight	Trost Love Cat	2 May 1605	early August
John Knight	Hopewell	18 April 1606	24 September 1606
James Hall	Four ships	29 May 1606	4 October 1606
Henry Hudson	Hopewell	1 May 1607	15 September 1607
James Hall	One ship	1607	1607
Henry Hudson	Hopewell	22 April 1608	26 August 1608
Henry Hudson	Half Moon Good Hope	6 April 1609	7 November 1609
Henry Hudson	Discovery	17 April 1610	6 September 1611
Thomas Button	Resolution Discovery	14 April 1612	September 1613
James Hall William Baffin	Patience Heart's Ease	20 April 1612	19 September 1612
Benjamin Jones William Baffin	Tiger Matthew Sea Horse Gamaliel Desire Annula Richard and Barnard	13 May 1613	6 September 1613
William Baffin	Thomasine	16 April 1614	4 October 1614
William Gibbons	Discovery	1614	1614
Robert Bylot William Baffin	Discovery	18 April 1615	1615

COMMANDER (OR PILOT)	SHIPS	SAILED	RETURNED
Robert Bylot William Baffin	*Discovery*	26 March 1616	30 August 1616
Jens Munk	*Enhiörnigen Lamprenen*	9 May 1619	21 September 1620
William Hawkridge	*Lions Whelp* and another vessel	early June 1625	1625
Luke Foxe	*Charles*	3 May 1631	1631
Thomas James	*Henrietta Maria*	3 May 1631	22 October 1632
Vitus Bering	*St. Gabriel*	14 July 1728	1728
James Napper Robert Crow	*Churchill Mushsquash*	7 July 1737	1737
Christopher Middleton	*Furnace Discovery*	June 1741	13 October 1742
William Moor Francis Smith	*Dobbs California*	20 May 1746	14 October 1747
Charles Swaine	*Argo*	4 March 1753	21 October 1753
Charles Swaine	*Argo*	2 May 1754	October 1754
Constantine Phipps	*Racehorse Carcass*	June 1773	September 1773
Richard Pickerskill	*Lion*	25 May 1776	October 1776
James Cook	*Resolution Discovery*	12 July 1776	
Walter Young	*Lion*	23 March 1777	26 August 1777
John Ross	*Isabella Alexander*	18 April 1818	14 November 1818
David Buchan	*Dorothea Trent*	25 April 1818	22 October 1818
William Edward Parry	*Hecla Griper*	11 May 1819	October 1820
William Edward Parry	*Fury Hecla*	8 May 1821	October
William Edward Parry	*Hecla Fury*	19 May 1824	October 1825
George Lyon	*Griper*	16 June 1824	10 November 1824
Frederick W. Beechey	*Blossom*	19 May 1825	1828
John Ross	*Victory*	23 May 1829	1833

COMMANDER (OR PILOT)	SHIPS	SAILED	RETURNED
George Back	*Terror*	16 June 1836	3 September 1837
Sir John Franklin	*Erebus* *Terror*	19 May 1845	

Search for Franklin Ships

Sir James Clark Ross	*Enterprise* *Investigator*	12 May 1848	6 June 1851
Henry Kellett	*Herald*	26 July 1845	November 1849
Thomas Moore	*Plover*	1 January 1848	1850
Robert Sheldon	*Nancy Dawson*	1848	1850
James Saunders	*North Star*	1849	1850
Robert Goodsir	*Advice*	1849	1849
E. J. De Haven	*Advance* *Rescue*	1850	1851
Horatio Austin	*Resolute*	1850	1851
Erasmus Ommanney	*Assistance*	1850	1851
William Penny	*Lady Franklin*	1850	1851
Alexander Stewart	*Sophia*	1850	1851
Sir John Ross	*Felix*	1850	1851
C. C. Forsyth	*Prince Albert*	1850	1850
Robert McClure	*Investigator*	1850	1854
Richard Collinson	*Enterprise*	1850	1855
William Kennedy	*Prince Albert*	1851	1852
Charles Frederick	*Amphitrite*	1852	1852
Edward Inglefield	*Isabel*	1852	1852
Rochfort Maguire	*Plover*	1852	1855
Sir Edward Belcher	*Assistance*	1852	1854
Henry Kellett	*Resolute*	1852	1854
Sherard Osborn	*Pioneer*	1852	1854
Leopold McClintock	*Intrepid*	1852	1854
W. S. J. Pullen	*North Star*	1852	1854

COMMANDER (OR PILOT)	SHIPS	SAILED	RETURNED
William Fawckner	*Breadalbone*	1853	
Lt. Elliott	*Diligence*	1853	
E. A. Inglefield	*Phoenix*	1853 1854	
Comm. Jenkins	*Talbot*	1854	
Comm. Kane	*Advance*	1853	1855
Leopold McClintock	*Fox*	1857	1859

Subsequent to Franklin Search

Roald Amundsen	*Gjoa*	16 June 1903	31 August 1906
Henry Larsen	*St. Roch*	23 June 1940	
Henry Larsen	*St. Roch*	22 July 1944	16 October 1944
O. C. S. Robertson	*Labrador*	1954	1954
T. C. Pullen	*Labrador*	July 1956	1956
T. C. Pullen	*Labrador*	1 July 1957	1957
William D. Anderson	*Nautilus*	22 July 1958	5 August 1958
James F. Calvert	*Skate*	1958	27 March 1958

Table of Contents

PART ONE

The Way to the Indies

	Chronological table	*vi*
1.	Conquerors of the Ice	*3*
2.	Cabots out of Bristol	*13*
3.	The Unknown Coast	*20*
4.	The Timid, the Lost, and the Hungry	*28*
5.	Hunt a Dragon, Bag a Bear	*35*
6.	The Great Dutchman	*44*
7.	All that Glitters	*62*
8.	Mariner and Scholar	*87*
9.	Frustration	*103*
10.	Mutiny	*114*
11.	In Hudson's Wake	*127*
12.	Beyond Hope Sanderson	*138*
13.	Three Came Back	*144*
14.	'North-West Fox'	*156*
15.	The Strange and Dangerous Voyage	*165*

PART TWO
Solving the Puzzle

16. Fiction and Fact   *181*
17. The Wild Irishman   *191*
18. The American 'Argo'   *211*
19. Old Hopes Revived   *221*
20. The Twin Attack   *235*
21. Opening the Door   *254*
22. Boothia Felix   *275*
23. The Passage Discovered   *294*
24. The Passage Traversed   *311*
    Notes   *319*
    Selected Bibliography   *333*
    Index   *341*

Maps

Novaya Zemlya   *39*
Davis Strait   *105*
Hudson Bay   *128*

Part One

The Way to the Indies

1

Conquerors of the Ice

W^{*hen*} the high fin and snub nose of the United States submarine *Nautilus* emerged from the cold blue-green water between Spitsbergen and Greenland on 5 August 1958, the dream of four centuries was realized. The sun was shining and the brilliant ice lay in a long white curve behind. *Nautilus* had pioneered a commercial route through the Arctic Ocean exactly fifty-two years after Roald Amundsen completed the first voyage through the 'Northwest Passage.' The third submarine *Nautilus* to be involved in Arctic exploration, her success might almost have been predicted accordingly. The first was, of course, Jules Verne's fictitious prodigy. The second was the conventional submarine in which the great explorer Sir Hubert Wilkins attempted to go to the Pole under the ice in 1931. The third is the first nuclear-powered ship ever constructed. A marvel of modern maritime engineering, she had already outperformed all existing vessels and hopes were high that she could make the passage. She could cruise submerged almost indefinitely at better than twenty knots, and she did not need to surface in order to recharge storage batteries; her power plant required no oxygen. Her highly special-

3

ized crew, carefully chosen from the already select United States Navy Submarine Service, lived in greater physical comfort than any explorers ever had before. They had everything from equipment to purify the air, with temperature and humidity control, to a Coke machine and high fidelity equipment.

In the summer of 1957 Commander William R. Anderson took *Nautilus* out for preliminary ice probes. In September she passed 87° latitude, but had to turn back when an electric power failure stopped the gyrocompass about 180 miles from the North Pole. Equipment had, however, been carefully checked during the run, and much valuable information about under-ice navigation collected. To supplement standard magnetic compasses and gyrocompasses, which grow increasingly erratic as a Magnetic Pole is approached, the Sperry Gyroscope Company developed a new gyrocompass, the Mark 19, for work in high latitudes. Inverted fathometers, or ice detectors, had been installed to measure the distance between submarine and ice, while sonar devices picked up the presence of ice lying on their course. Subsequently a television camera and screens were added for observing the under-surface of the ice, and also an inertial navigator — an elaborate electronic device, unaffected by terrestrial magnetism, which stores up data and gives a continuous reading on position.

So tested and equipped *Nautilus* was sent to the Pacific in 1958 and received orders to proceed to Portland, England, by way of the Arctic Ocean. Leaving Seattle 9 June, Commander Anderson attempted to take her west of St. Lawrence Island, which lies across the entrance to Bering Strait, but he was forced by ice to turn back and he proceeded around the island to the east. Continuing north through Bering Strait, he entered the shallow Chukchee Sea where, north of Cape Lisburne, Alaska, he was stopped by gigantic ice ridges projecting down so near the ocean floor that he was forced to retreat to Honolulu, arriving there 28 June.

Nearly a month later, 22 July, air reconnaissance showed the ice conditions considerably improved, and *Nautilus* headed north again. In the Chukchee Sea, she again met ice ridges which left a perilously narrow layer of water between the ice and the bottom of the sea. Anderson had hoped to find a way through to the deep waters of the main Arctic Ocean beyond, but was forced to turn east. Feeling his way to the Barrow Sea Valley, he settled into deep water and headed north. At 11:15 p.m. Eastern Daylight Time, 3 August 1958, *Nautilus* crossed the North Pole, and two days later surfaced beyond the ice — ninety-six hours after she disappeared beneath the icepack north of Point Barrow,[1] having traveled 1830 miles beneath the ice.

Seven days later, U.S.S. *Skate,* another nuclear submarine, under Commander James F. Calvert, arrived at 90° North, and then went on to visit the drifting observation station Alpha where members of the United States Air Force and civilians were collecting oceanographic and meteorological data in connection with the International Geophysical Year. *Skate* spent eleven days under the ice cruising over 2400 miles and surfacing nine times through polymyas in the pack. This remarkable voyage was followed by another in March 1959. This time Commander Calvert surfaced at the Pole on 17 March in order to hold services for Sir Hubert Wilkins and, in accordance with the widow's wishes, to scatter his ashes in the Arctic wind. The first man to fly across the Arctic from Alaska to Spitsbergen (in 1925), Wilkins had unsuccessfully attempted the sea route that the United States Navy now followed. *Skate's* extraordinary voyage — over 3000 miles during which time she surfaced ten times — ended 27 March when Calvert brought his ship out from the ice pack.[2]

The achievements of Commanders Anderson and Calvert and of their ships are among the great nautical accomplishments in history. *Nautilus* was given the first Presidential Unit Citation ever awarded to a naval vessel in peacetime. It reads in part:

> This voyage opens the possibility of a new commercial sea-
> way, a Northwest Passage, between the major oceans of the
> world. Nuclear powered cargo submarines may, in the future,
> use this route to the advantage of world trade.

Commander Anderson believes cargo submarines, especially
tankers, will ply the Arctic route, and that it will be the great
seaway of the future.[3] Commercial plane services now crisscross
the Arctic, and the strategic importance of the area is second to
none.

Now it is true, as the citation says, that the *Nautilus* voyage was
a Northwest Passage, although the idea of a passage through
continental North America or across its northern extremity was
the one that had traditionally captivated geographers and merchants and navigators. An aspect of the European geographical
awakening after the discovery of the New World, the search for
a passage resulted from the need for a short route to the fabulous
wealth of the Indies, and continued in response to men's desire
to increase their geographical knowledge long after it appeared
that the Passage could have no economic importance, being
frozen or ice clogged much of the year. Few, if any, other geographical premises have, over a long period of time, consumed
as much thought, money, and effort — not to mention the lives
— of as many intelligent and brave men. The English in particular seemed to have been obsessed with the idea. Yet if no silks
and spices arrived from the Indies by this route, other more basic
economic resources were discovered and exploited, which in total
value have exceeded many times over any anticipated luxury
trade to the East. Man's understanding of the geography and
climate of the Arctic was enormously extended; peoples and
cultures discovered; the biological sciences greatly enriched. And
now, perhaps, the primary purpose of the search too has been
realized.

In the past few years a navigable route has been opened by
three notable voyages, the most recent being that of the powerful

new Canadian ice-breaker *Labrador* under Captain O. C. S. Robertson, R.C.N., in 1954. A heavy, deep-draft ship that crunches heavy ice as a heel mashes an egg shell, she not only bulled her way through the Northwest Passage via Prince of Wales Strait but became the first vessel to circumnavigate North America on a single voyage. Two years later she enabled the three United States Coast Guard ships, *Storis, Spar,* and *Bramble,* to complete the passage. They sailed from the west coast of the United States to deliver supplies to the Distant Early Warning (D.E.W.) Line stations along the Arctic seaboard. They were met by *Labrador,* commanded by Captain Thomas C. Pullen, R.C.N., who had sailed from Halifax, Nova Scotia. The big ice-breaker crushed her way through Bellot Strait to the Coast Guard vessels and led them back out to open water — the first American ships to make the Passage.[4]

Labrador, with her 6500 tons displacement and thirty foot draft, was enormous compared with the Royal Canadian Mounted Police ship *St. Roch.* Superintendent Henry A. Larsen had been captain of *St. Roch* from the time of her construction in North Vancouver, British Columbia, in 1928. She was one hundred and four feet long, twenty-five feet beam, and thirteen feet draft, especially designed to carry supplies to the northern outposts of the Royal Canadian Mounted Police and for their patrol of the Arctic region. Her construction, therefore, was of the strongest, and she was sheathed outside with Australian gumwood to withstand the grinding ice. In the spring of 1940 Commissioner S. T. Wood of the Royal Canadian Mounted Police ordered Larsen, after he had completed his routine duties along the western Arctic coast, to proceed to Halifax, for duty in the eastern Arctic, by way of the Northwest Passage.

After a false start Larsen left Vancouver on 23 June 1940, and going through Bering Strait and rounding Point Barrow, proceeded with his duties as far east as Cambridge Bay on Victoria Island. To carry out further assignments he then retraced his route westward and wintered at Walker Bay near the southern entrance of Prince of Wales Strait. The following summer, after spending some time on police duties, he reached Gjöa Haven where he was forced to spend the winter of 1941–2. The next summer he worked *St. Roch,* with considerable difficulties, through the shoal-studded waters of Rae Strait and James Ross Strait, up Franklin Strait, through Bellot Strait and thence by Prince Regent Inlet and Lancaster Sound. He then ducked in back of Bylot Island and, entering Baffin Bay, continued south through Davis Strait out into the Atlantic, arriving at Halifax on 11 October 1942.

In 1944 Larsen took *St. Roch,* with a 300 horsepower motor replacing her 150 horsepower one, through the Northwest Passage by another route. Leaving Dartmouth, Nova Scotia, 22 July 1944, he returned once more to Lancaster Sound and sailing directly west worked his way through heavy ice across Melville Sound and entered Prince of Wales Strait. He survived a storm of hurricane force at the mouth of the Mackenzie River, and then proceeded around Point Barrow, through Bering Strait, and arrived back in Vancouver 16 October — a voyage of eighty-six days. By this remarkable performance Larsen and the schooner *St. Roch* became the first man and ship in history to navigate the Northwest Passage in both directions.[5] *St. Roch* has now been presented by the Royal Canadian Mounted Police to the city of Vancouver, where she is preserved in Stanley Park.

By these two successful voyages, Superintendent Larsen became the leading authority on the various navigable possibilities for a Northwest Passage. His opinions are summarized in the latest Hydrographic Office *Sailing Directions for Northern Canada.*[6] There are five possible routes of which only two are practical and only one for big ships. These are the routes sought by explorers for centuries, and both were navigated by Larsen in *St. Roch.*

In order to picture these channels more clearly in the mind's eye, let us consider the pertinent geographical features of the region for a moment. The ice pack of the Arctic Ocean fits the world like an askew skull cap. On one side it hangs down roughly 1400 miles from the North Pole toward Bering Strait, and on the opposite side reaches about half that distance west of Spitsbergen. If one looks at a globe or a Polar projection map of the world and visualizes the sea without ice, it is obvious that the Arctic, as an open, navigable ocean, would be one of the great sea lanes of the world — the principal trade route between Europe and the Far East — as geographers have postulated for centuries.

Let us now focus on the vast Canadian Arctic archipelago. At first glance the triangular area, its base stretching from the entrance of Hudson Strait to the mouth of the Mackenzie River and its apex at the northern point of Ellesmere Island off the northern coast of Greenland, looks like something shattered. A closer look will reveal some remarkable features. Just below the seventy-fifth parallel the fragmented islands are bisected by a waterway, running directly east and west between Baffin Bay and that part of the Arctic Ocean called the Beaufort Sea. A single channel, its names change like those of some Boston streets, at almost every block. Beginning at its eastern end this strait is called in succession Lancaster Sound, Barrow Strait, Viscount Melville Sound, and McClure Strait. For simplicity for the moment let us call it Channel A. Roughly five degrees south is another channel with many names which follows the continental coast from the Beaufort Sea to Rae Strait where it is stopped in its easterly progression by the Boothia Peninsula jutting out to the north. Beginning at the westerly end its names are Amundsen Gulf, Dolphin and Union Strait, Coronation Gulf, Dease Strait, Queen Maud Gulf, and Simpson Strait. Again for convenience, we shall call this Channel B. From Channel A four large channels lead south. From east to west these are (1) Prince Regent Inlet, with its continuation the Gulf of Boothia ending

in Committee Bay, (2) Peel Sound with its continuation Franklin Strait, (3) McClintock Channel, and (4) Prince of Wales
Strait.

The large islands bounding Channel A on its northern side
are, from east to west, Devon, Cornwallis, Bathurst, Byam Martin, Melville, Eglinton, and Prince Patrick. At the southwest
corner of Devon is the tiny but important Beechey Island. On the
south side, again from east to west, the islands are Bylot, Baffin,
Somerset, Prince of Wales, Victoria, and Banks. The southern
shore of Channel B is the continent of America. On its northern
side, this time from west to east, lie Banks, Victoria, and King
William Islands.

In the great series of British voyages of the nineteenth century
the eastern end of Channel A was rediscovered and its length
sailed to a little beyond 110° west. Simultaneously the southern
shore of Channel B was explored from its western end eastward
to about 95° west longitude. The problem remained to find a
connection between the two. For all practical purposes (1),
Prince Regent Inlet, is a blind alley. On its easterly side it is connected with Foxe Basin and Hudson Strait through the Gulf of
Boothia by ice-choked Fury and Hecla Strait. To the west it
connects with (2), Peel Sound, through narrow Bellot Strait,
separating the Boothia Peninsula from Somerset Island. This
was the route by which *Labrador* brought the Coast Guard vessels. The waters of (2) and (3), McClintock Channel, come together in and are connected with Channel B by Victoria Strait.
Victoria Strait and McClintock Channel are usually ice encumbered but, and this is most important, small vessels can
avoid the ice by going through the shallow channel separating
King William Island from the mainland. This is called James
Ross Strait and Rae Strait and meets the eastern terminus of
Channel B. This was the way Larsen took on his west to east
passage. Number (4), Prince of Wales Strait, is direct and,
cartographically speaking, uncomplicated, and was used by both

St. Roch and *Labrador* going from east to west. Thus a North-west Passage through this archipelago can theoretically be accomplished in several different ways.

These several ways, however, are reduced in number by practical circumstances, as Larsen has pointed out. Some waters are too shallow, some are usually ice clogged. The most direct, for instance, that of using Channel A the entire distance, is impractical because the heavy ice of the Arctic Ocean, forced by currents into its western end as into a funnel, accumulates in enormous amounts. The only practical routes, then, are those navigated by Larsen — the southern via Rae, James Ross, and Bellot straits for small craft, and Prince of Wales Strait for large ships. It will be noted that *Labrador* with her deep draft did not venture down among the shoals behind King William Island.

Looking briefly at the eastern approaches to the Northwest Passage, the first land usually raised on a voyage from England (and most of them originated there) toward the northwest is Cape Farewell, the southern tip of Greenland. Greenland is separated from northern Labrador and Baffin Island by Davis Strait and its continuation, Baffin Bay. About halfway up the west coast of Greenland is the large island of Disko, an important rendezvous point for explorers and whalers. The only exits out of northern Baffin Bay are Smith Sound leading north, and Jones and Lancaster Sounds leading west. At the southwestern end of Davis Strait are three parallel bodies of water bearing a striking superficial similarity; from north to south these are Cumberland Sound, Frobisher Bay, and Hudson Strait. The first two are inlets of Baffin Island; the third leads to Hudson Bay and the interior of the continent. To the northwest of Hudson Bay, Southampton Island is separated from the mainland on the west by a strait called Sir Thomas Roes Welcome (today shortened to Roes Welcome) and on the north by Frozen Strait. These two straits meet in Repulse Bay at the eastern neck of the Melville Peninsula. Off the Welcome Strait, Wager Bay penetrates the western shore, and to the south Chesterfield Inlet penetrates even further. To the northeast, Hudson Strait, where it enters Hudson Bay, is also connected by Foxe Channel with Foxe Basin. At the northern end of Foxe Basin, Fury and Hecla Strait leads to the Gulf of Boothia. As the map of the north unfolds through the work of the explorers whose names these geographical features bear, the importance of establishing these relationships will become apparent.

Another fact will also become clear. From the earliest recorded voyages to that of *Nautilus,* the leaders who pushed into the ice packs and across the frozen wastelands were bold men. Whether gallant Elizabethan sea dogs, fishermen, whalers, or careful Victorian explorers, their fortitude, courage, and endurance have almost without exception been exemplary. Among their crushed ships and through the tales of suffering, starvation, even cannibalism, in cold of unbelievable intensity, and amid storms of incredible fierceness, there shines a constant, admirable intrepidity and unsatiated curiosity, continuing until the Passage was proven, no matter how filled with ice or how precarious its navigation might be. And the wonder of it is that once a man had encountered those fields of ice and desolate coasts he should want to go back to them. Yet some of the greatest, Frobisher, Davis, Baffin and Hudson, Ross, Parry, Franklin, and others, returned again and again.

Note: The first voyage through the Northwest Passage from the Atlantic to the Pacific by a nuclear-powered submarine was recently completed by the U.S.S. *Seadragon.* The submarine sailed from Portsmouth, New Hampshire, entered Lancaster Sound, navigated through the Canadian Arctic islands, and emerged from McClure Strait. She went north to the Pole and then south to Hawaii through Bering Strait, the voyage ending 14 September 1960.

2

Cabots out of Bristol

*B*y the Papal Bulls of Alexander VI in 1493, Portugal and
Spain divided the newly discovered world and all parts
to be henceforth found. The agreement, adjusted and confirmed
the following year at the Treaty of Tordesillas between John II
of Portugal and Ferdinand and Isabella of Spain, gave Spain all
new and heathen lands west of a line drawn 370 leagues west of
Cape Verde and everything east of it to Portugal. To a great extent the two peninsular powers were anticipating discoveries.
Indeed the Spaniards had identified the Antilles as islands off
the Asiatic coast, and Columbus had thought Hispaniola was
Japan. The Portuguese in the early fifteenth century had been the
first to venture boldly into the Atlantic. They had discovered
Madeira, the Azores, and Cape Verde; they traded with England through the port of Bristol. But although Bartholomew
Diaz reached the Cape of Good Hope in 1486, they had not yet
crossed the Indian Ocean.

Nevertheless, the available evidence indicated that good sea
lanes to the Far East could be found across the Atlantic Ocean
and along the African coast, and developments in ship construc-

tion and navigation as well as increased knowledge of astronomy and geography favored such ventures. The high prices of Eastern goods provided the final and commercial incentive. For centuries the highly lucrative spice trade had been monopolized by the Venetians, whose ships met the western ends of the long caravan routes in the eastern Mediterranean. In 1453 the Turks captured Constantinople and strengthened their hold over Asia Minor, the Balkans, and the Levant. Not long thereafter they conquered Egypt and with it Alexandria, the principal spice port. While the Turkish conquest did not seal off the Eastern trade, because the Sultan could not control the hordes of pirates and freebooters swarming the eastern Mediterranean, commerce became increasingly precarious toward the end of the fifteenth century. The resulting high prices led the western seafaring nations to make bolder voyages into the Atlantic.

The Portuguese were the first to reach India by sea when Vasco da Gama succeeded in rounding the Cape of Good Hope in 1497. Soon after Christopher Columbus's first voyage, the Spanish realized that he had not reached Asia and that they must find a way through the land barrier. In 1520 Magellan found the way around it, discovering the strait which bears his name, and one of his ships completed the first circumnavigation of the world. Thus the two Iberian countries controlled the two known commercial sea routes to the Far East, Portugal having what may be called the Southeast Passage and Spain the Southwest.

The year before Diaz discovered the Cape of Good Hope, Henry VII was crowned King of England, an event destined to shake the maritime supremacy of Spain and Portugal. Henry was to be instrumental in creating a merchant marine and in encouraging overseas trade and exploration. Until this time the men of Bristol had been virtually the only seafarers in a predominantly agricultural country. There was good reason for this. In ancient times many Norsemen had settled in Bristol and, even after their explorations and settlements ended, vestiges of their knowledge lingered. The ships of Bristol's Society of Merchants went regularly to Iceland, trading English woolens for fish. They also maintained close commercial relations with Portugal and shared the Portuguese belief that there were islands in the Atlantic, especially to the west of Ireland. From Bristol started the first English explorations westward, encouraged by Henry VII's new regulations. He required that English goods be carried in English, Irish, and Welsh ships. He made commercial treaties with other countries and obtained fishing privileges in Scandinavian waters. While he respected the naval might of the Iberian countries, he obviously had no intention of being bound by a treaty to which he was not a part.[1]

When the news came of Columbus's discoveries, he may have had some regret that he had not acccepted the offer of that explorer's brother, Bartholomew, for an expedition to the Orient. The proposed fee had been exorbitant, however, and the King was favored with a second chance. Less than four years later John Cabot approached him with a plan for sailing west to Far Eastern riches.

Like his great contemporary Columbus, John Cabot was born in Genoa, but in 1461 as a youth of eleven he moved to Venice, where fifteen years later he became a citizen. It was from this prosperous Italian port that he traded to the eastern Mediterranean. At this time Alexandria was the principal port in the spice trade between East and West, but at Mecca too, where the long overland caravan trails terminated, western goods were brought to barter for the luxuries of the East. On one of his journeys Cabot went to Mecca and saw the silks and spices, the perfumes and precious stones. From the merchants he learned that quantities of these things came from the most remote regions of eastern Asia. Knowing that the world was round, he realized that it would be shorter, quicker, and therefore more profitable, to bring the Asiatic produce to the European market directly across the Western Ocean, as the Atlantic was then called. In about 1484 John Cabot decided to go to England. He explained his ideas to the merchants of Bristol and for several years sailed with his Bristol friends searching systematically for the islands purported to lie in the Atlantic which would, they thought, make convenient places for refreshment on a voyage to Asia. Their ships returned with nothing but watery wastes to report. Then, in the summer of 1493, they received the dramatic news that Christopher Columbus had reached the Indies by sailing west from Spain. They decided immediately to give up the island search and push straight across the North Atlantic for the Asiatic mainland.

To obtain official permission for such a voyage Cabot applied to King Henry VII for formal letters patent. On 5 March 1496 [2] the King generously granted:

> To our well beloved John Cabot citizen of Venice, to Lewis, Sebastian, and Santius, sonnes of the sayd John, and to the heires of them, and every of them, and their deputies, full and free authority, leave, and power to saile to all parts, countreys, and seas of the East, of the West and of the North, under our banners and ensignes, with five ships of what burthen or quantity soever they be, and as many mariners or men as they will have with them in the sayd ships, upon their owne proper costs and charges, to seeke out, discover, and finde whatsover isles, countreys, regions or provinces of the heathen and infidels whatsoever they be, and in what part of the world soever they be, which before this time have bene unknowen to all Christians.

The Cabots were bound to bring their cargoes from these voyages into the port of Bristol and to pay one-fifth of their net profits to the King. All goods, however, were to enter duty free and other men were forbidden to trade in the lands the Cabots discovered, without a license from the patent holders. Unauthorized trading would mean the forfeiting of ships and goods. The King's subjects were also instructed to give the Cabots every assistance possible, 'for their money,' in fitting out and supplying their ships for these undertakings.

On 2 May 1497,* John Cabot, perhaps accompanied by his son Sebastian,[3] sailed from Bristol on the ship *Matthew* with eighteen men including some Bristol merchants, among them possibly Robert Thorne the elder and Hugh Eliot. Working north and west, he beat to windward for fifty-two days against the prevailing westerlies and into the big, black, dirty seas of the North Atlantic. At five o'clock on the Saturday morning of 24 June, he reached land which he called *Prima terra vista,* and took formal possession in the name of King Henry VII. Cape Breton Island was probably his first landfall, but the exact location is not known. Sailing along Nova Scotia and beyond for three hundred leagues, Cabot noted the southwestward trend of the coast. He then sailed north, sighting two small islands and Newfoundland before heading downwind for Bristol, where he arrived 6 August. At no time did he see any natives, but he found their snares and traces of their laborious work on trees, and he picked up a fisherman's netting needle.

John Cabot never doubted that he had reached northeast Asia and that by sailing farther south he would arrive at Japan. He lost no time getting to Court, where he appeared 10 August. The King, pleased that his explorer had reached the country of the Grand Khan, gave him ten pounds 'to have a good time with,' granted him an annual pension of twenty pounds, and promised him ten ships on his next voyage. For about ten days John Cabot, dressed in silk, was the lion of London, where he was called the Great Admiral and crowds ran after him as he walked through the streets.

Early in May 1498 Cabot once more dropped down the Avon

---

* The Gregorian calendar (new style) was adopted by most of Europe in 1582, and the Protestant states of Germany in 1700. It was not adopted in Great Britain until 1752. Therefore, English dates before 2 September 1752 are old style. Add eleven days to old style dates to convert to new style.

River from Bristol and headed westerly on the Atlantic. Three hundred men manned his five ships, one of which was provided at the cost of Henry VII and the others by London and Bristol merchants. The fleet, laden with merchandise, was to sail south along the newly discovered coast to tropical latitudes and trade at Japan, China, and the Spice Islands. No one knows exactly how far the 1498 fleet sailed or how many ships returned. No populous and wealthy Oriental cities were found. There are good indications that from the Newfoundland region they followed the shoreline south almost to Chesapeake Bay. There is also evidence that John Cabot and his ship were lost on this expedition somewhere near Grates Cove north of Conception Bay, Newfoundland.[4] The survivors returned to Bristol, probably in 1499, and John Cabot never again appears in English records.

But although no ships returned laden with spices and silks, John Cabot's voyages, besides the increase in geographical knowledge, had one important result — the establishment of the Newfoundland fishery. His tales of the fish swarming so thick that they impeded his ship and of dipping them out with baskets lowered into the water were more than any fisherman could resist. The Bristol men at once saw that there would be no further need to import fish from Iceland since the waters off Newfoundland teemed with fish, theirs for the taking. Beginning almost immediately and continuing throughout the sixteenth century, English, French, Portuguese, and Spanish fishermen swarmed in those waters.

It seems probable that after the voyage of 1498 the English, like the Spanish, came to realize that the lands they had reached were not part of Asia but a new land between them and the desired continent. There are indications that, sometime before April 1509, Sebastian Cabot sailed from Bristol in search of a Northwest Passage around the newly discovered land. That there were three hundred men and but two ships suggests that he planned to establish a colony as a halfway point on the way to

Asia. No one knows his exact route, but he sailed north until the sea was full of icebergs and the days twenty-four hours long. He may have sailed up the east coast of Greenland, but he almost certainly explored the Labrador coast far north of his father's voyaging. He entered Hudson Strait and saw Hudson Bay, which he took for the Pacific, wide open before him. He reached 67½° North latitude where his crew, frightened of the ice, became mutinous and forced him to turn back. Refreshing his ships at the Land of the Baccalaos, he coasted south for an unknown distance and then returned to Bristol.[5]

The new king, Henry VIII, who had meanwhile acceded to the throne, had neither the inclination nor the money for further efforts to reach Cathay. There was one yarn about the trip that Cabot apparently liked to spin, and his friends repeated. Their greatest sport in the north, he said, was watching the well-fed bears wade into the water and catch the fish swarming near the shore. Because of this ample food supply the bears were never hungry and never molested the men. As there was, for the time being, no hope of pursuing the problem further in England, Sebastian Cabot kept his secret of the way to China and went off to Spain for the next thirty years.

3

The Unknown Coast

W^{hen} John Cabot made his second voyage in 1498 he may have had a Portuguese pilot named João Fernandez on board one of his ships. Fernandez, who lived on the island of Terceira, belonged to a class of small landowners called *llabrador*. Like most men in the Azores he was also a seafarer, and he was apparently trading with Bristol before John Cabot left on his first voyage. Between 1492 and 1495 Fernandez was making voyages toward the north, probably looking for islands, and perhaps reached Greenland.[1] In any case, Greenland was called Labrador for some years before the name got transferred to its present location, and it is said to have been named for a *llabrador* of the Azores who was sailing with the English.

There is also a possibility that João Fernandez sailed with Gaspar Corte Real in 1500. The Corte Reals were Portuguese noblemen and hereditary governors of the Azores. Gaspar sailed from Lisbon in June 1500 with two ships on a northern voyage of exploration. Sailing to the Azores he touched at the island of Terceira to take on fresh food and water, and then sailed north to Greenland. There he proceeded up the east coast until stopped by ice; returning, he rounded Cape Farewell, touched at the west coast and returned to Lisbon.

On his second voyage, which sailed 15 May 1501, Gaspar's three well-found ships, following a somewhat more westerly course, missed Greenland and made their landfall on the present coast of Labrador. Prevented from going northward by heavy ice and storms, they turned south and crossed the Strait of Belle Isle to Newfoundland. They found the country well populated and captured sixty of the Indians to carry home as slaves. Near the place where it is supposed John Cabot died, Corte Real met an Indian with a broken Italian sword and a boy wearing metal European earrings, which could only have come from John Cabot's expedition three years earlier. Gaspar's three vessels were separated, either deliberately or accidentally. On 8 October one ship arrived in Lisbon with seven natives on board; three days later a second ship with fifty more wretched, captive Indians came into port. But Gaspar Corte Real was not on either of them, and his ship did not return.

Determined to find his lost brother, Miguel Corte Real sailed forth with three ships on 10 May in the spring of 1502. Arriving on the Newfoundland coast, Miguel, when he saw the vast number of rivers, harbors, coves, and gunkholes where a ship could lie hidden, realized that the only chance for a successful search lay in dividing his fleet. A rendezvous was decided upon for 20 August. On that date two of the ships appeared but Miguel failed to show up, and vanished as completely as his brother Gaspar had. The king of Portugal sent out another expedition to search for the brothers, but it was similarly unsuccessful. King Manuel forbade Vasqueanes, Governor of Terceira, permission to lead another search.

Whether João Fernandez went with Gaspar Corte Real in 1500 or had reached Greenland on an expedition of his own is not clear. He apparently gave information to Henry VII on the desolate Land of the Labrador, and it seems probable that he was the first since the Norse voyagers to discover Greenland.

The lives of these early sixteenth-century explorers out of Bristol and Lisbon are greatly entangled. When Gaspar Corte Real was preparing for his second voyage, João Fernandez, with two of his countrymen, Francisco Fernandez and João Gonsalvez, was in England. With three Bristol merchants the Portuguese petitioned Henry VII for letters patent. Obtained on 19 March 1501, these were similar to but more extensive than those authorizing John Cabot's expedition. There is a hint that one of their purposes was the search for a Northwest Passage.[2] The Spanish Ambassador vainly protested these activities as he had John Cabot's voyages.

There is evidence that this group made a voyage in 1501 and again in 1502. In the latter year the King granted various sums of money 'to the merchants of Bristol that have been in the new found land,' and pensions to two of the Portuguese 'in consideration of the true service which they have done unto us, to our singular pleasure, as captains unto the new found land.' Between August 1501 and August 1502 Robert Fabyan, as recorded by Hakluyt, wrote:

> This yeere also were brought unto the king three men, taken in the Newfound Island, that before I spake of, in William Purchas time, being Maior: These were clothed in beasts skins, & did eate raw flesh, and spake such speech that no man could understand them, and in their demeanour like to bruite beastes, whom the king kept a time after. Of the which upon two yeeres after I saw two appareled after the maner of Englishmen, in Westminster pallace, which at that time I could not discerne from Englishmen, til I was learned what they were, but as for speech, I heard none of them utter one worde.[3]

The eating of raw flesh indicates Eskimos rather than Indians and so provides a clue of a voyage toward the Northwest.

After the 1501 voyage the name of João Fernandez disappears.

The other two Azoreans along with the Bristol merchants, under the name of the Company Adventurers to the New Found Lands, continued to make annual voyages through 1505. Although the voyages probably were primarily concerned with fishing, the king's patent enabled these men to explore and colonize the new country and, by implication, search for a way around it to Asia.

France, in the early sixteenth century, participated but little in finding a short way to the East. There was, to be sure, the attempt of Thomas Aubert, a Dieppe mariner, in 1508.[4] He is chiefly noted for bringing to France the first American Indians, seven of whom were exhibited in Rouen the following year. But in 1524 Francis I of France engaged the widely traveled and perhaps piratical Florentine Giovanni da Verrazano to sail for the new world. Francis, who once demanded to see the clause in Adam's will dividing the world between Spain and Portugal, had no more intention than Henry VII of recognizing such a division. It was Verrazano's declared purpose to reach Cathay by a westward voyage and to find a passage through any land across his course. Leaving the Desiertas Rocks, near Madeira, in the ship *Dauphine* on 17 January 1524, he sailed westward for twenty-five days with fair weather. On St. Valentine's Day he weathered a violent storm and altered his course northerly. After another twenty-five days he made his landfall in 34° N., which, if his reckoning was correct, is near Cape Fear, North Carolina. Because he failed to discover either Chesapeake Bay or Delaware Bay some historians contend that his landfall must have been far north of that.

He coasted south for about fifty leagues but, finding no safe anchorage, turned north. In a leisurely manner he worked his way along the coast, observing the trend of the shoreline and trading with the natives. He apparently mistook either Chesapeake Bay or Delaware Bay for a western ocean but missed the entrance to the bay. He concluded that there was a slender neck of land separating the Atlantic from the Pacific. A map made by his brother Jerome, which could only have been based on Giovanni's information, shows North America nearly bisected in this region by a great sea coming in from the west. Giovanni explored New York Harbor for the first time and named what is believed to be Block Island Louisa in honor of the King's mother. Anchored for fifteen days in Newport Harbor, Rhode Island, he explored the islands and country inland, traded for necessities with the Indians, and exchanged visits with their chiefs. The place delighted him, and he thought the natives lighter and more handsome than any people he had ever seen. He left with regret on 6 May.

Dauphine next landed in the vicinity of Portsmouth, New Hampshire. The Indians, who were more primitive there and dressed in skins, attacked him when he attempted to explore the countryside. As Verrazano continued northeasterly the rugged headlands and multitudinous islands of Maine reminded him of the Adriatic. Instead of exploring the land further, he continued to about 50° latitude and the New Found Land of the Breton fishermen. Provisions and stores nearly exhausted, he returned to France, arriving in Dieppe in early July. In his report to Francis I, Verrazano wrote: 'My intention in this voyage was to reach Cathay, on the extreme coast of Asia.' While he expected to find land blocking his way he did not doubt that it could be penetrated by some passage to the Pacific. He had not found the passage to the Orient, but he had pretty conclusively shown that it must be north of Newfoundland.

Spain, secure in her control of the known western way to the Indies, was nevertheless concerned by all this activity. If such a northwest passage existed it would provide a far shorter route. Precautions were taken: ships were sent up the Pacific coast to intercept any Portuguese or English vessels that might emerge from the passage and a Spanish expedition to the northwest was undertaken. They chose an experienced man. Estevan Gomez had sailed with Magellan as pilot on *San Antonio* but had deserted at the Strait and brought the ship home. He was a Portuguese who had been a pilot of Spain at the same time Sebastian Cabot was made Pilot Major in 1518. In February 1525 Gomez sailed with one small, armed ship and a year's provisions from Corunna, a Spanish port. His intention was to find a northern passage to the Moluccas — the Spice Islands. Such meager information as exists about this voyage and the evidence of Spanish maps indicate that Gomez sailed along the coast from Cape Breton possibly as far as Florida, having given what may have been the Hudson River the name Rio de San Antonio. It is said he returned by way of Cuba, where he refitted his ship. Gomez arrived at Corunna without a single ounce of spice but with a shipload of native men and women to be used as laborers. A helpful friend asked Gomez what he had brought and the Captain replied slaves (*esclavos*). To everyone's vast amusement the friend thought he had said cloves (*clavos*) and hastened to spread the great news at Court of the Passage's discovery.

Ten years later, on 20 April 1534, Jacques Cartier, a native of the Breton port, Saint-Malo, set out with two small ships of about fifty tons each and 162 men to seek a western route to the Indies. After making a good passage he reached Cape Bonavista, Newfoundland, 10 May. He then coasted northward to the Strait of Belle Isle where he crossed to the Labrador side. Finding it a forbidding land, he turned south and sailed through the Gulf of St. Lawrence, discovering Bird Rocks and Brion Island. He followed the shore of what he thought was the mainland (Prince Edward Island) westward to a bay (actually Northumberland Strait). He crossed this 'bay' and touched on the New Brunswick coast. Miramichi Bay he thought at first was the Northwest Passage. Here on 4 July he was surrounded by a great fleet of canoes full of Micmac Indians who he thought might attack him and fired his cannon to drive them away. He next tried the Bay of Chaleur; still no passage opened before him. Once more crossing over to the Labrador shore, he discovered a promising-looking strait, now called Mingan Passage, between it and Anticosti Island. Head winds and tides slowed his progress. As the season was getting late and supplies were low, he called a council, which decided not to pursue St. Peter's Channel, as he named it, but to return to France. Putting about, Cartier passed through the Strait of Belle Isle on 15 August and arrived 1 September at Saint-Malo after a good passage.

Impressed by Cartier's explorations and the possibility that the passage entrance was located, Francis I commissioned him to complete the exploration beyond Newfoundland. The following spring with *Great Hermina* (120 tons), *Little Hermina* (60 tons), and *Emerilon* a 'small galley,' Cartier sailed forth into contrary winds and severe storms. In late July the three vessels, separated by storm, rendezvoused at White Sands, Newfoundland, and from there sailed again through the Strait of Belle Isle. Cartier had with him two Indians from the previous voyage whom he intended to use as guides through St. Peter's Channel. As he passed beyond Anticosti Island he was cheered to see the water open out and, turning southward to the mainland, he explored westward to about Cape Chat. He then recrossed the St. Lawrence and followed the north shore back to Anticosti Island. Although the Indians informed him that the St. Lawrence was no strait but a river whose banks rapidly contracted and whose water became fresh, Cartier decided to see for himself and turned up river. As the banks of the St. Lawrence closed in and the water freshened, he passed the black Saguenay flowing out of its great gorge, and remarked the white whales — the beluga — which still play in the deep, dark waters near its mouth. He followed the river until stopped by the Lachine Rapids. He then wintered at Hochelaga, the present site of Montreal, where many of his company died. On 20 May he began his return passage taking along the Indian king, Donnacona. His souvenirs included a bundle of beaver skins, a string of wampum, and a red copper knife from the Saguenay. The ships passed south of Newfoundland this time, clearing Cape Race 16 June, and arrived at Saint-Malo, 1 July 1536.

Cartier's third voyage, begun 23 May 1541, does not concern us as the purpose was no longer to seek a Northwest Passage, but to find precious metals and diamonds, and to consider sites in the St. Lawrence region for French colonization. The voyage also stimulated the French fishing industry. Although Breton fishermen had been on the Newfoundland banks for nearly half a century, now fishermen came from all the French ports. In addition to his enormous contribution to geographical knowledge, Cartier gave the first extensive accounts of the Iroquois and Algonquin Indians.

Like the other very early voyagers, Cartier had expected to sail to Cathay without great difficulty. Following John Cabot's discovery, Corte Real, Verrazano, Gomez, and Cartier each expected to find a broad strait. With Cartier's voyages it became obvious that the Atlantic seaboard of North America was unbroken. Then thoughts and exploration turned toward the Arctic, to the region of Hudson Strait, and higher latitudes. Then too the search became the special concern of the English.

4

The Timid, the Lost, and the Hungry

While the continental Europeans were exploring, hoping to find passes through the long Atlantic seaboard of North America, the English were not idle. But their three efforts following the Cabots were peculiarly unrewarding. Something of the comic opera and considerable tragedy emerge from the few surviving facts about these expeditions. From the little that is known of an abortive voyage begun in 1517, certain reasonable conjectures can be made. Sebastian Cabot, along with Thomas Spert, a noted mariner, shipowner, onetime master of the 'great ship' *Henri Grace à Dieu,* and first master of Trinity House, is said to have been acting in an advisory capacity for the venture, one which had the moderate interest of and some backing by Henry VIII. A fleet was outfitted under the command of John Rastell, brother-in-law of Sir Thomas More. Rastell, with two London merchants, William Howting and Richard Spicer, apparently bore most of the expense and ventured cargoes. The purposes of this voyage to Newfoundland are not wholly clear. One was certainly fishing; another, perhaps, was to try out More's Utopian theories, as tools and equipment for a colony were among the cargo. If Cabot was associated with the venture he might have had in mind a colony supported by fishing to act as a base for pushing through the Northwest Passage to Cathay. The evidence indicates that some such scheme was in the back of Rastell's mind.

Several naval vessels were outfitted at London but only two, *Barbara* and *Mary Barking,* are known by name. While the expedition had the backing of the King, it was opposed by the Earl of Surrey, then Lord Admiral, who did not want ships diverted from the Channel. He, through Spert, contrived to delay the expedition by conspiring with John Ravyn, purser of *Barbara* and owner of *Mary Barking*. Ravyn managed delays for ship repairs and stores at Dartmouth, Plymouth, and Falmouth, and succeeded in ending the voyage at Cork, Ireland. By then the season was well advanced, and Ravyn with hired accomplices locked Howting in his cabin, threatened to kill Rastell and Spicer, and absconded with part of the cargo. The ships were sailed back to England and two years later Rastell brought suit against Ravyn to recover the value of the goods that had been taken from him, and apparently won.[1] So ended, through intrigue in high places, what was intended to be a great expedition combining fishing, colonization, and a search for the Passage.

Whatever Cabot's connection with the 1517 fiasco, it is certain that, still Pilot Major of Spain, he was visiting in England in 1520–21, attempting to whip up interest and support for a voyage to Asia. He was so sure that he knew where the Passage through North America lay that with a sufficiently well-prepared expedition he expected to sail through to Eastern riches. The King supported him, as did Cardinal Wolsey. The King offered a Royal Navy ship, asked the London Merchant Companies to furnish five other vessels, and guaranteed to furnish all supplies and take the risk of the ships' loss.

But the London Merchant Companies were not enthusiastic and the records of the Draper's Company show that they did not favor the risk. They claimed that Sebastian Cabot, who was to command the expedition personally, had never been in those regions, but whether they meant to Newfoundland or Cathay is not clear. They also argued that no other English mariners had experience in those waters and should the ships get separated there was increased danger of loss. The opposition was great, and the King became diverted by the outbreak of a new war with France. Sebastian Cabot returned to Spain and opened secret intrigues with the Council of Ten of his native city of Venice to obtain backing for the venture. His lack of success ended his attempts to sail into the broad blue sea he had seen so briefly beyond the western end of Hudson Strait. Soon he would sail to South America and explore the River Plate for Spain, but in his old age, he was once more in England thinking of the same rich goal by another direction.

Although Henry VIII had shown little curiosity in northwest passages when Sebastian Cabot returned in 1509, he became sufficiently interested to materially assist the abortive projects of 1517 and 1521. With the pressure of war removed, he finally managed in 1527, to dispatch an expedition to find the Northwest Passage. Richard Hakluyt, the great historian of English voyages, had difficulty obtaining much information about the 1527 expedition. He once asked Martin Frobisher about it and got a vague yarn about a great, but unnamed, mathematician who was also canon of St. Paul's who went on the voyage, and that the name of one of the two ships, which sailed from the Thames on 20 May 1527, was *Dominus Vobiscum*.[2]

Samuel Purchas, writing in 1625, had more accurate information in the form of two letters written by members of the expedition in August 1527 from the harbor of St. John's, Newfoundland.[3] The first was written to the King on the third of the month 'in bad English and worse writing' by John Rut, master of *Mary of Gilford*. The second letter was written (in Latin) to Cardinal Wolsey by one who signed himself 'Albertus de Prato' and who may have been Frobisher's canon of St. Paul's or the Italian pilot of the expedition. Purchas unfortunately prints only the framework of the letter and omits the body because he says it contains the same information as Rut's.

The two ships had sailed from Plymouth 10 June and continued in company until 1 July, when they were separated in a storm. Rut continued a northerly course for two days to 63° N. latitude. Finding no land, deep soundings, and dangerous quantities of ice, he turned southward, and after a four-day run reached the coast near St. Lewis Sound, Labrador. After putting fresh water aboard and fishing for ten days he sailed to St. John's Harbor which, in case of separation, was the agreed rendezvous with the other ship *Samson*. Rut closed his letter by saying that after revictualing by fishing he would push on to those islands he had been commanded to reach, which probably means the Spice Islands and Japan. He may, however, have been referring to the West Indies.

The two ships probably never met again. From Spanish sources we know that one of them appeared in the West Indies later in the summer and was thus the first English ship in those waters. On 19 November the ship spoke a Spanish caravel at the Island of Mona, where she remained two days. She reached Santo Domingo on the 25th, and requested and was refused a pilot home. The Spaniards then tried to capture her, but she escaped from the harbor and three or four days later, when the inhabitants refused to sell her anything, raided the Island of Ocoa for provisions. She then sailed for England, but nothing is known of her arrival. I am inclined to think the ship may have been *Mary* with Rut, as Frobisher thought that *Samson* foundered in a storm. It is also known that the Italian pilot on *Mary* was killed and that John Rut was trading to France in *Mary* a year or so later. The whole affair may, as Williamson surmises,[4] have been hushed up for reasons of state.

In all the early accounts of New World voyages and Arctic

explorations it was assumed that the voyage of John Rut resulted
from two letters of Robert Thorne's, one written early in 1526
to Edward Lee, the English Ambassador to Spain, and the other
to Henry VIII. We now know that this was not the case, as Rut's
voyage was too far advanced to have been influenced by the
Thorne writings and the letter to the King was never received.
The two letters are known only from copies of copies kept by
Thorne.

Robert Thorne, onetime mayor of Bristol, was a prosperous
and influential merchant residing in Seville, and a friend of Sebastian Cabot. Shrewd and imaginative, he managed to have two
Englishmen, Robert Barlow and Henry Latimer, a pilot, accompany Cabot when he sailed in 1526 for the Spice Islands by the
Strait of Magellan. Thorne reasoned that such experience would
prepare them for going with an English expedition, by way of
the Pole, and they could then take over when the ships arrived in
the Eastern waters. This fitted in with his views of the course
Henry VIII should pursue to expand his realm overseas and to
find a passage to Cathay. Thorne, from his Spanish residence,
saw rich cargoes from the East and the New World pouring into
Spain and Portugal, and felt, as a true Englishman, that his country should share in this wealth. In his two famous letters he out-
lined exactly how the English could share in this lucrative trade.
Interestingly enough, Robert Thorne says that he inherited his
taste for exploration from his father who was also a Bristol merchant and who, 'with another marchant of Bristow named
Hugh Eliot, were the discoverers of the New Found Lands . . .'
We have already pointed out that Robert Thorne the elder and
Eliot may have been two of the merchants who accompanied
John Cabot on one of his voyages.

As Thorne saw it, to sail directly over the North Pole to Cathy
was 2000 leagues shorter than to follow the routes of Spanish and
Portuguese ships. Foreseeing the objection that ships taking such
a course might encounter some difficulties with ice, he remarked that '. . . there is no land unhabitable nor sea unnavi-

gable.' He further pointed out the advantage that English woolens might very profitably be sold to the inhabitants of the cold regions through which the vessels must sail. He evidently intended to put his theories to the test and went so far as to purchase the ship *Savior,* planning to send her over the pole under the command of Roger Barlow, who was still without experience in Far Eastern waters. Failing to get through the Strait of Magellan, Cabot had instead explored the River Plate. Thorne's plans ended with his death in 1532 and Barlow, instead of bucking the ice, wrote, in 1540–41, the *Brief Summe of Geographie,* a work not published until 1932.

The final voyage in this early series, as well as one of the most puzzling and fantastic, took place in 1536. It was long considered to be one of the expeditions seeking the Northwest Passage, but Miss E. G. R. Taylor believes it to have been no more than a fishing voyage on which the Captain, a smart promoter, sold passage to a number of wealthy young men of London for a sightseeing tour of the frozen north; and that their adventures and hardships existed mostly in their imaginations as a result of the soft life they had previously led.[5] I am not wholly convinced that she is right. Captain Robert Hore, accompanied by many fine gentlemen and substantial men, began the voyage with great enthusiasm.

The tale was told by Thomas Buts, the last survivor of the expedition, whom Hakluyt rode 200 miles to interview, and it was reported by one Oliver Dawbeny to Richard Hakluyt of the Middle Temple, a cousin of Richard Hakluyt the author of the voyages. About 120 men including thirty gentlemen, embarking on the ships *Trinity,* of 130 tons, and *William,* sailed from Gravesend the end of April. The crossing took more than two months, but eventually they raised Cape Breton. They sailed northeast across Cabot Strait to Penguin Island off southern Newfoundland. They dined for some time on the flesh and eggs of the Great Auk as well as on some of the many bears, which they found 'no bad foode.' They chased a native boat ashore and followed the Indians into the woods. They found a boot and mitten near a hastily deserted camp fire, but the Indians did not reappear. Although no ice was encountered the expedition soon had other serious problems. Their food gave out. For a time they subsisted on such roots and herbs as they could gather, and by the ingenious expedient of stealing the fresh fish from an osprey's nest that the hardworking fishhawk brought to its unfortunate young. The officers were worried by the loss of men sent ashore to find food. Each party returned shorthanded, reporting companions captured by natives or killed by wild beasts. The sailors who went ashore were accused by those aboard ship of killing game, feeding themselves, and holding out on those left aboard. One of the latter, deciding to go ashore for himself, came upon a sailor eating a piece of meat and when he asked what he had the other replied, 'If thou wouldest needes know, the broyled meate that I had was a piece of such a mans buttocke.' When this shocking news was brought to the Captain he 'made a notable Oration' condemning the cannibals to everlasting hell. But the hunger continued and soon it was agreed to draw lots to see who should be dined upon. But before this decision was effected an unsuspecting French ship arrived on the scene. The Englishmen thereupon captured the Frenchmen, took over the ship and its victuals, and sailed for England, going far enough north to see many icebergs. The men were so emaciated and aged by their fearful experience that when they arrived Sir William and Lady Buts did not recognize their son Thomas until they examined a birthmark on his knee. Some months later the Frenchmen complained to Henry VIII of their treatment at the hands of his subjects. After examining all the evidence he decided that his subjects had suffered enough distress and, moved with pity, dealt out no punishment, but handsomely reimbursed the Frenchmen for their losses out of his royal purse. For the forty years after Richard Hore's return Newfoundland was left to the fishermen.

5

Hunt a Dragon, Bag a Bear

Discouraged by their failure to reach the East by way of a Northwest Passage, the English turned their attention to the Northeast. In the days of King Alfred, a Norseman named Othere lived far north on the Norwegian coast. About the year 870 he became curious to see just how far north the land extended. Coasting north for three days, he passed the farthest limit of the whale hunters of his time and then sailed for as many days more. The land turned east and, after waiting for a fair wind, Othere followed it for four days. As the coast then turned south, he again waited for the wind and sailed for five days until he came to the mouth of a great river where the land was inhabited. He returned, and sometime later told the tale of his voyage to King Alfred. Besides being curious to see the country, Othere said he went there chiefly 'on account of the walruses, because they have very noble bones in their teeth . . . and their hides are very good for ship ropes.' There is no doubt from Othere's clear and simple account that he was the first man to round the North Cape and discover the White Sea. Because King Alfred wrote it down, Othere's story was remembered.[1]

It is rumored that the Portuguese in 1484 sent an expedition to attempt to reach India by the northeast and that a Genovese, Paolo Centurione, who died before it could be put into effect, suggested a similar plan to Henry VIII in 1525. The idea simmered among the merchants, who were looking for new markets for their woolens.

Ever opportunistic, Sebastian Cabot returned in 1549 to England where he received a pension of £166.13.4 from Edward VI, and in June 1550 a further grant of £200. Three years later the newly incorporated Association of Merchant Adventurers, also called the Muscovy Company, made Cabot Governor for life and pressed plans to search north of Europe and Asia for a passage to the Orient.

The experienced Sebastian planned the expedition well. His instructions for the project while occasionally of a childish nature, at least to modern eyes, are in general sensible and good, and could be used by any well-conducted expedition. Great care was taken in selecting and preparing the ships and in enlisting competent officers and men.

Three vessels were fitted out at an expense of £6000: *Bona Esperanza* (120 tons) for the flagship, *Edward Bonaventure* (160 tons), and *Bona Confidentia* (90 tons). Sir Hugh Willoughby, a proven leader, was chosen as Admiral, and Richard Chancellor was Pilot Major and second in command. Chancellor was no common seaman: a Bristol man, he had been carefully trained for such work on a voyage to the Levant sponsored by Sebastian Cabot; a mathematical genius, he had worked closely with John Dee as a student of navigation and had improved the navigational instruments of his day. Chancellor's sailing master on *Bonaventure* was Stephen Borough, and he had two other good men in Stephen's younger brother William, later to become Comptroller of the Navy in the reign of Elizabeth, and Arthur Pet. No pains nor expense were spared to make this a successful expedition and the merchants of the Company never doubted that it would reach the Indies. In fact, so sure were they that the ships were sheathed in lead (probably the first metal sheathing on ships' bottoms in England) to protect the hulls against worms, which they understood were very destructive in tropical waters. Everyone who might contribute a bit of useful knowledge to the venture was consulted, from Dee to two 'Tartars' employed in the royal stable who were of no help whatsoever.

Sir Hugh Willoughby with thirty-five men including six merchants embarked on *Esperanza;* Chancellor with two merchants and forty-eight other men was given *Bonaventure;* and *Confidentia* was placed under the command of Captain Cornelius Durfoorth with twenty-eight men including three merchants. On 20 May 1553 the fleet was towed by boats down the Thames from Ratcliffe. Although the King was ill and unable to be present, the fleet made a brave show before the Court and great crowds of people at Greenwich. The ships fired a salute and the sailors cheered the hilltops to the echo. Thus, with rejoicing crowds and a fair wind, the first great organized English expedition departed.

Sailing north along the coasts of England and Scotland the fleet crossed over to the Norwegian shore which they raised in 66° latitude — the very part of the coast from which Othere began his voyage to the White Sea nearly seven hundred years earlier. They continued northward, exploring the coast as they went, until mid-September when *Bonaventure* was separated from the other two vessels in a storm. This was disastrous for Willoughby, because Chancellor was the principal navigator and pilot. The two ships sailed far to the north and east, seeking their consort without success. They fell in with a barren and inhospitable land believed to be Kolgujev Island and then turned back to the mouth of the Varzina River on the Kola Peninsula, where Willoughby decided to winter. Parties of men were sent out in different directions for several days without finding any sign of inhabitants. To judge from the date of Sir Hugh Willoughby's will and other papers, the men stayed alive until January 1554. But sometime thereafter, having no knowledge of successful Arctic wintering, all aboard the two ships froze to death or died of scurvy. They were discovered by Russian fishermen the following spring. The shocking tale quickly became clothed in legend. It was said that all the men were frozen to death and when they found Sir Hugh, he was seated at a table in his cabin, pen in hand and paper before him. Many of his companions were seated around; some eating, others opening lockers or performing shipboard duties. This, of course, was not true, but the story of the derelict ships and the ghastly scene was frequently repeated, and it is believed to be the source of the legend of *The Flying Dutchman,* the ship that forever sails the seas with a ghostly crew.*

Richard Chancellor in *Bonaventure* put into Vardö (Wardhouse) after the storm and waited seven days for the other two ships. When they failed to appear he decided to push on, and sailing north came to a place where there was 'no night at all, but a continuall light and brightnesse of the sunne shining clearly upon the hugh and mighty sea.' He turned south and finally reached the mouth of the Dwina River on the White Sea where the city of Archangel now stands, but where he found only a small monastery. The people were friendly and hospitable and immediately sent off a message to Ivan the Terrible about their extraordinary visitors. The Czar invited Chancellor and his companions to Moscow where they were entertained and passed the winter. While this voyage failed to reach its goal of far eastern Asia, it resulted in the establishment of regular commercial relations between England and Russia, to the immense profit of both countries and to the merchants of the Muscovy Company. Previous to this time trade between England

---

* My suspicion is that, as the tale grew with the years, the Willoughby tragedy and the enforced wintering of the Dutch explorer Barents became confused — hence *The Flying Dutchman.*

and Russia had been conducted by way of the German cities that controlled the Baltic.

Chancellor made a second voyage with *Bonaventure* and *Philip and Mary,* sailing down the Thames in early July 1555. Coasting Lapland, he found Willoughby and his ships and salvaged the ships' papers and merchandise. On this voyage he was accompanied by George Killingworth as agent for the Muscovy Company to Moscow. As they were being entertained by the Czar, Ivan reached out across the table and stroked Killingworth's beard, passing the end of it to the Metropolitan beside

NOVAYA ZEMLYA

him who blest it and remarked, 'This is God's gift' which it undoubtedly was for 'at that time it was not only thicke, broad,
and yellow coloured, but in length five foote and two
inches . . .'

On the return trip Chancellor attempted to bring back Willoughby's ships, *Esperanza* and *Confidentia*. With him came
the first Russian Ambassador to England. The return voyage
from Russia was a disastrous one. The four ships were separated by severe storms, and three of them sought shelter on the
coast of Norway where *Confidentia* was lost with all hands.
Esperanza fared no better for, although she apparently survived
the winter there, she disappeared on her crossing to England.
Only *Philip and Mary* arrived safely in London, on 18 April
1557. Poor Chancellor in *Bonaventure* worked his way into
Pitsligo Bay, Scotland, an anchorage open as a bootjack, where
his ship dragged her anchors and was driven on the rocks by the
tempest. Chancellor made a heroic attempt to save the Ambassador and succeeded, but he and seven Russians and several of
his crew were drowned 7 November 1556, and the wreck was
looted by the wild Scots.

While Chancellor was absent on his last voyage the Muscovy
Company decided to continue the attempt to reach Cathay and
sent out his former sailing master Stephen Borough in the ninety
ton pinnace *Searchthrift,* with instructions to penetrate to the
northeast as far as possible. As Borough with his tiny vessel
waited at Gravesend on 27 April 1556 ready for sea, Sebastian
Cabot, Governor of the Company, and a party of ladies and
gentlemen came on board,

> and the good olde gentleman Master Cabota gave to the poore
> most liberall almes; and then, at the signe of the Christopher,
> hee and his friends banketted, and made mee [merry] and them
> that were in the company great cheere; and for joy that he had
> to see the towardness of our intended discovery, he entered
> into the dance himselfe amongst the rest of the young and lusty
> company.[2]

On this gay note Sebastian Cabot disappears from history, and two days later Borough sailed.

Passing the North Cape on 23 May, he was led by a Russian vessel to the Petchora River. He then proceeded eastward and was enclosed by great ice 'which was a fearful sight to see,' but the first whale was an even more terrifying sight.

> On St. James his day, bolting to the windwardes, we had the latitude at noon in seventy degrees, twentie minutes. The same day, at a south-west sunne, there was a monstrous whale aboord of us, so neare to our side that we might have thrust a sworde or any other weapon in him, which we durst not doe for feare hee should have overthrowen our shippe; and then I called my company together, and all of us shouted, and with the crie that we made he departed from us; there was as much above water of his backe as the bredth of our pinnesse, and at his falling downe he made such a terrible noise in the water, that a man would greatly have marvelled, except he had known the cause of it; but, God be thanked, we were quietly delivered of him.[3]

In August, in company with a fleet of Russian fishing boats, he reached the south end of Novaya Zemlya and attempted to pass to the eastward of Vaygach Island, but was turned back by a severe storm on 3 September. He wintered at Colomogro, where he abandoned his plan to push on to the River Ob the following season, and returned to England, bringing the first information about Novaya Zemlya and the Samoyeds to western Europe.

After Cabot's death John Dee became the active champion of Northeast and Northwest Passages, and over a score of years after Borough's return he instigated the only other English expedition to the Northeast. Another of Chancellor's comrades, Arthur Pet, was given command of *George,* with Charles Jackman, veteran mate and pilot of Frobisher's voyage to the Northwest, as Captain of *William.* As before, these two barks were fitted out by the Russian merchants who had been prospering with a steady trade to Archangel, and the two men were instructed to attempt to complete the Northeast Passage to China.

Richard Hakluyt the elder, acting as an adviser to the Muscovy Company, compiled a set of sound instructions for the Captains' guidance. On the way to China they were to note if the northern lands east of Novaya Zemlya were populous, as this would be a potential market for warm woolen cloth. It was also important that they bring back descriptions of the climate and soil, especially if suitable for colonies, to see whether there were trees suitable for masts and if tar, pitch, and hemp were available for ships. They were to observe the geographical features of the land and find out whether or not there were good harbors and suitable building stone. If a strait was found it was to be surveyed and all hands were to be sworn to secrecy. Care was to be taken not to lose a man as there were fewer than twenty on both ships. If the expedition succeeded in reaching Kambalu, the capital city of the Grand Khan, they were to bring back samples of all products of the country, including a man for whom a hostage might be left. They were also to note the local architecture, clothing, furnishings, agriculture, and especially the type and size of the ships, forts, weapons of all kinds, and armed forces, both horse and foot. Hakluyt compiled a long list of the manufactured products which the English had available for trade and suggested that samples of all of them be taken along. And, finally, he emphasized that everything exhibited as samples of trading commodities should be first-class products, for shoddy goods create an ill opinion.[4]

Armed with these practical instructions Pet and Jackman left Harwich on 30 May 1580, sailing north and east as far as Vaygach Island, where they found plenty of wood and water. Pushing on into the Kara Sea, the first western Europeans to do so, they spent sixteen to eighteen days in heavy ice with a constant thick fog. They returned through the Strait of Vaygach amid ice, snow, and fog, and on 22 August parted company. Pet in *George* doubled North Cape the last day of the month and on 26 October arrived safely in the Thames at Ratcliffe. Jackman in *William* wintered on the coast of Norway and left in February in company with a Danish ship and was never heard of again.

The Merchant Adventurers in this series of voyages never achieved their hope of finding the Chinese dragon but they did make the acquaintance of the Russian bear. The Pet-Jackman voyage was almost the last of English sea expeditions to the Northeast. But a few years later a great Dutchman and his comrades were making heroic explorations in that direction.

6

The Great Dutchman

The Dutch were interested observers of the English attempts at the Northeast Passage. Like their commercial rivals across the North Sea, they too were prevented from entering the rich Far Eastern trade by Spanish and Portuguese supremacy on the sea. In 1584 Philip II of Spain, who had acquired sovereignty over Portugal, prohibited the Dutch from trading there. The source of their India goods thus cut off, it was no coincidence that Olivier Brunel, a Brussels adventurer, led the first Netherlands Arctic expedition that year.

Brunel was a man of vast experience in the Russian trade, which came about in this way. In 1565 the Dutch had established a commercial station at Kola in Lapland (near the present Murmansk), following by twelve years the settlement of the English Muscovy merchants on Rose Island at the mouth of the Dwina River. The English hoped to exclude other nations from their lucrative Russian trade, but the tenacious Dutchmen, from their base at Kola, tracked them into the White Sea. Following their discovery of where the English were trading, the Dutch sent Olivier Brunel on a Russian ship to Kholmogory, a town around the monastery of St. Michel, near the English settlement which later became the thriving city of Archangel. His instructions were to learn the Russian language and negotiate for commercial relations. The English, soon hearing of the intruder, persuaded the Russians that Brunel was a spy, and he was imprisoned. Several years later two Russian merchants, Jakor and Grigory Anikiew of the famous commercial house of Strogonoff, interceded in his behalf and he was released. Brunel then entered the employment of the Anikiews and as their commercial agent made overland journeys and coasting voyages to the eastward; trading with the Samoyeds, crossing the Petchora, penetrating Siberia at least as far as the Ob River, and becoming well acquainted with conditions in the Polar Sea. But all during his years in Russian service, while his knowledge and experience were increasing, Olivier Brunel never lost sight of his original purpose — to establish direct commercial relations between Russia and the Netherlands. He constantly pointed out the desirability of such a trade to his employers and finally persuaded them to send agents with him to Holland. For several years he made journeys between the two countries and at last, in 1577, brought one of the Dutch merchants to Russia. So successful were his efforts that within a few years ships were sailing annually from the Netherlands by way of Kola to a flourishing Dutch factory at Archangel, where the English soon joined them.

The 1580 expedition of Pet and Jackman inspired the Russians, who had far more accurate knowledge of the Siberian coast than the English and whose commercial maturity was rapidly developing, to attempt a voyage to Cathay themselves. They commissioned a Swedish shipbuilder in the employ of the Strogonoffs to build two ships on the White Sea for the projected Northeast effort and Brunel was sent to Antwerp to enlist officers and sailors to man the vessels.

However, Brunel decided that his own country rather than

his employers should benefit from his extensive knowledge of the Arctic. Leading Dutch merchants were sold on the idea and approached Prince William the Silent for support and financial assistance. The Prince favored the expedition but refused national funds. Disappointed but not discouraged, the merchants proceeded with their plans. The first Netherland Arctic voyage was fitted out at private expense; and in 1584 the enterprising Brunel with a ship from Enkhuizen sailed for the Empire of Cathay by way of the north. But neither yare ship, rich cargo, nor experienced leader brought success to the venture. Brunel, in attempting to force a passage of Pet's Strait, wrecked his ship in the shallow waters of the Petchora estuary. Pointedly, and with good reason, avoiding his former Russian employers, he made his way back to western Europe where he entered the service of the King of Denmark to search for the lost Greenland colonies. Afterward he may have sailed on one of the English expeditions to the Northwest. Holland's first Arctic explorer took no part in the three important expeditions of his countrymen which followed where he had first ventured.[1]

The trade of the Netherlanders with Russia prospered and they became powerful commercial rivals of the English in the White Sea. They still desired many of the Eastern products formerly obtained in Portugal and so, as their knowledge of northern waters and ice conditions increased, they once more thought to extend commercial relations to China and India by way of the Northeast Passage.

In 1593, led by Balthasar de Moucheron, a successful trader to Russia, merchants of Middleburg and Enkhuizen agreed to fit out a vessel from each town to sail to the Far East by the Northern Ocean. Middleburg contributed *Swan* under the command of Cornelius Nay, an experienced pilot and master in the Russian trade, accompanied by François de la Dale, who had lived in Russia, as supercargo and interpreter. *Mercury* of Enkhuizen commanded by Brant Tetgales, another skillful seaman, was selected as the second ship and her supercargo was Jan Huygen van Linschoten, a remarkably traveled young man. Linschoten had returned to his native town of Enkhuizen the previous September after five years' residence in Goa, where he had gone on a Portuguese vessel. During his stay there he became acquainted with a fellow townsman named Dirck Gerritsz, who had lived in India for twenty-five years and who had made voyages to China as a ship's gunner. It was Linschoten's ambition to visit China and Japan but lack of funds prevented it. Upon his return to Europe he wrote an excellent account of his travels and was in the process of getting this published when he was invited to sail on this expedition with instructions to keep a full journal of the voyage. He immediately grasped the opportunity, for if he could not reach his heart's desire from India, perhaps he could get there from the North.

Stimulated by the activity of the other towns, the merchants of Amsterdam decided to get in on the act. They fitted out a third vessel (named *Mercury* like the Enkhuizen entry, to the confusion of historians) and placed her, with a pinnace, or fishing boat, under the command of William Barents. This seafaring burgher of Amsterdam had never commanded an expedition, and this was the only occasion when he sailed to the Arctic as a captain. His colleagues praised him not only as a pilot and navigator but also as the best of seamen and a man of infinite resources, who faced danger with courage and endured hardship with fortitude and good humor.[2] As there were diverse opinions concerning the best route to follow, it was agreed that Barents should go easterly around the north of Novaya Zemlya, while the other two vessels attempted to penetrate the Kara Sea by Vaygach Island. Nay was given command of the whole squadron which sailed from the Texel on Sunday, 5 June 1594. By the twenty-third of the month the ships had all arrived

at Kilden on the coast of Lapland and five days later Barents
sailed for Novaya Zemlya. The others waited until 2 July and
then took their departure for Vaygach. It was agreed that in case
the two parts of the expedition should be unable to meet beyond
Novaya Zemlya, that they would rendezvous again at Kilden
and wait for each other there until the end of September.

Barents first sighted Novaya Zemlya on 4 July and on the
seventh was at Williams Island where he and his crew found
vast quantities of drift wood and many walruses, a good road-
stead for ships to lie, and the wreckage of a Russian ship. Here
too they encountered a great white bear which they shot, 'but the
beare shewed most wonderful strength,' and attempted to escape by swimming. The sailors pursued in a boat, lassoed the
animal, and pulling him up to the stern hoped to capture the
beast alive to carry to Amsterdam as a curiosity. The bear, however, had other ideas and began to climb over the transom as
frightened Dutchmen scrambled for the bow. Fortunately,
when the bear was half into the boat, the loop around its neck
caught on the rudder. There it hung and was killed with a pike,
the huntsmen contenting themselves with its fleece. From a
nearby island, where they found two large crosses set up by Russians, they sailed on the tenth to Cape Nassau.

For the next twenty-five days Barents battled against head
winds and ice, putting his ship about eighty-one times, and sailing over 1500 miles to the Orange Islands and back to Cape
Nassau. On the night of the thirteenth the ship was forced back
by an ice field stretching as far as the eye could see. But Barents
again struggled forward beyond Ice Point, where his men found
certain gold stones (probably iron pyrites), and finally reached
the Orange Islands on the last day of July. His men would sail
no further. Having made the first exploration of the west coast
of Novaya Zemlya, they began their homeward voyage.

At the Orange Islands they had found a herd of some two
hundred walruses, morses, or seahorses as they were variously

called. So impressed were they by the girth and numbers of the beasts that Gerrit De Veer the chronicler of Barents's voyages wrote in admiration:

> This sea-horse is a wonderfull strong monster of the sea, much bigger than an oxe, which keepes continually in the seas, having a skinne like a sea-calfe or seale, with very short hair, mouthed like a lyon, and many times they lie upon the ice; they are hardly killed unlesse you strike them just upon the forehead; it hath foure feet, but no eares, and commonly it hath one or two young ones at a time. And when the fisher-men chance to find them upon a flake of ice with their yong ones, she casteth her yong ones before her into the water, and then takes them in her armes, and so plungeth up and downe with them, and when shee will revenge herselfe upon the boats, or make resistance against them, then she casts her yong ones from her againe, and with all her force goeth towards the boate; whereby our men were once in no small danger, for that the sea-horse had almost striken her teeth into the sterne of their boate, thinking to overthrowe it; but by means of the great cry that the men made, shee was afraid, and swomme away againe, and tooke her yong ones againe in her armes. They have two teeth sticking out of their mouthes, on each side one, each beeing about halfe an elle long, and are esteemed to bee as good as any ivorie or elophants teeth, specially in Muscovia, Tartaria, and there abouts where they are knowne, for they are as white, hard, and even as ivory.[3]

Coasting southward along Novaya Zemlya, eight miles south of St. Lawrence Bay, they saw a cross upon a point and found the remains of a Russian ship, forty-four feet long on the keel. Three wooden houses stood nearby and six sacks of rye meal were found buried in the ground. There were crosses and heaps of stones, piles of pipe staves for packing salmon, 'and by them stood five or six coffins, by graves, with dead men's bones, the coffins standing upon the ground all filled up with stones.' Grateful for the sacks of rye, they named this sheltered harbor Meale-Haven.

Meanwhile the other two ships were sailing eastward, where they found the mid-July weather as warm as Holland in dog days and the mosquitoes many and ravenous. At the south end of Vaygach Island they landed to examine 300 to 400 crudely-carved wooden figures, their faces turned toward the east. These ill-made figures sometimes had five to seven broad faces with projecting noses and holes for eyes and mouth carved on a single post. Another cache of better made idols with eyes and nipples of metal were found stored in a house. While the Dutch were examining these curious carvings a man armed with a bow drove up in a reindeer sledge and shouted. Thereupon more sledges with about thirty armed men drove out of a valley and attempted to surround the Dutchmen who hastily fled to their boat and shoved off under a shower of arrows. This bloodless battle is the only recorded conflict between northern natives and Northeast explorers.[4] Once friendly relations had been established with the Samoyeds, the Dutch received a good deal of important information from them about the Kara Sea and ice beyond the Strait.

Leaving Idol Point and sailing through Pet's Strait and beyond for over 200 miles, Nay and Linschoten found the Kara Sea deep blue, ice free, and full of whales. There were no obstructions or difficulties and, noting that the coast trended to the southeast toward Cathay, they considered the way clear; on 11 August they decided to return home with the good news. Three days later they returned through Pet's Strait (now called Yugor Schar) and the following day fell in with Barents sailing south.

Happy with the results of their exploring and convinced that the passage was there to be sailed through, they sailed for home together, where they arrived in mid-September. Barents's men, to lend substance to their yarns, exhibited in Amsterdam a great sea horse they had killed on the ice off Novaya Zemlya. (It must have smelled most gloriously by that time.)

The reports submitted by Barents and Linschoten were very

different in character. Linschoten's extremely optimistic account immediately stimulated the merchants, substantially backed by Prince Maurice of Orange and the States General of the United Provinces, to send out to China a larger, better equipped fleet the following year. A forty-ton yacht from Rotterdam went along for the sole purpose of returning to Holland with the good news as soon as the fleet rounded Cape Tabin or broke through beyond the ice with open water before them to the southeast.

The splendid fleet of seven vessels, ranging from forty to three hundred tons, that sailed from the Texel on 2 July 1595 was the best equipped and most costly the Dutch had yet sent out. The ships were handsomely laden with supplies for eighteen months and trade goods in abundance. Manning the fleet was one of the most talented groups of skillful seamen and experienced traders that could be assembled. Once more Cornelius Nay in *Griffin* of Zeeland, accompanied by his former flagship *Swan* from the same place, was named Admiral. Reliable Brant Tetgales as Vice-Admiral commanded the new war-pinnace *Hope* that had been contributed by Enkhuizen along with the veteran *Mercury*. William Barents, the ablest navigator of them all, was named Pilot Major of the fleet and sailed with the new *Greyhound* of Amsterdam accompanied by another ship, probably his old *Mercury*. Rotterdam supplied the little yacht to act as herald. Again the irrepressible Linschoten and capable François de la Dale were aboard as supercargoes. They were joined, among others, by Jacob van Heemskerck, Jan Corneliszoon Rijp, and Gerrit De Veer. But well-found ships and able, talented men were not enough. The timing was bad and they were unfortunate in the year, for the previous winter had been one of unusual severity in the north. Arriving on the late date of 19 August at Yugor Schar, they found the ice stretching so far that it looked like a continent and 'was most frightful to behold.' For nearly a month they made repeated attempts to penetrate the Kara Sea and continue their voyage eastward, but with little success. Some encouragement came from the Samoyeds, who told them that after five days sailing easterly they would round a point and beyond it a great sea stretched to the south-east. This information agreed with their own theories but, 'the weather being mistie, melancholy and snowie,' they made no progress. The commanders bickered and argued, frustrated by their inability to get around or through the ice. Barents, particularly, tried desperately to make some headway but it was impossible.

On 6 September a depressing incident further discouraged the men already dismayed by endless ice. A party was sent ashore on States Island to seek for rock crystal and as two of the men were resting

a great leane white beare came sodainly stealing out, and caught one of them fast by the necke, who not knowing what it was . . . cried out . . . Who is that that pulles me so by the necke? Wherewith the other, that lay not farre from him, lifted up his head to see who it was, and perceiving it to be a monsterous beare, cryed and sayd, Oh mate, it is a beare! and therwith presently rose up and ran away.

The beare at the first faling upon the man, bit his head in sunder, and suckt out his blood, wherewith the rest of the men that were on land, being about 20 in number, ran presently thither, either to save the man, or else to drive the beare from the dead body; and having charged their peeces and bent their pikes, set upon her, that still was devouring the man, but perceiving them to come towards her, fiercely and cruelly ran at them, and gat another of them out from the companie, which she tare in peeces, wherewith all the rest ran away.

On board Barents's ship 'we beheld the cruell spectacle of our two dead men, that had beene so cruelly killed and torne in pieces by the beare.' A landing party was quickly armed to go to the rescue and kill the animal, but 'the beare still [went on] devouring her prey, not once fearing the number of our men, and yet they were thirtie at the least.' Thereupon three of the bravest went forward and shot at the bear and missed. Then one went closer and shot her between the eyes

> and yet shee held the man faste by the necke, and lifted up her head, with the man in her mouth, but shee beganne somewhat to stagger; wherewith the purser and a Scotishman drew out their courtlaxes (cutlasses), and stroke at her so hard that their courtlaxes burst, and yet she would not leave the man. At last William Geysen went to them, and with all his might stroke the beare upon the snowt with his peece, at which time the beare fell to the ground, making a great noyse, and William Geysen leaping upon her cut her throat.[5]

The next day they buried their dead, skinned the bear that they might take the skin to Amsterdam, and departed.

By 15 September the prospects of further exploration were hopeless. The commanders met together in Nay's cabin and after prolonged discussion agreed to sign a protest drawn up by Linschoten stating that they had done all that was humanly possible to accomplish their mission without success and that now, for the safety of their ships, crews, and cargoes, they should sail homeward. The ships all arrived in Holland at different times between late October and mid-November, and thus the most elaborate and expensive expedition failed in its objective and made no new discoveries.

Although the States General lost its enthusiasm for further expeditions, it offered a handsome reward for the success of any privately financed venture. The undaunted merchants of Amsterdam fitted out two ships under the command of Jan Corneliszoon Rijp and Jacob van Heemskerck, who acted as supercargo, with William Barents again as chief pilot. Great care was taken in selecting the crew; unmarried men receiving preference to prevent the temptation of returning to wives and children prematurely. Leaving Amsterdam 10 May 1596, they attempted to sail through the Vlie on the thirteenth but were beaten back by head winds, and Rijp's ship ran aground. She was gotten off without serious injury and they finally cleared the Vlie five days later.

The first day of June they reached the latitude where there was no night, and on the fourth saw a spectacular parhelia in the sky. During this part of the voyage Rijp and Barents were in continuous disagreement over the course sailed; Barents maintained that they were too far to the westward, and Rijp claimed that if they did not go to the west, the previous voyages showed they would fall in with impenetrable ice. Barents was unconvinced and wished to try again close inshore around the northern end of Novaya Zemlya, but Rijp had his way. Neither cared about attempting the passages by Vaygach again. On 5 June they mistook their first floating ice for swans, an illusion swiftly dissipated. By the next day they could not make headway through it. Later the ice opened up and they sailed between two beautiful island-like bergs with grass-green water in between.

Four days later an island about twenty miles long was discovered. On landing the next day they gathered birds' eggs and nearly broke their necks sliding down a high snow covered hill. A name for the new island became obvious when on

> The 12 of June in the morning, wee saw a white beare, which wee rowed after with our boate, thinking to cast a roape about her necke; but when we were neere her, shee was so great that we durst not doe it, but rowed backe again to our shippe to fetch more men and our armes, and so made to her againe with muskets, hargubushes, halbertes, and hatchets, John Cornellysons men comming also with their boate to helpe us. And so beeing well furnished of men and weapons, we rowed with both our boates unto the beare, and fought with her while four glasses were runne out [two hours], for our weapons could doe her little hurt; and amongst the rest of the blowes that we gave her, one of our men stroke her into the backe with an axe, which stucke fast in her backe, and yet she swomme away with it;

but wee rowed after her, and at last wee cut her head in sunder with an axe, wherewith she dyed; and then we brought her into John Cornelysons shippe, where wee fleased her, and found her skinne to be twelve foote long: which done, wee eate some of her flesh; but wee brookt it not well. This island wee called the Beare Island.[6]

And so it is called to this day, but for many years the English referred to it as Cherie Island in honor of Sir Francis Cherie who sent Stephen Bennet to the north in 1603 to trade and discover.

Sailing northerly they saw drifting toward them a dead whale, 'that stouncke mounsterously; and on it there sate a great number of sea meawes.' Continuing through cold mist amidst unseen ice, they discovered Spitsbergen on 19 June. On the western shores of the island they found the nesting grounds of the barnacle goose, whose eggs, until then people had thought grew in Scotland on trees overhanging the ocean, dropped into the water and developed into young geese. Thus was disproved one of the most extraordinary folktales in natural history, believed by even the most serious people until that time.* The explorations continued until 29 June when both ships sailed back to Bear Island.

The discovery of Spitsbergen, which was thought to be a part of Greenland for many years thereafter, was the greatest accomplishment, but far from the climax, of this voyage. After the return to Bear Island on 1 July Rijp and Barents decided to separate; the former returning for further explorations to Spitsbergen, while Barents sailed for Novaya Zemlya, where he arrived over two weeks later, hoping to round its northern end, find the sea free of ice, and sail on to China.

* In the Middle Ages there was considerable dispute as to whether fowl were fish or flesh. Most of the common people and many churchmen contended that fowl were fish and therefore could be eaten on fast days. Since geese were the commonest food fowl, the myth may have arisen to help justify eating them as fish.

He spent the next month working against ice and head winds, and arrived at the Orange Islands 15 August after nearly losing his ship when a berg to which they were moored 'with one great brake . . . burst into foure hundred pieces at the least.' Barents achieved his first objective in rounding the northern tip of Novaya Zemlya, but he was unable to force his ship farther eastward. On the twenty-fifth, the situation hopeless, they decided to return to Holland. But they had waited too long, for the Arctic clutched them firmly.

With time running out, the courageous and tough-minded Dutchmen ironically named their bay prison Ice Haven, and methodically set about making plans for an Arctic wintering. In early September a howling northeast snowstorm drove the ship ever higher up on the ice which 'burst and crakt with great force.' They wondered that the ship could withstand such pressure for De Veer says 'that there drifted icebergs by us, as big as the salt mountains of Spain,' and they soon decided to build a house to winter in rather than trust themselves to the ice-bound vessel. With the ice solidly closed in, the ship, her rudder torn away and thrust up onto heavy ground ice, 'We were forced,' says Gerrit De Veer, 'in great cold, povertie, miserie and griefe, to stay all that winter.'

Northern Novaya Zemlya is a treeless land, but luckily the men located an immense store of driftwood which provided them with logs for house construction and fuel in abundance for the long cold months ahead. Their most skilled workman, the ship's carpenter, died but, nevertheless, by combining drift logs with planks and timbers ripped from the ship, a solid square house slowly rose in the chill wilderness. In the center of the roof was a wooden chimney, and inside bunks were built for each man. There were days so bitter that work stopped and the men could only huddle around the shipboard fire. Throughout the construction, the moving of stores from ship to house, and the eight-mile journeys to accumulate the vast, vital piles of firewood, they were smitten by frequent storms while severe wind and dreadful cold cut them to the marrow. Constantly harassed by silent, hunting polar bears, the men worked in groups with their weapons ready. That the Dutchmen's hopes for eventual escape were high is shown in the fate of one prowling polar bear: for 'we tooke the dead beare, and ript her belly open; and taking out her guts we set her upon her forefeet, so that she might freeze as she stood, intending to carry her with us into Holland.'

The men suffered greatly from the smoke below decks in the ship where they were forced to remain much of the time to keep warm, so half of them moved into the house about the middle of October before the interior was finished and the others followed near the end of the month when all was completed and supplies, arms, and other necessities were transferred. Two small, open boats with all their gear were brought near the building as insurance against the loss of the vessel during the winter.

By early November the sun had disappeared for, although it still rose above the horizon, the weather was so thick it could not be seen. As the sun vanished so did the cruel bears. Their place was taken by little white foxes, which became an important food supply. They were trapped and eaten all winter and their skins were made into warm caps. The entire party nearly died in December when, because of the extreme cold, it was decided to make a fire of coal which had been brought from the ship and to stop up the chimney and every crack around the doors. So they all went to sleep in great comfort but almost suffocated from coal gas fumes and barely managed to open the doors and clear the chimney in time.

In spite of their hardships their spirit and courage remained high and their health remarkably good, and at one point they amused themselves by playing golf on the ice. At times they barely kept from freezing. Bear-fat lamps lighted the room, their clock froze up, and they regularly turned an hour glass thereafter. But they bathed regularly by making a steam bath out of a wine cask. On Christmas Eve they opened the door and saw wide, clear water, but another northeaster came on and the ice shut in again. Christmas they lay in their house with a wild storm raging and listened to the little foxes run over the roof, and Twelfth Night was celebrated by drinking wine and making meal pancakes. The snow had piled up to such an extraordinary depth by 5 January, that one door was opened and a room dug in the snow like a vault which was used as a toilet and disposal place for garbage. By the twenty-first the foxes began to disappear and it was reckoned that the bears would soon be abroad again. On the twenty-fourth Gerrit De Veer, Jacob van Heemskerck, and another walked to the seaside and saw the sun once more, but when they returned to the house and told William Barents he would not believe them, for he reckoned it fourteen days too soon. There has been much discussion over this observation, which can only be accounted for by an unusual refraction, for the sun could not have been seen until 9 February.[7]

As the sun rose slowly higher the cold became more intense and the storms more frequent. For a time they abandoned any attempt to keep a door free, and left and entered the house through the chimney. On 15 April, a fair day, seven men went aboard the ship to inspect her condition. On the way meeting a bear and finding its den hole in the ice, one of the men crept in, 'but not too farre, for it was fearefull to behold.' They also saw that 'the ice was in such a wonderfull maner risen and piled up' that it was 'as if there had bin whole townes made of ice, with towres and bulwarkes round about them.'

In late May they began excavating their small boats from the snow and again had to be vigilant for the prowling bears. By 12 June the boats' gunnels had been raised and other alterations made for voyaging in the open ocean. The boats were dragged over a smoothed ice roadway to open water and preparations were made to depart in them, as the ship was still fast in the ice.

William Barents wrote a letter telling how they came out of Holland to sail to the kingdom of China, had been forced to winter here, and were now sailing in open boats, after dwelling ten months on Novaya Zemlya. The letter was placed in a powder horn and hung in the chimney.

The boats were stowed with provisions and on the fourteenth William Barents and a sailor who were ill were drawn on sleds, carried aboard, and they sailed off east northeast. Two days later they made the Orange Islands and van Heemskerck, who was in one boat, called to Barents in the other and asked how he did. He answered that he was quite well and hoped to be able to run again before he reached Vardö (Wardhouse). Then Barents said to De Veer, 'Gerrit, are we about the Ice Point? If we be, then I pray you lift me up, for I must view it once againe.'

It was hard going. Cold and wet from frequent head winds, sometimes dragging their boats over intervening ice to reach open water, they worked their way slowly southward along the coast. Claes Andrianson the ill sailor became worse, and on 20 June said he could not hold out. Thereupon William Barents, whom they had thought was less sick, said he did not think he would live much longer than Andrianson. Barents and De Veer then continued to talk about their course and finally Barents said, 'Gerrit, give me some drinke,' and no sooner had he quenched his thirst than he died, and the sailor died shortly thereafter. Barents's death saddened them, for not only was he their sole pilot but he more than any other had sustained their courage and guided them with his wisdom.

As they pushed on south, they supplemented their diet by raiding nesting colonies for birds and eggs. A month to the day after Barents's death they were surrounded and nearly capsized by a herd of walruses, but escaped with a strong wind. By 28 July they were nearing the southern end of Novaya Zemlya, and sailing past what was then known as St. Lawrence Bay they came upon two Russian vessels with about thirty men on shore

— the first people they had seen since separating from Rijp thirteen months before. The Russians were friendly, particularly as there was mutual recognition between some of them and van Heemskerck and De Veer who had entertained them on board ship at Vaygach on the previous voyage. The next day the Russians loaded their ships with barrels of train oil dug out of the shingle beach where it had been hidden, and set sail for Vaygach.

The courageous, scurvy-sick Dutch followed after in their open boats but soon lost sight of their new friends in the mist. Held up by the ice and strong winds, they were forced to land on a small island where they found an ample supply of spoon wort or scurvy grass, and they began to recover almost immediately after eating it. Although they were still hungry, weary, and in peril from sea and weather, the worst was over. Working their way along the coast, obtaining food from the increasing number of Russian fishermen, they crossed over the mouth of the White Sea and arrived at Kola 2 September, where they were taken rejoicing aboard the ship of the same Jan Corneliszoon Rijp from whom they had separated at Bear Island the year before. The two boats were set up as a monument at Kola and the men arrived in Holland 29 October. Two days later the twelve survivors of the original seventeen went to Amsterdam jauntily wearing the same clothes and the white fox-skin caps they had worn on Novaya Zemlya. Jacob van Heemskerck, the commander of the expedition, died heroically ten years later, on 25 April 1607, at Gibraltar, where the fleet he commanded defeated the Spanish, who never again could prevent the Dutch sailing anywhere on the high seas.

Two hundred and seventy-five years after William Barents and his party lived through the first successful Arctic wintering, Captain Elling Carlsen of Norway entered Ice Haven, 7 September 1871, and there found the fallen down house. He spent several days searching about, excavating a great many relics which were later purchased and exhibited at The Hague in a reconstruction of Barents's house. On 17 August 1875, another Norwegian, Captain M. Gundersen, a walrus hunter in the schooner *Regina* collected a few more relics at Ice Haven, including a manuscript Dutch translation of the narrative of the English expedition of Pet and Jackman. Charles L. W. Gardiner, an English yachtsman, recovered still more of Barents's relics the following year, including the letter signed by van Heemskerck and Barents which was still in the powder horn where they had left it.

The results of the three Dutch voyages, in which William Barents played a leading role, were insignificant in terms of their real objective. But their contributions to knowledge of the Arctic were enormous. Not only were Bear Island and Spitsbergen discovered, and the entire western shore and northern end of Novaya Zemlya explored, but knowledge of weather and ice conditions and the habits of northern birds and animals was greatly increased. The first successful Arctic wintering provided useful experiences for future explorers. But no longer was it necessary or desirable for the Dutch to seek further for a Passage by the inhospitable North, for the same year that van Heemskerck and his companions returned from their Ice Haven winter, Cornelis de Houtman, who had found his way around the Cape of Good Hope, brought the first Dutch fleet to the Netherlands from the East Indies. No more was the Northeast Passage seriously considered as a commercial route to China. As a piece of geographical exploration it thwarted men for many years, when it was finally forced by the resourceful Norwegian Arctic explorer A. E. Nordenskiöld in 1878, in his carefully planned, well-executed voyage in *Vega* during his circumnavigation of Europe and Asia.

7

All that Glitters

For forty years after the voyage of Richard Hore no further attempts were made to search for the Northwest
Passage. In other areas, however, the subjects of Elizabeth I had
been asserting England's maritime supremacy. Then simultaneously, as so often happens, several Englishmen were stirred
with the dream of finding a commercially profitable passage
by the Northwest to the Indies.

Among them was the young and ambitious Humphrey Gilbert. In the late summer of 1553 he had returned from service
with the Earl of Warwick at Le Havre where, it has been suggested, he first acquired his interest in America and in the
Northwest Passage. Two years after his return he petitioned the
Queen for a patent, offering to undertake 'the discoveringe of a
passage by the Northe, to go to Cataia, & all other the east partes
of the worlde' with the provision that he and his brothers Sir
John and Adrian would be given monopoly rights of trade
through the passage and a percentage of the customs on all goods
brought back that way for ninety-nine years. A similar docu-

ment presented a short time earlier by Anthony Jenkinson probably prompted Gilbert's petition.

Jenkinson, an indefatigable traveler in the service of the Muscovy Company, had made notable overland journeys to Persia in attempting to develop trade to China and the East Indies across Russia. He had failed to reach those lands, and his journeys had convinced him that the overland route was impracticable. His thoughts then turned to Stephen Borough's explorations to the Northeast, and he persuaded himself that a water route could be found in that direction. Jenkinson considered the existence of a passage by the northwest much less certain.

The two petitions were brought before the Queen, who, in a typical gesture, summoned both men before her in late 1565 or early 1566 to argue their respective views. D. B. Quinn neatly sums up the scene:

> Jenkinson asserted, firstly, that a fisherman of 'Tartaria' had told him he had sailed far to the east and believed that there was a passage. Gilbert replied that this was not expert evidence. Secondly, Jenkinson said that a unicorn's horn, which must have come from the Far East, had been found on the northern shores, of which Gilbert said that it could not have been a unicorn's horn and was probably the horn of an animal found in the north. The third point was that there was a continuous westward flowing current, which Gilbert said was due to rivers flowing into the north. The issues were trivial, but Gilbert, if he reports the discussion correctly, succeeded in displaying some geographical knowledge.[1]

The gifted Gilbert's arguments convinced Jenkinson that the Northwest offered the better chance, and the two men made a joint appeal for royal privileges. Then Jenkinson went to Russia, where he wrote to Sir William Cecil, later Lord Burghley, complaining that they had not heard about the petitions and asking Cecil to make sure that if the royal grants came — which they in fact never did — they should not be for Gilbert alone. Meanwhile the energetic partner of whom he was so distrustful wrote to his elder brother, Sir John Gilbert, the now famous letter, 'A discourse of a discoverie for a new passage to Cataia,' which circulated in manuscript but was not published until ten years later.[2]

Some of Gilbert's arguments in his discourse were similar to those used by Cabot and Thorne. He pointed out, for instance, the benefits of direct trade with the Far East, the possibility of trade with the American Indians, the by-passing of Spanish and Portuguese enterprises, and the advantages of establishing a station as a halfway point near the west coast of North America 'about Sierra Nevada.' He also was one of the first Englishmen to suggest colonizing America for its own sake. It was this idea too that eventually became his major concern; he seems to have given up the notion of exploring for the Northwest Passage personally, although still interested in the possibility of its usefulness.

After writing his 'discourse' Gilbert left England to fight in the Irish wars, but returned in December to present a new petition to the Queen. He was now willing to undertake discovering the Passage alone under the auspices of the Muscovy Company, provided he had certain large benefits and one-tenth of all the lands discovered. The Company offered to back him if he would conform to their regulations. The Spanish Ambassador, getting wind of Gilbert's proposal, wrote Philip II of these plans which, if successful, might be prejudicial to Spanish commerce. Fortunately, perhaps, for Spain, Gilbert would not accept the terms of the Muscovy Company and returned to Irish service, where he remained until 1570.

No one knows how much Humphrey Gilbert's letter influenced others. The idea of renewing the attempt at the Northwest was currently being discussed in political and commercial as well as in academic circles. One of its enthusiasts was Captain Martin Frobisher.

Born about 1539 in Doncaster (Yorkshire), the fourth of five children, he was schooled and cared for by his uncle, Sir John York, a London merchant and Master of the Mint. At fifteen he was sent to the Guinea coast of Africa and was one of the few survivors of a fever that decimated the crew. Cargoes of pepper and gold brought back from Benin assured the financial success of the venture. So began the career which kept the Yorkshireman at sea for the rest of his life in varied activities, from the Newcastle coal trade to the capture of Spanish ships and flagrant piracy in the English Channel. Arrested for piratical acts, he was never tried and was released after a short imprisonment. In all of his activities he seems always to have had some sort of commmission from the Queen or a foreign monarch. Frobisher, apparently through his uncle, was highly regarded at Court and widely acquainted with the wealthy merchants. In 1572 Elizabeth I forbade her subjects to accept foreign commissions, and Frobisher probably gave up his sea-roving at that time, but before then he paid little attention to the ownership or nationality of the ships he captured. On one of his Guinea voyages he had heard from the Portuguese of the existence of a Northwest Passage and the theory nagged at him for many years. When Frobisher finally offered to lead an attempt at such a passage, the time was obviously right. He aroused prompt and enthusiastic support at Court, among the merchants, and with other navigators experienced in northern travels. Among his influential supporters were Lord Burghley, Treasurer of England, the Secretary of State Sir Francis Walsingham, Robert Dudley Earl of Leicester, the Earl and Countess of Warwick, and the Queen herself.

In December 1574, Elizabeth I gave Frobisher a letter to the Muscovy Company, which had sole rights to the use of a northern passage east or west. Many years having elapsed since they had attempted to find such a route, they were instructed to license Frobisher to do so. The Company refused. Thereupon the Queen ordered them either to undertake it themselves or to give Frobisher permission. In short, they could either fish or cut bait. At the time the Director of the Company was Michael Lok, an acquaintance of Frobisher's though some seven years his senior. Besides being a wealthy and prominent merchant, he had practical experience in navigation and was a student of geography. He had voyaged to the Levant as a ship's captain, had traveled widely throughout Europe, and spoke several languages. Like many of his merchant contemporaries he had resided in Spain and Portugal for several years and marveled at the riches coming into the ports of those countries. Although himself an enthusiastic believer in the possibilities of the Northwest Passage, his colleagues were not. So it was that the Privy Council in February 1575 gave permission to Frobisher, Lok, and a group of other merchants and adventurers.

Lok and Frobisher immediately and energetically set about raising funds and seeking advice. Practical information was acquired from the most experienced Arctic explorer of the time, Stephen Borough. His brother William Borough, now Comptroller of Her Majesty's Navy, who also had sailed to the Northeast, drew up a chart with rhumb lines on which to plot new discoveries. He superintended the outfitting of the ships. Dr. John Dee, official geographical and mathematical adviser to the Muscovy Company since the death of Sebastian Cabot, wrote out advanced instructions for Frobisher and his sailing master Captain Christopher Hall on 'the Use of Instruments of Navigation' and 'in the Rules of Geometry and Cosmography.' For geographical information they consulted Richard Willis, the historian and Richard Eden's literary executor, who had translated and published in 1553 Peter Martyr's *Decades of the Newe Worlde,* as well as Richard Hakluyt of the Middle Temple. It

was doubtless to obtain further information that George Gascoigne, a poet and relative of Martin Frobisher, called on Sir
Humphrey Gilbert in 1576.

He came away with the manuscript of Gilbert's 'discourse'
which he pubished in April the same year without the writer's
consent. It was essentially the same manuscript that had been
circulating for the previous decade with a few additions — the
most important being a curious story which Gilbert heard from
a Spaniard named Salvaterra in Ireland in 1568. Salvaterra
claimed that eight years before, Friar Andro Urdaneta of Mexico had shown him 'a Sea Carde' of a voyage he had taken from
the Pacific through the Northwest Passage to Germany. He had
shown this chart to the King of Portugal who had advised him
not to publish it as it would aid the English. On this tenuous evidence of the existence of an inter-ocean strait Salvaterra offered
to accompany Gilbert on a voyage to find it. There was, of
course, some confusion, as in 1560–61 Urdaneta was explaining
to Philip II that certain Frenchmen had discovered the Passage
through America at 27° N. coming into the Pacific between
40° and 50° N., and in 1565 Urdaneta made a voyage to the
Philippines from where he returned to Spain via Central America the following year. Whether it was intentional or not, the
publication of Gilbert's discourse vivified interest in Frobisher's
projected voyage. Through conversation and gossip Frobisher
and Lok had stimulated enormous enthusiasm and secured
many informal and verbal pledges to help in the venture.

The Muscovy Company, upon the Queen's orders, neither
helped nor hindered. The Russian trade was profitable, so they
saw no need to venture capital in further attempts to reach
richer regions by a most precarious and hitherto unproved
route. Lok would have benefited had he heeded the advice of
his colleagues for, when after several months only £875 had
actually been raised, he pledged himself to underwrite all expenses of the expedition beyond that amount.[3] He believed

that the East Indies could be reached in this way, and if no Passage was found the voyage would pay off in new fishing and whaling grounds.

Two barks named for the Archangels, the newly built twenty-ton *Gabriel* and the twenty-five ton *Michael,* were procured. A pinnace of about seven tons was to sail with the two vessels for the purpose of surveying uncharted waters and exploring in the vicinity of new coasts. (It may be noted that the Pilgrim's *Mayflower* alone had nearly four times the combined tonnage of Frobisher's ships.) Small though the barks might be, they were well equipped, supplied, and victualed. The medicine chest held every drug then available. The extremely interesting list of charts, maps, and nautical instruments shows how abundantly the scientific and navigational needs of the expedition were provided for. Dr. Dee had done his work well. There were, for instance, twenty compasses and eighteen hour glasses, both cross staff and astrolabe were provided, and there was a meridian compass for finding the variations of the Pole, and other instruments.[4] Most important, because of the influence it had on the geographical reports of the expedition, was the 'mappe universal,' the latest and best available of the great Flemish geographer Gerard Kaufmann, inventor of the map projection (later systematized by Edward Wright the mathematician) which bears his more familiar name, Mercator. He was the most respected man in his field and a close personal friend of John Dee's.

Without showing the influence of his cartographical aids the geographical results of the Frobisher expeditions cannot be understood. Mercator's map unfortunately included the new features of an earlier work known as 'the Zeno map.' Briefly, the story of the Zeno map is this. The Zeni was one of the noble and powerful families of Venice for generations. In December 1558 a small book consisting of three parts was compiled by Nicolo Zeno and published in that city. The first two parts, corroborated from other sources and substantially correct, tell of the travels of Caterino Zeno, Venetian Ambassador to Persia in 1471–3. It is the third section that created a sensation in geographical circles throughout Europe. In it Nicolo Zeno included fragments of letters and documents allegedly written by his ancestors, the brothers Nicolo and Antonio Zeno, concerning their voyages in the service of a northern chieftain in the late fourteenth century. This section was accompanied by their map drawn in 1380, which shows Greenland, Iceland, sections of North America named Estotiland and Drogeo, and a large island called Frisland south of Iceland. Greenland was shown not only much farther north than it actually is, but connected with Europe and running in a more eastward and westward direction, due to the extreme compass variation in the northwestern Atlantic which, unless taken into account, hopelessly distorts the geography. Frisland is shown in the latitude of southern Greenland but about 20° farther east.[5] Nicolo Zeno, the younger, claimed that these and many more documents had always been in his family, but that as a child, not knowing their worth, he had destroyed them. Now he printed such fragments as survived, filling in what he could remember of the pieces destroyed. The truthfulness of the account was not questioned and the accompanying *Carta da Navegar* was accepted as genuine by the two leading cartographers of the last half of the sixteenth century — Gerard Kaufmann and Abraham Ortelius. By placing Frisland on their maps they created a confusion in the geography of the North Atlantic that lasted for about two hundred years, and some of the remnants persisted even into the last century. Scholars have disputed the genuineness of the Zeno narratives and chart. It is now thought that there is some basis of fact, but that Nicolo the compiler, through ignorance or chicanery, so muddled fact and fiction that they are difficult to separate.[6]

Frobisher was ready for sea at Ratcliffe by 7 June 1576. Christopher Hall, an excellent pilot, was sailing master of *Gabriel,*

and Owen Griffyn commanded *Michael*. The entire company
consisted of thirty-five men. Among them as purser sailed
Nicholas Chancellor, son of Richard, who had not followed
his father's maritime career but had been sent to Russia as an
apprentice accountant for the Muscovy Company. As they
dropped down the river the pinnace smashed her bowsprit and
foremast in a collision with an anchored ship. They stopped at
Deptford for repairs, and shortly after noon the next day at
Greenwich, where Frobisher went ashore to take his leave of
the Queen. The gallant fleet proceeded down the Thames and
on 12 June passed Gravesend, only to be forced by headwinds
into Harwich. After several days they got clear of the coast but
Michael was leaking so badly that they wisely put into the Shetlands on the twenty-sixth to correct the nuisance and to fill the
water casks. While there, Frobisher and Captain Hall wrote Dr.
Dee that some of his careful instructions were mathematically
over their heads.[7] Pushing westward from the Shetlands on 11
July they saw rising to the west northwest the coast of Greenland near Cape Farewell 'like pinnacles of steeples, and all
covered with snow.' This they thought was Frisland as the latitude of 61° was correct according to their chart. Frobisher
wanted to land but was prevented by icebergs driving along the
coast and thick fog rolling in from the sea.

Two days later they were hit by a furious tempest which nearly
ended the voyage then and there. *Gabriel* was thrown on her
beam ends and, with the crew panic-stricken, Frobisher himself
worked his way forward and took the pressure off her by releas-
ing the foresail halliard. The foreyard broke and the ship was
lightened further by the loss of the main topmast. The mizzenmast too was cut away. It took all Frobisher's magnificent lead-
ership to prevent the terrified crew from cutting away the
mainmast as well. The ship righted herself, but with the open
well deck full of water she wallowed, no longer answering her
helm. Driving before the furious wind for a day until it abated,

Gabriel weathered the storm, but the pinnace and her four men were lost. This sample of North Atlantic weather was too much for Owen Griffyn who took *Michael* back to England, where he reported that Frobisher was lost.

Far from having foundered, Frobisher was pushing his battered craft westward to what he and Hall believed to be the coast of Labrador, where they raised a prominent headland 'of a marvelous great height' which they named Queen Elizabeth's Foreland. Actually it was Resolution Island, across the mouth of Hudson Strait from Cape Chidley. They needed repairs. Ice encumbered the coast; for days they beat up and down seeking an anchorage. At last the ice disappeared, and on the first land they reached Hall caulked the ship and made other repairs. A broad opening into the land with a good channel was entered 11 August. As they sailed westward for sixty leagues they believed they had found the Passage. Frobisher was sure that he had a long extension of Asia on his right hand and North America on his left, that the sea was open to Cathay, and that he was justified in following the precedent of Magellan at the other end of America by naming his channel Frobisher Strait.

His hopes high, Frobisher landed to make observations and to get a view of the straits westward. Large deer fled before him as he made his way to the top of a high hill and saw what appeared to be a school of porpoises or seals in the distance. As they swam closer, to his astonishment the creatures turned out to be strange little men 'in small boates made of leather.' For the first time the English had encountered Eskimos in their kayaks. Fascinated, they watched the skillful maneuvers until they realized that the natives were heading for their boat and were about to cut them off.[8] Hurrying to the boat, they arrived just in time to prevent this disaster. Later in the day Hall again went ashore where the Eskimos had landed, gave each of them a needle, and persuaded one man to come on board ship by leaving one of the crew as hostage. After a meal of ship's meat and wine, which the Eskimo did not like much, he was returned to his companions. The good treatment he had received enticed nineteen others — the entire party — to come aboard. After friendly relations were established and confidence gained on both sides, the Eskimos brought meat and fish to the ship and shocked the English by eating it raw. They eagerly exchanged bear and seal skins for looking glasses and other trinkets, and imitating the sailors, climbed about the rigging, did acrobatics and stunts of their own, and thoroughly enjoyed themselves. Hall noted that the women had blue marks on their faces and that they looked like Tartars — another proof that Asia was near.

Frobisher and Hall landed again the next day, 20 August, to make further investigation. From the hilltop Frobisher had seen afar off two headlands which he believed marked the western end of his Strait. Because of the strong tides running 'and for many other good reasons they judged the open water beyond the headlands to be the West Sea, whereby to pass to Cathay and to the East India. And on this syde of the sayd headlands they saw many islands not far asonder.' [9] Nearer at hand they also saw the ruins of twelve old stone houses with large quantities of whale bones lying about. They judged the buildings to be work houses, an indication that European whalers had been there, and that this was a station for trying out blubber. In a valley not far away they came upon three skin houses and a skin boat (*umiak*) full of men nearby. At the point of a partisan Frobisher forced one of the Eskimos to take him 'into their houses and there saw their manner of foode and lyfe, which is very strange and beastly.'

Anxious to continue on to Cathay, Frobisher bargained with an Eskimo to pilot him through the straits. After payment of a bell and a knife, one of the natives apparently agreed and indicated it would take two days. If he at all comprehended the arrangement he must have meant it would take that long to reach the end of the Bay. Frobisher brought his new pilot aboard ship to look around and later in the day ordered five of the crew to set him ashore, cautioning them not to land but to return immediately to the ship. The sailors, however, had smuggled some trade goods along and, after landing their guest, pulled around a point where they could not be seen from the vessel. Frobisher saw the boat reappear beyond the point with only two men in it and signaled for them to pick up the other three and return at once. Again the boat vanished behind the point and from that moment neither boat nor men were ever seen.

The next morning they sailed up and down as near the shore as possible blowing a trumpet and firing a gun but nothing was seen. The following day they continued the search and finally saw fourteen native boats approaching, one with twenty men. Their ship was made ready for attack with boarding canvas set up and a cannon ready. These precautions were unnecessary for the Eskimos would not come near the ship, but Frobisher enticed one man by holding out a bell toward him as an offering. As he came closer, the Admiral tossed it short into the water. The Eskimo was greatly agitated at this loss, and as Frobisher held out a second bell he came in close and reached for it. As he did so, Frobisher, exhibiting his tremendous strength, grabbed him by the wrists and lifted him, kayak and all, onto the deck. The infuriated native bit off his own tongue but lived in spite of it; his companions fled. For the next four days they hung around, hoping to be able to exchange their hostage for the sailors but nothing more was seen of the Eskimos.

Handicapped by the loss of their only boat and five seamen, it was now impossible to continue the exploration of the straits which they were sure would lead through to the South Sea. By 1 September they again sighted Frisland (Greenland) and coasted it for six days. On the seventh they were hit by another severe storm and nearly lost a man overboard. He clung to the foresheet and held on until Frobisher himself hauled him to safety. On 1 October they put into Yarmouth, and the next day

anchored at Harwich to refresh their sick and weak men. On
the ninth *Gabriel* arrived at London, receiving a joyful welcome.
Their strange man and his boat 'was such a wonder onto the
whole city . . . as seemed never to have happened the like great
matter to any man's knowledge.' It was noted that his legs were
shorter in proportion to his body than a white man's, that he
was in 'countenance sullen or churlish and sharp withall' which
is not to be wondered at, and he was judged, as Hall had opined,
to be of the 'Tartar nation.' The unfortunate Eskimo did not live
long for he caught a cold at sea and died shortly after arriving
in England.

Questions from friends and backers poured in. After they had
heard the tales and marveled at the adventures they wished to
see what had been brought back from the new country. The
only thing Frobisher could produce was a piece of black stone
which one of the adventurers' wives was inspired to throw in
the fire where it seemed to burn; so she took it out and quenched
the flames with vinegar and the stone 'glistened with a bright
Marquesset of golde.' The glistening properties of the sample
stone raised hopes of opportunities in the straits greater, perhaps, than those of the Indies. Lok took the ore to three different reliable London assayers, each of whom told him the stone
contained no gold. But Lok became obstinate about it. He had
made up his mind that the ore was gold and he eventually
found in London an Italian assayer named John Baptista
Agnello, who told him what he wanted to hear. Agnello had
Lok bring him more samples of the ore three different times
and after each occasion produced small amounts of gold powder
which he said he obtained from the ore. Lok asked him how
he could do it when the Government assayers had failed and
Agnello cunningly replied, 'It is necessary to know how to flat-
ter nature.' [10] Lok reported these results to the Queen and her
Secretary of State, Sir Francis Walsingham, but cautiously did
not mention it to Frobisher. Walsingham was suspicious and

remarked that alchemists had tried these things on the Queen before. He took samples and had his suspicions confirmed by reliable assayers.

It seems inconceivable that in the face of the best scientific opinion of his day Lok could be so taken in and deceived. However, he was convinced and asked the Queen to allow him to send a ship for more ore at his own expense. He already had had to make up a deficit of more than £738 in wages and other expenses of the first expedition. But with the talk of gold in the air, there was no difficulty getting Frobisher and the other adventurers to back another venture; with discoverers' rights in the productive gold mine they expected not only to offset the losses of the first trip but to gain vast profits.

On 17 March 1577 the Crown granted a charter to Lok, Frobisher, and their group to form the Cathay Company. Lok was appointed Governor of the Company for life, and Frobisher the High Admiral. The Queen herself contributed £1000 and the two-hundred-ton ship *Aid*. *Gabriel* and *Michael* were fitted out to accompany the larger ship. The Company planned to send one hundred and twenty men, including thirty miners as well as assayers, carpenters, and other craftsmen. Six criminals, who might thus earn their freedom, were to be set ashore on Frisland to study the people and country; they would be picked up on the return voyage. The original purpose was not forgotten for, after landing the miners and other workmen and leaving *Aid* to be loaded with ore, Frobisher was authorized to take one of the smaller vessels and explore the straits westward for not more than a hundred leagues from his westernmost point of the first voyage. Some men were to be left to winter at Frobisher Strait and, if there was not sufficient ore for mining, Frobisher could use his discretion about sailing on to Cathay with the two small ships and sending *Aid* back to England.

In the case of the first voyage the only account we have by a participant is the log of Christopher Hall. For the second voyage we have two good narratives, that of George Best and one by Dionyse Settle, a gentleman on the trip. Best, who was Frobisher's lieutenant and historian of three voyages, was killed in a duel some six or seven years later by Oliver St. John, afterwards Viscount Grandison. Others with Frobisher on *Aid* included his former master Christopher Hall and, as mate, Charles Jackman who later disappeared on Pet's homeward voyage. *Gabriel* was commanded by Captain Edward Fenton and *Michael* by Captain Gilbert Yorke, a kinsman of Frobisher.

On Whitsunday, 26 May 1577, the three ships dropped down the river from Blackwall to Gravesend and two days later put into Harwich. There they received orders to discharge any men above one hundred and twenty; fourteen men, including the criminals, were put ashore. The expedition arrived 7 June at the Orkneys, where the islanders fled from their cottages in fear that they were about to be attacked by pirates. The next day the ships headed west with 'a merrie winde.' A few days later they fell in with three English fishermen bound home from Iceland and sent letters home by them. For the next twenty-six days they sailed and saw 'many monsterous Fishe, and strange Fowle,' drift wood, and 'many Great fir trees floating in the sea.' The fourth of July they sighted Greenland, as before guarded by huge islands of ice, and in the approximate position of Frisland on the Zeno map. They noticed that the icebergs were fresh and concluded correctly that it was not sea ice, although this also freshens as it ages. While becalmed they cast over an unbaited hook and caught a halibut large enough to feed the entire company. After trying unsuccessfully for four days to land on Greenland, a wind arose and enabled them to leave that foggy coast. On 16 July, having weathered a storm that took the topmasts off *Michael,* they sighted Queen Elizabeth's Foreland, North Foreland or Hall's Island, and the entrance to Frobisher Strait. That they hit their goal speaks well for their navigation.

Frobisher lost no time getting about his business, for two days later the two assayers were put ashore on the small island where he had picked up the first ore. No ore could be found there but quantities were located on other islands. Going a couple of miles inland into the barren, rugged, still partly snow-hidden wilderness, the Admiral and his party ascended the highest nearby hill where they solemnly sounded a trumpet, knelt and prayed, and then built a cross of stones and named the eminence Mount Warwick in honor of Lord Ambrose Dudley, Earl of Warwick. No sooner had they left the mount than it was occupied by Eskimos waving a flag, 'mowing like Bulls,' and apparently wanting to establish communication with their visitors. The English mooed right back at them and blew their trumpets, which so delighted the natives that they laughed, skipped, danced, and greatly rejoiced. To open trading negotiations two men from each party met on neutral ground, where pins and needles were exchanged for bow cases, but further invitations were mutually declined.

Frobisher and Hall thought to take a hostage and perhaps obtain information concerning the five missing men of the previous year. Meeting two of the bolder Eskimos unarmed, a few trifles were exchanged and the English then attempted to seize the two men. But the Eskimos were too quick for them and ran off with the Admiral and master in hot pursuit. When the natives reached their weapons hidden behind a rock Frobisher and Hall had to flee, and even then an aboriginal arrow hit Frobisher ignominiously in the backside. The wound was slight and face was somewhat regained by a Cornishman, 'a good footeman,' who overtook one Eskimo whose arrows were spent, and being also a good wrestler 'shewed hys companion such a Cornish tricke, that he made his sides ake agaist the grounde for a moneth after.' He captured the native alive and brought him back to the ship.

While Frobisher and his party were thus occcupied ashore

the cook overheated the galley stove while a workman was fix-
ing its chimney and set *Aid* on fire. The blaze was extinguished
with difficulty. As if this were not enough, all three ships nearly
foundered in a sudden storm and heavy ice that night while
Frobisher and Hall were still ashore, and were saved only by
the magnificent seamanship of the mates and master gunner.

The next few days were spent trying to find a safe anchorage.
As they sailed back and forth seeking harbors and exploring
the islands and countryside along both shores of the 'strait' for
ore, numerous geographical features were named. The beach
wrack of one small island produced a dead narwhal. The tip of
its tusk was broken off revealing a hollow interior which
prompted a scientific experiment. Spiders were placed inside
the hollow horn where they died at once, proving conclusively
to the Elizabethan seamen that the creature was a true sea unicorn, for the unicorn's horn was a powerful antidote for all
poisons, and all spiders were considered poisonous.

Eager to load his ships, Frobisher eventually located a good
anchorage hard by a sufficient store of ore on 29 July. But the ice
forced him out, cutting the cable of *Gabriel* and nearly driving
her ashore, where almost twenty tons of ore had to be abandoned as the barks pulled farther up the sound to a safer anchorage. On a small island they found an Eskimo tomb containing a human skeleton and, beneath a stone, a cache of fish,
sleds, bridles, kettles, skins, bone knives, and other objects. Their
prisoner demonstrated how dogs were harnessed and indicated
that they had a large variety of dogs for pulling sleds and a
small fat kind for eating.

Finally, on the twenty-ninth, under Countess of Warwick
Island, a safe harbor was found where there was ample ore
gleaming golden in the pale, northern sunlight. The miners
were set to work and Frobisher, discovering houses and inhabitants on the nearby mainland, set out to get news of his five lost
men. The natives fled and the officers examined the abandoned

tents, finding several garments and shoes which had belonged to the lost Englishmen. Thus encouraged, they left a note in the tent, but no other sign of the lost sailors was ever found.

One pitched battle was fought with the Eskimos at a place named Bloody Point, where half a dozen natives were killed and one of the Englishmen wounded. The Eskimos when wounded, rather than be captured, leapt from cliffs into the sea. The only ones taken were two women — one of whom was young with a baby, and the other so old, deformed, and ugly that they removed her boots to see if she were cloven hooved. Although she was not, they decided not to take any chances, and she was released. The younger woman with her child was held to provide companionship for the Eskimo taken earlier, and it was considered doubtful if one would have survived the voyage to England without the other.

Frobisher, from his continual meetings with the natives, understood that some of his men were still alive and wrote them another letter, waiting three days for the return of the Eskimo messenger who was to deliver it. No contact was made. Thus the time he had intended to spend exploring the Strait was taken up by these humanitarian efforts.

A full cargo, two hundred tons of ore which Jonas Shutz — a German assayer friend of Agnello's brought along as the expert — said was rich, was put aboard 20 August. Everyone was exhausted, ice was now beginning to make, and it was judged wise not to tarry longer. On the twenty-third the little fleet set sail homeward with a fair west wind. Six days later they ran into a heavy northeaster and, although life lines were strung along both sides of the vessel, young William Smith, master of *Gabriel,* and the boatswain were swept overboard the following day, at the height of the storm. The boatswain caught hold of a line and was pulled back aboard but he lost his grip on Smith's hand which he had managed to grasp and the master drowned. Extraordinarily enough, Smith, who was in good spirits that morning, told his captain that the night before he had dreamed that he and the boatswain were swept overboard and that the boatswain had him by the hand but could not hold on.

During the calm following the storm it was discovered that the rudder of *Aid* was broken in two and barely hanging in place. Twelve hardy men working in pairs were sent overboard into the icy water to strengthen it. Luckily, the ocean stayed calm. The repairs got them across the Atlantic, but the rudder was still giving trouble and the ship steered badly when they made the open road of Padstow in Cornwall. They limped into Milford Haven 23 September. So pleased was Elizabeth I with Frobisher that he was eagerly received at Court, entertained and complimented, and awarded £100 by the Queen. She named his newly discovered land south of the Frobisher Strait *Meta Incognita,* the Unknown Goal.

Everyone was encouraged by this second voyage. The Eskimos attracted a great deal of attention although they died within a month or so. The Company members were asked to pay the mariners' wages and, as after the first voyage, Michael Lok paid the largest share. But no one seemed worried for tests on the ore indicated that a profit of five pounds a ton might be realized. There was also increased hope that the ultimate passage to Cathay would be found. The ore was placed under quadruple locks in Bristol Castle and the Tower of London. On the strength of the reports by Agnello it was not difficult to persuade the adventurers to finance a new expedition or to attract new investors to the Cathay Company. With all this enthusiasm based on two hundred tons of rock, a large and elaborately equipped expedition was formed under the direct supervision of the Crown. Ten times as much ore would be brought back, and a colony established to continue working the mines, study the climate and country, and, perhaps, act as a base for pushing on through the passage to the Pacific.

A fleet of fifteen vessels was assembled with quantities of supplies. One hundred and twenty colonists were on board with a fort built in sections to be assembled for their wintering.* Carpenters, miners, smelters, soldiers were assembled. The experienced men and officers of the previous voyages were retained. The ships ranged in size from the four-hundred-ton *Thomas Allen* of Vice Admiral Captain Yorke, twice the size of Frobisher's *Aid,* to the little *Moon,* even smaller than the veteran *Michael* and *Gabriel,* which were making their third Arctic voyage. George Best, this time as Captain of *Anne Frances,* again wrote the story of the expedition. The experienced Edward Fenton sailed as Lieutenant, third in command of the expedition, and Captain of the *Judith.* Many other veterans of the earlier voyages were again aboard. Christopher Hall was once more chief pilot and Charles Jackman was pilot 'for the discoverie' — evidently for passage searching. The other ships were *Hopewell, Bear, Thomas* of Ipswich, *Emmanuel* of Exeter, *Frances* of Foy, *Emmanuel* of Bridgewater, *Salamander,* and the bark *Dennis.*

Investors rejoicing, the ships sailed from Harwich 31 May 1578. Off the Irish coast they came upon and aided a Bristol ship which had been looted by French pirates and left with dead and wounded men. Crossing the Gulf Stream which set them to the northeast, they sighted Frisland 20 June. For the first time Frobisher was able to get ashore on what we now know was the southern end of Greenland, which he named West England. Here he found Eskimo tents and belongings, including a box of nails and a trivet, and noted that the inhabitants resembled those of Meta Incognita. Three days later they set sail for Frobisher Strait with a fair wind through a sea filled with porpoises and whales. *Salamander* struck one of the latter so hard that the ship lost all headway. The beast uttered a great noise and was found floating dead two days later.

The success or failure of Arctic expeditions has often depended on luck with weather and ice conditions in particular

* Perhaps the earliest record of a prefabricated building.

seasons, as these vary greatly from year to year. The year 1578 was apparently one of the worst. When the fleet arrived off Queen Elizabeth's Foreland 2 July, it found the Strait clogged with ice. Contrary winds and dangerous ice separated the ships. For weeks they struggled under the most discouraging conditions imaginable. The bark *Dennis,* laden with supplies for the wintering colony and two sides of the fort, was sunk by an iceberg but without loss of life. Eventually Frobisher worked his way into what he believed to be his Strait where the trend of the land was right but the tides and current surprisingly strong. Christopher Hall stated flatly that he had never seen that land before, but Frobisher sailed up it for sixty leagues before naming it Mistaken Strait and turning back. He regretted that he could not pursue this strait further as it gave evidence of being the long-sought passage. Actually they were in Hudson Strait and had they continued would have entered the Bay. Returning along the northern shore of Hudson Strait, *Gabriel* was sent to explore a channel through Queen Elizabeth's Foreland which she proved to be an island (Resolution Island) by entering Frobisher Bay.

This voyage demonstrates the tremendous ability of Martin Frobisher as a commander for, although the men grumbled under their hardships, only those in *Thomas* deserted and returned to England. In spite of ice and July snowstorms alternating with breathless heat, the mines were opened up at Countess of Warwick Island; there, and from another island called Best's Blessing, cargoes were taken on. When it was found that a house large enough to accommodate all members of the expedition could not be constructed with the timber that remained after the loss of *Dennis,* Captain Fenton volunteered to winter with sixty men. The carpenters found too little time remaining to erect a wooden building large enough for the reduced number of men. They did, however, build a small house of lime and stone, where the timber for the fort was buried, along with surplus supplies, to use the following year and to make more cargo space for ore. The clergyman Wolfall regretted he would not have the opportunity to spend the winter, for he had made the voyage filled with a missionary zeal to spread the Gospel among the Eskimos. He celebrated the first communion service of the English Church in the New World.

With holds full of ore the fleet worked out of the Bay, intending to wait outside for *Emmanuel* of Bridgewater to complete her cargo. Suddenly a storm arose, scattering the vessels so quickly that Frobisher, who was on *Gabriel* at the time, could not get back to his own ship and made the voyage home on the small one. Anchored on a lee shore within the Strait, *Emmanuel* made a remarkable escape from the coast. She was one of the small, sturdy vessels known as a buss (used especially in herring fishing) and is usually spoken of as *Buss* of Bridgewater. Coming home alone she reported a large island in 57° latitude, sailing along its coast from near mid-day 12 September to the following afternoon. Thus the fictitious Island of Buss made its first appearance. The ships all arrived in English ports about 1 October. It is really remarkable and speaks highly of Frobisher and his officers that a voyage involving so many ships and men could be consummated in such a difficult season in those latitudes with the loss of only one ship, the desertion of another, and the death of about forty men from scurvy, exposure, and various accidents.

By the time Frobisher got home Michael Lok was in financial trouble. Some of the ore had been assayed and found worthless. Lok was ruined and thrown into debtors' prison. The Cathay Company collapsed amid bitter recriminations between Lok and Frobisher.[11] An extraordinary document entitled 'The Abuses of Captain Frobisher against the Company' was drawn up in an attempt to discredit the one principal who had done his job well. Frobisher replied with equally passionate and hotheaded charges. Apparently his losses were heavy also, for while he was away his wife Isabel, a woman of some means when she was married, asked Walsingham for help to keep herself and her children from starving. Frobisher recouped his losses more quickly than Lok and others did, perhaps returning to piracy for a couple of years, after taking part in an expedition against Ireland under Sir William Winter. Thereafter he remained in the Queen's service; he was knighted for his distinguished part in defeating the Armada in 1588, and died a hero's death from a wound sustained fighting the Spaniards at Brest.[12]

The mica and other worthless rocks so laboriously brought across the Atlantic were used as road building material or dumped in the harbor at Dartford, and so ended the first great commercial operation of the English in the New World. Unfortunately too the mining operation sidetracked the original purpose of the voyages. Although Frobisher had wished to explore further on his second and third voyages, and while he observed that the Mistaken (Hudson) Strait might be a better passage than his original discovery, his first duty to the Company was to load his ships and get them safely home. This he did.

It is an extraordinary quirk of history that the Frobisher voyages, so well-conceived and successfully carried out, not only intensified but actually created a cartographical confusion that was not clarified for over two centuries. Surely this is an unequaled record, for after most expeditions coasts have been more precisely charted and seas less mysterious. Nevertheless, Frobisher and his officers knew the way to the Strait and had no great difficulty finding it again on successive voyages. As Stefansson has observed, the Frobisher expeditions were well above many that came later in correctness of observation and interpretation.

The confusion resulted from the dependence on the Zeno map, the inability to figure longitude accurately,* the great variation

---

* Longitude could not be reckoned exactly and easily until the invention of Harrison's chronometer in 1762. Previously longitude could only be determined by rather complicated astronomical observations which most captains were incapable of making.

of the compass needle in those regions, the mistaking of mist and ice for land, and the misinterpretation of their observations by later explorers and cartographers. John Davis, who commanded the succeeding series of voyages, concluded that Frobisher had first sighted Zeno's Frisland and then arrived at Greenland. He therefore showed Frobisher Strait cutting off the southern tip of Greenland, and so it remained on the charts long after Frisland was proved nonexistent. Frisland on the Zeno chart was approximately in the latitude of the southern tip of Greenland. Therefore, when Frobisher sighted the southern end of Greenland, he assumed it was Frisland and that the real Greenland was farther north as shown by Zeno. When he reached his Strait he concluded that America was on his left hand and a projection of Asia on his right. Actually he was more nearly correct than Davis, for as we have seen he was in Frobisher Bay on Baffin Island, and his Mistaken Strait into which he sailed for two hundred miles on his third voyage was Hudson Strait. The belief of Frisland, actually a duplication of Iceland, persisted many years. Curiously enough, on the map of Michael Lok compiled from data collected on Frobisher's voyages, Frisland is located south of Greenland with no definite north coast, and it duplicates almost exactly in outline the southern end of Greenland. Frobisher Strait, although distorted, is shown where it should be, in North America.

The second geographical red herring was dragged out of the Atlantic when the buss *Emmanuel* sighted an unknown island on her voyage home. It was reported by a passenger Thomas Weirs, whose statement was printed by Hakluyt in the first edition of his famous *Principall Navigations* in 1589. The discovery was mentioned briefly by George Best eleven years earlier in his history of the Frobisher voyages. Doubtless something was sighted, but whether it was an ice floe, fog, or a part of the Greenland coast is not known.[13] However, the Island of Buss, aided by false reports, developed until, in Seller's Atlas of 1670, it

is shown with a definite coastline, named harbors, and mountains. As no one ever saw it again it was assumed to have sunk
and was referred to as the Sunken Island of Buss well into the
nineteenth century.

Frisland and Buss, among the many phantom islands of the
Atlantic, complicated the geography and obscured Frobisher's
discoveries. In fact, the site of his voyages and mining operations
was not known until 1862 when the American explorer Charles
Francis Hall found among the Innuit Eskimos of Baffin Island
legends of the coming of European ships and of men digging in
the ground that agreed exactly with the Frobisher narratives.
The white men had come, said the Eskimo, for three successive
years; first with one ship, then with three ships, then with many
ships. Since their traditions were correct in these details, it can be
assumed that they were also correct in their account of Frobisher's men 285 years before. The five men captured by the
Innuit lived with them for two winters. Then they dug up the
timbers buried on the third expedition, built a boat and sailed
for home early in the season, and were lost in the ice.[14] The
Eskimos took Hall to the remains of the stone house and the
mine workings. Hall found many relics which he collected and
sent to the Smithsonian Institution in Washington and to the
Royal Geographical Society in England. Ironically enough, and
although the relics are meticulously listed and were exhibited
at the Philadelphia Exposition in 1876, not one of them can be
found in either London or Washington.[15]

8

Mariner and Scholar

The geographical evidence brought back by Frobisher indicated that he could have sailed on unhampered had he not been obliged to load his ships with ore. The financial debacle of the Cathay Company, wiped out by its investments in the ill-advised mining activities of Frobisher's last two voyages, for a time discouraged further explorations to the Northwest. General belief in the existence of a Passage was not shaken, however, and before the close of the sixteenth century another series of voyages was made to find an open waterway through rocky northern shores and floating ice to the warm South Sea.

In the seven years between the return of Frobisher's fleet and the launching of the next attempt, a man who was to influence and encourage English geographical exploration more than any other became important. The Reverend Richard Hakluyt, while he never made a voyage himself beyond crossing the Channel, was advisor, historian, planner, and promoter for English adventurers from 1582, when his first book was published, until his death in 1616. Younger cousin of the Middle Temple lawyer of the same name, who probably first inspired his geographical interest, Hakluyt was thirty years old when his *Divers Voyages touching the Discovery of America* appeared.[1] In this work he printed a short, rather vague statement of a Portuguese friend concerning the probability of a Passage in 58° North latitude based on a story that João Cortereal, a relative of the explorers of the same name who went to the Northwest eighty years before, had found an ice-free passage in that latitude. This statement is otherwise unconfirmed. More important, Hakluyt's introduction, after giving his reasons for believing in the Passage, which are similar to those held by Thorne, Gilbert, and others, urged its exploration—not entirely for the trade riches which would accrue, but for geographical knowledge and the glory of God as well.

Two years later, at the request of Sir Walter Raleigh who had just obtained a charter for a colony in the New World, Hakluyt wrote *The Discourse of Western Planting* to urge the Queen to support discoveries and expand her realm in the western world. The *Discourse,* a hastily written, diffuse document, was read by Walsingham, Raleigh, the Earl of Leicester, and other influential expansionists before it was consigned to the archives.[2] While this document is concerned primarily with colonization, one chapter is devoted to the possibilities of using the colonies as bases to search both by land and by sea for the Northwest Passage. No really new arguments for its existence are put forward. Hakluyt drew on previously published works including Gilbert's 'Discourse' and a pamphlet written in 1583 by Sir George Peckham. Sir George, an amiable knight and merchant, had been one of the principal financial backers of Gilbert's last colonizing attempt. His businesslike scheme was for a colony in Newfoundland to be supported by fishing. Ships would take settlers out and bring fish back. The colonists were to catch and cure fish for export and, without the vast expense necessary to outfit an expedition specifically for the purpose, might have 'the great hope and likelihood of [finding] a passage beyond the

Grand Bay [Gulf of St. Lawrence] into the South Sea . . .'[3]

Even though the first great mining venture in the New World had been a failure, the fishing banks continued to provide a profitable source of revenue. The English were beginning to see the New World as more than a barrier to Far Eastern riches. Thoughts of colonies to secure natural resources and to serve as supply depots in case the Passage was found began occurring to some. Sir Humphrey Gilbert had shifted his interest to colonization and, three years before he died, granted his rights to royalties from discoveries north of 50° latitude to his old friend, Dr. John Dee.

Dee, the teacher of so many men who had navigated both to the northeast and northwest, retained his interest and belief in the Passage and still hoped for financial gain from that direction. He apparently did little with his grant until the evening of 23 January 1583 when Adrian Gilbert, Sir Humphrey's younger brother, and Sir Francis Walsingham called on him simultaneously, and 'so talk was begonne of Northwest straights discovery.' Secretary Walsingham was still interested in the possibility of a navigable Northwest Passage, and impressed by their conversation Dee invited them, together with their associate John Davis, to meet at the house of the Clerk of the Privy Council Robert Beale the following night. There, with talk supported by charts, Davis, Dee, and Gilbert must have sold the idea of another expedition to their political friends and incidentally to themselves. On 6 March Dee, Gilbert, and Davis met with representatives of the Muscovy Company who still held primary rights in the Northwest. The results of the meeting are unknown, but plans continued to be made and drafts of applications for patents or charters were written.[4]

We now come to one of the most fantastic episodes in the entire history of exploration plans. Dr. Dee believed in communication with spirits, a fashionable intellectual amusement of many prominent Elizabethans including the powerful Earl of Leicester. Dee had studied the occult for some years and, as a matter of fact, Adrian Gilbert and John Davis had dabbled with him in these experiments. Having recently become acquainted with Edward Kelly, a young Irishman who seemed to possess extraordinary powers as a medium, Dee spent much of the spring and summer of 1583 communicating with the other world. One of the spirits named Madini was especially talkative, and Dee through Kelly asked it about Adrian Gilbert's abilities to convert the infidels on the projected voyage, about the feelings of Secretary Walsingham and Lord Burghley toward him, and other intimate questions. He was told the latter gentlemen were turning against him, although the remarks about Gilbert were noncommittal. His faith in his old friends thus shaken by Madini, Dee decided that the Continent offered wider opportunities for his study of necromancy and left England in September. John Dee, one of the finest mathematical minds of the time, never again recovered his academic respectability. After his departure a mob, enraged by his séances, wrecked his library and laboratory although many of his manuscripts, books, and instruments were saved.[5]

His rights were transferred to Gilbert and Davis, and his place was taken by Sir Walter Raleigh in a proposed corporation of January 1584, 'the colliges [colleagues]of dyscovery of the north west passage.' When the patent was finally granted on 6 February, it was to Adrian Gilbert alone to discover a passage to China and the Moluccas by the north, northeast, or northwest.[6] Two months later Raleigh obtained a grant for colonizing in Virginia and dropped out of the Northwest venture.

Support for a voyage came from two sources: the Devon port of Exeter and London. The merchants guild of Exeter met 6 January 1585, and we learn from its minutes that a request for support from Sir Walter Raleigh for his voyage to Virginia was refused by its members 'as they were adventurers already with Mr. Adrian Gilberte in a voiage unto China they will not adventure anie more in anie suche voiages untill they see that voiage ended or some successe thereof.' The London group was headed by the greatest single investor in the undertaking, William Sanderson. He was an enormously successful merchant adventurer, a patron of geographical studies always interested in the North, and a member of the Fishmongers' Company. Perhaps of equal significance in this undertaking, he had married a niece of Gilbert's and Raleigh's. He played the part to the Davis voyages that the unfortunate Lok had acted in the Frobisher expeditions. The project also had the important blessing of Secretary Walsingham and the Privy Council.

It is probable that, throughout the several years of meetings and discussions between the various people involved, it had been always intended that their associate Captain John Davis should be in command of the expedition. He also was a friend of Sanderson, who recommended him highly as a navigator and as captain and pilot for the voyage. John Davis was more than a business associate of Adrian Gilbert. He was a west countryman who had shared his boyhood with Gilbert and his brothers, his neighbors at Sandridge, where he was born. In their village of Stoke Gabriel a few miles above Dartmouth, Davis was married in 1582, and his eldest son Gilbert baptized the following year. We know nothing of his seafaring experiences before his first Arctic voyage, but he was obviously already a skilled pilot and captain. Despite the London backing, this was a west country enterprise.

On 7 June 1585 two vessels, gaily and euphoniously named *Sunshine* and *Moonshine,* sailed from Dartmouth with Davis in command. An account of this voyage was written by Sanderson's nephew John Janes, who sailed with Davis as clerk and super-cargo. There were altogether aboard the fifty-ton *Sunshine* thirty-five men, and nineteen more sailed in her thirty-five-ton consort. After putting into Falmouth, they were forced by contrary winds into Grimsby at the Scilly Islands and held there. Captain John Davis was not a man to waste his time, however. While the wind blew in his teeth for twelve days he charted the Scilly Islands. Janes tells us that

> The Captaine, the Master and I went about all the Ilands, and the Captaine did platte out and describe the situation of all the Ilands, rockes and harboroughs to the exact use of Navigation, with lynes and scale thereunto convenient.

The wind came fair and easterly on the twenty-eighth enabling them to clear the Scilly Islands and stand to sea. After the first of July the sea swarmed with life. Porpoises were harpooned and caught 'and it did eate as sweete as any mutton.' Whales were seen in abundance. Then, on the nineteenth, they were enshrouded in thick mist and fog, the tide ran strong to the northward, and they 'heard a mighty great roaring of the Sea, as if it had bene the breach of some shoare,' but they could see nothing. Soundings showed 300 fathoms and better so Davis and Janes explored in a boat, leaving instructions for a gun to be shot off every half hour until they returned. Soon they discovered that all the racket was made by islands of ice grinding together. Landing on the ice which surrounded them, they filled their boat with it for fresh water and returning to *Sunshine* altered their course toward the north, hoping to double the land.

When the fog scaled off the following day

> wee discovered the land, which was the most deformed rocky and mountainous land that we ever sawe. The first sight whereof did shewe us as if it had bene in forme of a sugar loafe, standing to our sight above the cloudes for that it did shewe over the fogge like a white liste in the skye, the tops altogether covered with snowe, and the shoare beset with yce a league off into the Sea, making such yrksome noyse as that it seemed to be the true patterne of desolation, and after the same our Captaine named it, The land of Desolation.

Davis's 'land of Desolation' was on the southeast coast of Greenland, probably near Cape Discord. Attempting to land the next day he was stopped by ice two miles from the shore. His crew fished the black, thick water without success and the men of *Moonshine* pulled a sixty-foot tree out of the sea, in which there was a quantity of driftwood. But the ice was everywhere to the north and to the east so Davis put about and coasted the land southwesterly. Keeping well off, he finally altered his course to the northwestward and sailed for four days. Then again land was sighted on 29 July in 64° bearing northeast. He had rounded Cape Farewell, the southern tip of Greenland, and was at the entrance of the fiord which he named Gilbert Sound, where the capital Godthaab is now situated.

Exploring the coast and admiring the many fine sounds and roadsteads, Davis concluded that the land was an archipelago. The first indications of inhabitants, a child's shoe and bits of clothing, were found on a small island where they landed for wood and water. When Davis and his party climbed a hill on another island they heard a noise like the howling of wolves, and saw some Eskimos. Like Frobisher's men, the English howled back at the screeching aborigines. Captain William Bruton of *Moonshine,* in an inspired moment, brought all ship's musicians ashore. As they struck up the band the English began dancing and put on such a good performance that communication was soon established with ten canoes of Eskimos who came to enjoy it. The following day the number of canoes increased to thirty-seven, and the Eskimos put on a little drumming and dancing of their own. Trade was brisk. The handy kayaks delighted the sailors who bought five of them as well as assorted clothing; they also experimented with native weapons and paddles. Vast stores of driftwood of all sorts lined the shores but the only growing trees were dwarf birches and willows. The sea was alive with seals and 'the cliffs were al of such oare as M. Frobisher brought from meta Incognita.'

The wind came fair, enabling them to sail northwest to 66° 40′ where they anchored under a mountain with cliffs shining like gold. They named it Mount Raleigh. Davis had crossed

his Strait to the Cumberland Peninsula of Baffin Island. Here
at the mountain's foot he named Exeter Sound, and to the north
and south, Cape Dyer and Cape Walsingham. The men killed
two polar bears with guns and boar spears, but there was little
else about the country to recommend it. 'The coast is very moun-
taynous, altogether without wood, grasse or earth, and is only
hugh mountaines of stone, but the bravest stone that ever we
sawe.'

As they coasted southward following the trend of the shore,
the crew began muttering about their small food allowance.
Davis increased it. Rounding a southerly point, which was
named Cape of God's Mercy (now shortened to Cape Mercy),
the two ships entered Cumberland Sound on 11 August and
sailed northwestward for sixty leagues. Again many signs of
inhabitants were found. On landing the explorers were met by
twenty dogs and, thinking they were about to be attacked, shot
two. Wooden and bone sleds, the heads of animals, and a freshly
killed seal all proved that natives were not far off, but none
were seen.

From the tide, the color of the water, the presence of whales
which seemed to come from the westward, and the increasing
depth of soundings, Davis concluded that Cumberland Sound
was very possibly the long-sought Passage. After two days' discussion of whether or not to begin the return voyage, they decided to continue their explorations. But the wind turned to the
northwest, dead ahead. There it stayed, and Davis, believing the
water passages continued between many islands, finally turned
and sailed before it. One more brief landing was made while
riding out some foul weather; then they made sail for England,
and Baffin Island dropped behind them on the twenty-sixth.
They sighted southern Greenland 10 September and a few days
later the ships were separated by a storm. They arrived in Dartmouth within two hours of each other on 30 September.

Within three days of his return John Davis wrote Sir Francis
Walsingham that he believed there was no doubt of the Passage,

that the water was deep and ice free, and indicated that he was available for another try. His optimism apparently inspired confidence, for in six months funds had been raised and ships provided. Again the same combination of merchants furnished the backing, only this time the Devonshire men contributed the larger share. This expedition was better equipped, for, in addition to *Sunshine* and *Moonshine* (the latter owned by William Sanderson), were the fine 120-ton *Mermaid* and the ten-ton pinnace *North Star*.

They sailed from Dartmouth 7 May 1586 and separated 7 June near Greenland in the latitude of 60°. Davis ordered *Sunshine* under Richard Pope, her master's mate on the first voyage, to explore the east Greenland coast accompanied by *North Star*. Davis with the other two ships proceeded to his old anchorage in Gilbert Sound. There they assembled a pinnace, which had been brought in parts on the deck of *Mermaid,* for exploring inshore. Once more the Eskimos came in their boats and the two groups, recognizing each other, rejoiced. Davis distributed knives as presents. Sometimes as many as a hundred Eskimo kayaks gathered about the English ships. They brought quantities of skins, seals, deer, and hare, as well as fish. The natives also helped the Englishmen launch the pinnace and advised them about the terrain. In the pinnace Davis explored ten miles or more up several of the fiords and channels. Landing frequently he found the land desolate, mountainous, and, well inland, snow covered. Near the water, however, there was some grass and moorland.

As the relationship with the Eskimos became more familiar, sporting contests were held. The English were superior in leaping but the Eskimos seem to have had the edge in wrestling although west countrymen were noted as excellent wrestlers. But this familiarity soon brought out the thievish character of the natives. They cut cables for the iron and made off with weapons and oars, clothing, and finally an anchor.

On 7 July Davis took the pinnace and went on an exploring

trip for four days, penetrating to the head of the fiord and following various channels. On his return to the ships he found that the natives had stolen the anchor and were also boldly pelting the crews with sling stones. He attempted to make peace but, when the boatswain was knocked down by a rock, he lost patience and pursued the Eskimos with gunfire. When they in turn tried to make peace, he seized one of the men as a hostage for the return of the anchor; but the ruse was unsuccessful and the Eskimo later died.

Davis, who himself wrote the account of this voyage that was published by Hakluyt, gives an excellent account of the native culture. He remarks that the Eskimos practiced witchcraft (a subject with which he had some familiarity) and that fortunately it did not work. He also compiled a remarkably accurate list of native words, considering his brief contact with the Eskimos and the difficulty of writing down words of an unknown language. These are the first ethnological notes of any consequence made about the Greenlanders.

Attempting to sail farther north, Davis was surprised to find his way blocked by enormous ice beyond 63°, where the year before the same sea had been clear. For a week he coasted along the pack through fog which formed heavy ice on sails and rigging. Men began to fall ill and become discouraged. Here Davis exhibited both the humanity and the courage which was typical of the man. Removing all the sick to *Mermaid* and revictualing *Moonshine* from her, he sent his largest ship home and continued exploring with healthy volunteers in the smaller vessel. He had learned that small craft were far superior to large ships for Arctic exploration. During the transfer of men and supplies, which took place on the Greenland coast near Sukkertoppen, the weather was very hot, and for the first time they made the acquaintance of the ravenous northern mosquitoes.

After *Mermaid* departed with the sick and useless, Davis crossed over to Baffin Island near Exeter Sound. Curiously enough, although he made approximately the same landfalls as the previous year and again crossed the mouth of Cumberland Sound, Davis apparently did not recognize anything. This seems almost inconceivable in a man of Davis's ability, yet he made no attempt to sail up Cumberland Sound where he had been so hopeful toward the end of his previous voyage. Instead he continued south, missing Frobisher Bay and Hudson Strait, to the Labrador coast in 57°. Here he admired the land and the great quantity of game birds. After sampling the fishing, which he found excellent even with poor equipment, he continued south and expressed hope of a passage at a place, probably the Strait of Belle Isle, which a head wind prevented him from entering. On the Newfoundland coast his men caught and cured fish, but five young sailors bringing the last of the fish aboard were surprised by Indians, whose behavior was in sharp contrast to the Eskimos of Greenland. The natives killed two of the crew with arrows and wounded two others so severely that Davis was doubtful if they would live. One with an arrow through his arm escaped by swimming. After a severe storm during which they considered cutting away the masts, Davis got off the coast and returned to England. He arrived in early October, relieved to find that *Mermaid* had brought her ailing men back safely.

When the fleet separated, *Sunshine* and *North Star* had been ordered to explore up the eastern coast of Greenland to the eightieth parallel. We learn from the account of Henry Morgan, purser on *Sunshine,* that the two vessels made northerly for two days when they were turned easterly by ice whose edge they followed to Iceland. Arriving there on 12 June, they remained five days during which they received some fresh lamb from an English vessel. They arrived at the agreed rendezvous at Gilbert Sound 3 August. Passing their time alternately playing football and fighting with the natives, they waited until 31 August. Davis, of course, never came back that way. On the homeward voyage the pinnace *North Star* was lost in a storm just as Frobisher's pinnace had been lost on his second voyage. *Sunshine* arrived in the Thames at Ratcliffe on 6 October.

The Exeter merchants were discouraged but Sanderson and his associates decided to send Davis on a third voyage. Nevertheless they felt it prudent to cushion their investment with commercial fishing. Veteran *Sunshine* was once more fitted out, along with *Elizabeth* of Dartmouth and the lapstreak-built pinnace *Ellen* of London. The expedition got under way 19 May 1587 when the ships left Dartmouth. Both John Janes and Davis have left brief accounts of the voyage. It did not begin auspiciously. *Sunshine* was leaking like a sieve, taking 500 strokes of her pump per four-hour watch to keep the water down. A packet of letters to be sent home on the ship *Red Lion,* met at sea, fell short, and the lead-heaving weight carried them to the bottom. The pinnace *Ellen,* whose owner had praised her sailing qualities highly, 'was like to a cart drawed by oxen' and had to be towed by *Elizabeth.*

Davis, undismayed by the ill luck, fixed *Sunshine*'s leaks as best he could and made straight for Greenland. Without sighting its southern tip he came on 15 July to his old anchorage in Gilbert Sound. Here his crew immediately set about putting together another pinnace from parts brought with them, but the Eskimos stole the upper strakes for the nails, so they were forced to hoist the mutilated craft aboard one of the ships to use later for fishing. There was now a good deal of friction with the natives, and arguments between Davis and the fishermen who wanted to load their ships now that the season was wearing on. Finally, on 21 June, a rendezvous on the Labrador coast having been agreed upon, two ships left for the fishing grounds, while Davis in the cranky little pinnace *Ellen* headed north along the shore, naming it London Coast.

By 30 June Davis had reached 72° 12′, finding the sea clear and open to the north and west. Here at the high headland which he named Hope Sanderson, a famous landmark for all Arctic explorers who have followed him, he was stopped by head winds. Turning westward he came up against the famous middle pack of ice in Baffin Bay which forced him steadily southward as he attempted to get past it. Ice and head winds forced him back to Greenland but he eventually crossed Davis Strait and reached its western shore at Mount Raleigh 19 July. He recognized Cumberland Sound and sailed up it to the end where he saw a whale swimming westward into a channel between the islands. By 29 July he had worked his way out of Cumberland Sound and was once more coasting south.

As he passed the mouth of Frobisher Bay, Davis renamed it Lumley's Inlet, not recognizing it as the scene of his predecessor's adventures. He then crossed the entrance of Hudson Strait and was impressed with the same great rushing and running tide mentioned by Frobisher. Ice was driving out of the Strait and Davis crossed with some peril. The northernmost tip of Labrador was raised 1 August, and named Cape Chidley for Davis's good Devonshire friend John Chidley, who died in the Strait of Magellan on an attempted voyage of circumnavigation. In trying to find a harbor in 54° *Ellen* struck a rock, but the resulting leak was repaired the next day. There being no sign of the two fishing vessels which had actually sailed for home sixteen days after parting company, Davis headed for England 15 August with little wood and only half a hogshead of fresh water. He arrived in Dartmouth exactly one month later. Immediately upon his return, Davis wrote to Sanderson

> Good M. Sanderson, with Gods great mercy I have made my safe returne in health, with all my companie, and have sailed threescore leagues further then my determination at my departure. I have bene in 73 degrees, finding the Sea all open, and forty leagues betweene land and land.
> The passage is most probable, the execution easie, as at my comming you shall fully know.

> Yesterday, the 15 of September, I landed all wearie, therefore
> I pray you pardon my shortnesse.
>   Sandridge, this 16 of September, anno 1587.
>   Yours equall as mine owne, which by triall you shall best
>   know,
>   John Davis.

Davis seems already to have forgotten the middle pack — two hundred miles of ice eight feet thick — which forced him back.

Just as Frobisher had failed so Davis failed after three courageous attempts to find the Northwest Passage. But knowledge of the land and its inhabitants was greatly increased by his efforts. He was more fortunate that his predecessor in that his discoveries were recorded on one of the most famous globes ever made.

William Sanderson was intensely interested in geography as well as trade. When Davis returned with a chart showing his new coasts, Sanderson commissioned Emery Molyneux, one of his protégés, to make him a pair of large globes incorporating the latest discoveries. Davis gave Molyneux all his data and worked closely with him, attempting, unsuccessfully, to reconcile his discoveries with Frobisher's. Frobisher, as we have seen, relied on the Zeno map published in 1558 and so mistook southern Greenland for Frisland. Davis knew it was not Frisland, but, unable to identify it with Zeno's Engroenland (Greenland), named it Land of Desolation. As there is no indication of longitude in any of the Frobisher accounts, Davis assumed, since he had not seen the Greenland coasts between 61° 30′ and 64° 15′ N., that Frobisher Strait was there. Davis's original chart has not survived, but his discoveries were preserved for posterity while Frobisher Strait was transferred to southern Greenland on the Molyneux Globe. This globe and its celestial mate were the first ever made in England, and they can still be seen in the Middle Temple, London. The influence of the Molyneux Globe on cartography lasted for many years. Almost until the nineteenth century, Frobisher Strait continued to bisect southern

Greenland. Davis's discoveries were also preserved on the 'New Map' made by Edward Wright.

Davis not only left his name on his Strait, but also on an instrument of navigation. He was one of the developers of the back staff which replaced the cross staff for observing the height of the sun. It was more accurate and easier to use, as the sun did not have to be looked at directly, and in its elaborated form is known as the Davis quadrant. Davis, on his third voyage, also kept a traverse book which was an improvement on earlier systems and set the form for entering the necessary information concisely in log books thereafter.

Despite his failures, Davis was sure he could sail to Cathay and wished to continue the search. Sanderson promptly undertook to arrange a fourth voyage: he tried to interest Sir Thomas Smith, later a great name in New World ventures; in June 1588 he presented a plan to the Exeter guild of merchants who were unresponsive, having invested heavily in the previous expedition. Further deterrents to the undertaking were the death of Sir Francis Walsingham in 1590 and, more important, the war with Spain. John Davis was, in fact, among those fighting the Armada, as commander of the dispatch vessel *Black Dog* for Lord Admiral Howard.

With the defeat of Spain, since interest in a Northwest venture could not be rekindled immediately, Davis took command of *Desire* for an expedition to the South Seas with Sir Thomas Cavendish. This was the vessel in which Cavendish had circumnavigated the globe from 1586–8. Davis went with the understanding that he would have his own pinnace to search 'that Northwest discovery upon the backe partes of America.' Cavendish was forced to turn back in the Strait of Magellan, and his ships became separated. Sir Thomas, who died on the return voyage, condemns Davis in a letter written on his death bed for deserting him and causing the failure of the expedition. Davis seems innocent of these charges for he lost his commander in thick weather and made every attempt to find him again.

It was during his efforts to find Cavendish that Davis discovered the Falkland Islands.

As Davis the seaman struggled with the elements, Davis the scholar was probably working on two important books during his cruising. In 1594 he published *The Seamans Secrets,* and in May the following year *The Worldes Hydrographical Description.*

The Seamans Secrets, one of the most important early English works on navigation, was, as he wrote in his dedication, the direct result of Davis's Arctic voyages:

> In those Northwest voyages where Navigation must be executed in most exquisite sort, in those attempts I was enforced to search al possible meanes required in saying by which occasion I have gathered together this breefe treatise.[7]

In his other book Davis sets forth both the objections and reasons for a Northwest Passage and reviews the history of the search. He concludes that America is an island, summarizes his three northern voyages, and gives accounts of the people, climate, and resources of Greenland and other places he visited.

Davis was never able to go back to his northern exploring, but his experience there served him well. After serving in the expeditions of the Earl of Essex to Cadiz and the Azores in 1596 and 1597, he went as chief pilot with the Second Dutch Fleet to the East Indies. On his return to England in August 1600 he found the East India Company preparing the first English expedition to the East Indies and accepted the position of pilot major in Captain James Lancaster's ship *Red Dragon.* His third voyage to the Far East was as pilot for Sir Edward Michelbone on board the 205-ton *Tiger.* It was on *Tiger* that John Davis was killed in late December 1605 by Japanese pirates. Thus this brave, enterprising scholar, inventor, writer, and mariner, was committed to the warm waters he tried so desperately to reach by the cold and elusive Northwest Passage.

9

Frustration

Fifteen years went by after Davis returned from his third voyage before another try was made to confirm that optimistic mariner's hopes. There was no further reason to continue seeking a northern passage to the Orient, for the English were now sailing to India and the East around the Cape of Good Hope. Still, it was obvious to anyone who looked at a globe that the long journey around the Cape could be eliminated if one sailed the shorter distance north of America.

In a charter of 1600 the newly organized 'Worshipful Fellowship of Merchants of London Trading into the East Indies' — the East India Company — had been granted exclusive rights to trade in the Orient. The Company did not intend to overlook any possibility that a northern, open-water channel existed, particularly as this was maintained by geographers and experienced seamen. In fact it was a navigator, George Weymouth, who kindled their interest and so led to their decision for an expedition. In a conference with Weymouth in September 1601, it was decided that two pinnaces of fifty and forty tons with a crew of thirty would be sufficient. However, the Muscovy

Company still held monopoly rights to trade through the northern passages, and, although it did not intend further attempts at discovery, it did not want to encourage those of any other group. This obstructionist attitude had also been evident when Frobisher was making his plans. When negotiations between the two companies failed, the East India Company appealed to the Privy Council. As the undertaking was considered for the country's general good, permission was received to proceed.

It was estimated that £3000 would be sufficient capital for the venture. Two sturdy fishing vessels called flyboats, *Discovery* and *Godspeed,* were obtained and provisioned for sixteen months. Captain Weymouth was to receive five hundred pounds if he discovered the Passage and nothing if he failed. The west country still produced, as always, the greatest number of good sailors and Weymouth journeyed to Devon to hire most of his crew. It was agreed that, after finding a passage toward China, he should proceed on his course 'soe longe as he shall finde those seas or any pte [part] thereof navigable and any possibilitie to make way or passadge through them.'[1] Neither he nor any of his men was to turn back toward England until they had spent at least one year from the time of departure attempting to perform their task. Letters from the Queen to the Emperor of China insured their amiable reception when they reached Asia.

Leaving Ratcliffe, the two ships sailed boldly down the Thames 2 May 1602, and on 18 June southern Greenland was sighted. Like Davis, Weymouth noticed

> blacke water as thicke as puddle, and in sailing a little space the water would be cleare againe. Seeing this change of water, so often to be thick, and cleare againe so suddenly, we imagined it had beene shallow water: then we sounded, and could fetch no ground in one hundred and twenty fathomes: and the Sea was so smooth, that we could discerne no current at all.[2]

DAVIS STRAIT

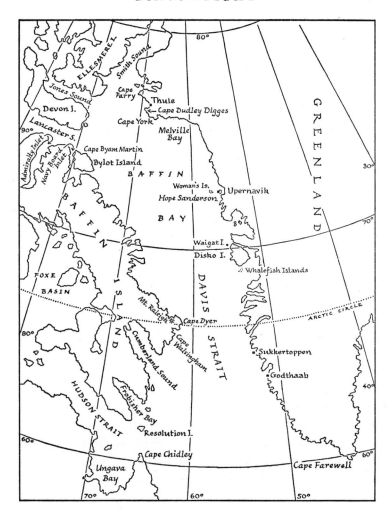

Ten days later they sighted Cape Warwick near the entrance of Frobisher Bay. It is impossible to follow Weymouth's course from his abbreviated journal. He evidently beat up and down the coast between 55° and 63°, plagued by storm, ice, and cold weather. He noticed the same currents and overfalls in Hudson Strait mentioned by his predecessors, and apparently penetrated the Strait for some distance. The cold, foggy weather iced up his lines and sails, which made working the ships difficult and discouraged the crews.

So downcast were they, in fact, that on the night of 19 July, while Weymouth slept in his cabin, the men conspired to bear up the helm and sail for England. The Reverend John Cartwright the chaplain and William Cobreth master of *Discovery* acted as spokesmen for the mutineers. Cartwright had been sent along especially since he had traveled extensively in Persia and the East and it was thought his experience would be helpful when the ships reached China. There was no violence but Weymouth could not alter the situation in two days of talking. The course was changed and Weymouth, coming out of his cabin, demanded of all the ship's company, 'Who bare up the helme?' And they answered, 'One and All.' After enduring a violent storm which ended in a whirlwind on the coast of Labrador they sailed home, arriving in Dartmouth 5 August 1602.

The voyage, far from living up to the brave words of the agreement, was a failure and the East India Company was justifiably annoyed. An inquiry into the mutiny and early return was held. On the testimony of John Drew master of *Godspeed,* among others, Cartwright was found to be the instigator of the mutiny. As punishment he was ordered to surrender a gown which had been given him to wear upon his presentation to the Chinese Emperor. Weymouth conducted himself well during the hearings. He was exonerated and it was determined that 'being very competant' he should command a second voyage the next season. The idea was abandoned, however. Later George Weymouth in 1605 explored the New England coast.

Weymouth's voyage, while in itself accomplishing nothing, began the first great period of concentrated effort to penetrate the Northwest Passage. For the first three decades of the seventeenth century there was an expedition probing the channels of the northern coasts nearly every year. No voyage was undertaken in 1604, but in 1605, 1606, and 1607, Christian IV of Denmark sent out three successive expeditions. The purpose of these voyages was to locate the lost Scandinavian colonies of Greenland rather than to find a Passage. Nevertheless they cannot be overlooked, since most of the explorers involved were similarly associated with the English northwestern voyages.[3] Not only did the English have the experience the Danish King needed in his search for the lost settlements but also there was a close family connection, James I being his brother-in-law. Many Scots were employed in Denmark at this time, including David Balfour a shipbuilder for the Danish Navy, and Andrew Sinclair who conducted the Danish King's English correspondence. Another Scot, John Cunningham, already a Captain in the Danish Navy, was selected to command the 1605 expedition. After his retirement he served until his death in 1651 as Governor of Vardö (Wardhouse), a trade depot in northern Norway. *Trost,* a ship newly built by Balfour, was Cunningham's flagship and James Hall, a native of Hull, was engaged as chief pilot and first mate. Besides *Trost,* two other Danish naval vessels were equipped for the voyage; *Red Lion,* under Captain Godske Lindenow, a well-known Danish officer who later became chief of the dockyard at Copenhagen, was an old, slow, and somewhat cranky ship, but the pinnace *Cat* was another new, fast vessel, commanded by the Englishman John Knight. Both Hall and Knight were employed because they had had Arctic experience at some previous time. From Hall's knowledge of Davis Strait and conditions there, it is nearly certain that he must have been on one of Davis's voyages.

The three ships left Copenhagen 2 May 1605 and had an uneventful voyage to Greenland, where they ran into the usual ice and mist and where, like many other Arctic voyagers, they noticed the black, thick water. As they sailed through the waters where Buss Island had been reported, they kept watch for that imaginary land. Hall concluded that it must have been laid down in the wrong latitude. The ships were separated by fog and after locating each other again Hall gave a Sea Card or chart to Peter Kieldsen, Master of *Red Lion,* to help him find his way should they again be separated.

Dodging icebergs of immense size as they sailed up Davis Strait, they finally came up against the middle pack and coasted along it easterly to the Greenland coast. The ice was too much for the Danes in *Red Lion,* and on 11 June they shot off a gun and deserted their two consorts. They touched briefly on the coast farther south, and then sailed home. Hall, leaving *Trost,* explored to the northward in the pinnace as far as Disko Bay, and made several detailed maps of sections of the shoreline. He rejoined *Trost* 10 July and after setting two unfortunate criminals ashore, who had been brought from Denmark under this sentence, they sailed for home carrying off four Eskimos, one of whom was so obstreperous that he had to be shot.

One month later *Trost* came sailing into Copenhagen exhibiting a big map of Greenland on her prow. Hall's maps and reports were well regarded and he was rewarded with a permanent appointment in the Danish Navy. The old colonies had not been found, but Hall had brought something with him besides natives. Hopes were entertained, based on samples of alleged silver ore which he produced, that Greenland would have great mineral wealth. Once more northern rocks were producing a delusion of riches.

Lindenow, after leaving Cunningham, had picked up two

Greenlanders who had mean dispositions, bit like dogs, and greedily ate anything they could get hold of. The three taken by Cunningham, on the other hand, were far more civil in their ways and soon became friendly with the crew. Possibly the shooting of their companion influenced their behavior. Lindenow's Eskimos, nevertheless, had been sufficiently civilized by the time the King and Queen came aboard *Red Lion* on her return to race in their kayaks and hold their own against a sixteen-oar boat. The King was so impressed that he had a kayak built with holes for two men, the first interest in a type of craft and sport now very popular in Europe. The Spanish Ambassador had just arrived in Copenhagen, and on being shown the Eskimos, their implements, and an exhibition of the three cutting figures in a kind of dance in their kayaks, he was so delighted that he sent them large sums of money which they immediately spent on fancy clothes, hats with ostrich plumes, swords, and spears. Decking themselves out in this finery they marched 'like Greenland Grandees' to the castle. In the spring they attempted to escape, but were recaptured by peasants and afterward watched more carefully.

It is a pattern in these early Arctic voyages for the sponsors to send out a larger and more elaborately equipped expedition on the second attempt — especially if the first had found supposedly valuable ore. And yet, as we have seen with John Cabot, Frobisher, Davis, and Barents, the larger the ships, the greater the fleet, the more expensive the preparations, the more meager the results. Christian I followed the pattern, imposing a special tax to finance the next expedition. Two additional ships were assigned to go with the original vessels. *Eagle,* a man-of-war of one hundred tons or almost twice the size of *Trost,* was commanded by Captain Hans Bruun who has left a journal of the trip. The other was a forty-ton vessel bought in Scotland, appropriately named *Gilliflower,* under Captain Carsten Richardson. Curiously enough Cunningham and Lindenow now exchanged places, Lindenow being named Commander of the expedition aboard *Trost* as flagship, and Cunningham sailing in his colleague's position as Captain of *Red Lion*. There are indications that the Danish officers were jealous of being out-ranked in their own navy by the British. John Knight had re-turned to England and little *Cat* had a new captain. James Hall was again pilot to the fleet. All Copenhagen was excited about the expedition, but no one more than the Eskimos who were to be returned to their homes. Unfortunately, they all died on the voyage out.

On the outward passage Hall thought he saw the Island of Buss, but the weather was thick and he was mistaken. Only two of the ships, *Trost* and *Eagle,* reached the same part of the Greenland coast as before. The others apparently never arrived at all. From the day of their arrival, 27 July, until 10 August when they left, most of the time was devoted to load-ing 'silver ore.' The day before leaving Greenland a young man who had been on the first voyage but who had committed some misdemeanor was put ashore with supplies and equipment. No sooner was he left alone than the Eskimos, perhaps remember-ing their kidnaped kinsmen, literally tore him limb from limb. The Danes, feeling that the victim was receiving his just punishment, made no attempt to rescue or avenge him. Later in the day, however, a group of natives came out to the ship and five or six of them with their boats were captured. Four Eskimos lived to reach Denmark, 4 October, but none of them ever saw Greenland again. The Eskimos had been taken with the intention of using them as interpreters and intermediaries on future expeditions. As none of them ever returned to Green-land their kidnaping had just the opposite effect and indeed sealed Hall's fate seven years later.[4]

No geographical discoveries were made on the 1606 expedi-tion. The ore was worthless; the old colonies had not been found; and the whole expedition was a bitter disappointment.

Christian IV was concerned that the ancient settlements were not located and determined to try again with a far more modest expedition. *Trost,* the best ship of the lot, was retained and command given to Carsten Richardson, who later distinguished himself on foreign service in Poland and Hungary. A smaller vessel called *The Greenland Bark* served as consort. Hall, making his third Arctic voyage for the Danes, was in sole charge of navigation, and he prepared himself particularly to accomplish his task by studying everything he could find on the old colonies, including Frobisher's voyages which, it will be remembered, were thought to have been to southern Greenland.

The 1607 expedition left the Danish capital on 13 May, taking the same route as the previous year. After taking a beating in particularly foul weather, running short of water, and attempting unsuccessfully to reach Iceland, the crews refused to go on. The ships were put about, and 25 July they were home again.

Meanwhile the East India Company, undaunted by Weymouth's failure and still hoping to cut the sailing time to the Orient, had decided to finance another expedition. They were joined by the Muscovy Company. In command was Hall's former colleague John Knight with Olivier Brunel who, it will be remembered, pioneered the Dutch explorations to the Northeast.

They sailed from Gravesend in the forty-ton bark *Hopewell* on 18 April 1606.[5] After being held up for a fortnight in the Orkneys by contrary winds, they had an uneventful crossing, except for sailing through a mass of dead cuttlefish, until they hit unusually heavy ice off southern Greenland. From 3 until 19 June, when he raised the coast of Labrador, Knight and his men worked their little bark among the ice, sometimes sailing, sometimes rowing through open channels, sometimes fending off ice, sometimes tying up to it, and once nearly crushed. On one monstrous, dirt-covered island of ice they found tracks of men, children, deer, and dogs. They pushed on until 19 June when they raised the coast of Labrador not far from the present town of Nain. Still the ice plagued them and they were unable to reach shore until two days later, when they ran on a submerged rock but got off without serious damage, and put a shallop together on a nearby island. On 23 June came a gale. The ship was warped into a cove with great difficulty. The following day, ice driving before the storm tore away the rudder and the ship, half full of water, was grounded in the cove to save the food and clothing. The wind had abated by the twenty-fifth, and they set about pumping out the ship and repairing the leaks.

The next day Knight and his brother, accompanied by Edward Gorrell the mate, Olivier Brunel, and two others, well armed with pikes, swords, and muskets, took the shallop and rowed to an island six miles distant. Landing about 10 a.m., Knight left Brunel with a trumpeter to guard the boat and asked them to wait until 3 p.m. Brunel watched the others walk inland and disappear over the top of a hill. He waited until eleven o'clock that night. No one ever saw them again.

Searching parties were sent out, but not a sign of the shore group could be found. Two days after Captain John Knight walked into oblivion the crew were pumping and repairing ship when about fifty Indians appeared and attempted to seize the ship's boat. Eight men with the boat led by the ship's mascot, a large dog, advanced toward the natives who fled before their bold approach. The ship was finally floated on the thirtieth, but she still leaked badly and was without a rudder. After a jury rudder was rigged, with pintles made out of iron bands from the Captain's chest, the vessel became manageable. Hope was abandoned for Knight and his companions. The ship cleared the coast 3 July, but was still so leaky that the pumps could not keep up with the water rising in the hold, due principally to a large hole under the forefoot which could not be repaired from the inside. To stop it, the main bonnet was quilted with oakum — a process called thrumming — which was passed over the leak outside. With these temporary repairs, the exhausted crew finally got the vessel to Fogo Bay, Newfoundland. There, with the aid of friendly fishermen, she was sufficiently repaired to cross the Atlantic. The hopelessly crippled expedition arrived at Dartmouth 24 September 1606, probably under Olivier Brunel who kept the journal after Knight's disappearance.

The importance of these rather fruitless voyages of Weymouth, Hall, and Knight lies not in any vast increase made in geographical knowledge, although Hall made more careful and detailed surveys of several localities than any of his predecessors, but in the continuity of exploration to this quarter of the world and in the experience it gave personnel. Slowly men were learning how to handle ships in ice — learning about the currents, prevailing winds, sudden storms, fog, heat, and cold of the high latitudes, and how to cope with them.

As Luke Foxe has pointed out in writing of Weymouth, 'Hee neither discovered nor named anything more than Davis, nor had any sight of Groenland, nor was not so farre North . . . yet these two, Davis and he, did (I conceive) light Hudson into his Streights.' [6]

10

Mutiny

*O*ne of the most brilliant names in the great Jacobean era of discovery is Henry Hudson. His life before he set out on his first voyage is a mystery. Everything we know about Henry Hudson occurred in the last four years of his life. Yet during that brief period he visited all the known northern regions of his time, from the extreme northeast to the northwest, and he saw much that no other explorer had seen.[1] Certainly Hudson was a navigator of wide experience, perhaps already in the employ of the Muscovy Company when that rejuvenated group of merchant adventurers retained his services to sail to Cathay straight over the North Pole — Robert Thorne's old suggestion.

Hudson left Gravesend on this bold venture on 1 May 1607 in the small bark *Hopewell,* probably John Knight's old ship, manned by a crew of ten men and a boy. The boy was his second son John, who accompanied him on all his voyages. He reached the east coast of Greenland in about 70° intending to follow it north. But the land bent farther eastward than he anticipated and in 73° he reached impenetrable ice. Skirting the ice, seeking and hoping for a rift or opening, Hudson followed this solid barrier as far as Spitsbergen, where he explored parts of that island group discovered by Barents eleven years before. A prominent point was named Hakluyt's Headland after the great geographical compiler and advisor to expeditions. Hudson on this voyage reached the neighborhood of 81°, the farthest north anyone had sailed up to that time. He also made important observations on the dip or inclination of the compass needle and the color of Arctic sea water. Finding it impossible to sail north across the Pole, Hudson hoped to round the northern tip of Greenland and return via Davis Strait, but this too was equally impractical. On his return voyage he discovered Jan Mayen which he named Hudson's Tutches. This voyage, so unsuccessful in its avowed purpose, had an important economic consequence. The explorer's accounts of the infinite numbers of whales and morses, as walruses were then called, in the seas around Spitsbergen stimulated the English and Dutch whaling industry. Just as the reports of Cabot over a century before resulted in the cod fishery based on Newfoundland, so Hudson now gave impetus to the northern whale fishery based on Spitsbergen.

The following year, 1608, Hudson made a second voyage for the Muscovy Company, this time to the northeast, a direction they had always favored. He was unsuccessful in his attempts to pass either to the north or south of Novaya Zemlya, but proved that the Kostin Shar was a bay in that island, rather than a strait as Barents had supposed it. Feeling that he was not prepared to sail into the Kara Sea by Vaygach Island, he decided to return westerly if he had a favorable wind, cross the Atlantic, 'and to make triall of that place called Lumley's Inlet [Frobisher Bay], and the furious over-fall by Captain Davis, hoping to runne into it an hundred leagues, and to returne as God should enable mee.'[2] The wind was not favorable and this expedition, which accomplished very little, was the last to receive the Muscovy merchants' support. It did, however, produce one observation of rare interest. On 15 June, on the outward passage in about 75°, two sailors, Thomas Hilles and Robert Rayner, made a curious report. Hudson writes:

> This morning, one of our companie looking over boord saw a mermaid, and calling up some of the companie to see her, one more came up, and by that time shee was come close to the ship's side, looking earnestly on the men: a little after, a sea came and overturned her: from the navill upward, her backe and breasts were like a woman's, as they say that saw her; her body as big as one of us; her skin very white; and long hair hanging downe behinde, of colour blacke: in her going downe they saw her tayle, which was like the tayle of a porpoise, and speckled like a macrell.[3]

It had been a difficult voyage.

After Hudson's lack of success in penetrating the ice, either to the north or to the northeast, the Muscovy merchants lost interest. Hudson did not. Like Davis he stubbornly believed that somewhere in that cold northern vastness there must be a channel to China. He had not long to wait to find others who were sufficiently interested in the possibility of a northern strait to make use of his experience and unshaken belief. The Dutch East India Company was as interested in finding and gaining control of a northern passage to the East as its English counterparts. The directors of this company were aware of Hudson's explorations and had followed his adventures with great interest. They were, therefore, more than a little intrigued by this navigator who had sailed farther north than any man before his time, to within ten degrees of the Pole itself. Now, through the Dutch Consul in London, Emmanuel van Meteren, they invited Hudson to come to Amsterdam to consult with them and learn his opinion about future northern explorations. After hastily attending the christening of a grandchild, a daughter of his eldest son Oliver, he accepted the invitation.

It is obvious that Hudson was more than a sea captain with a bent for northern exploration. Like Davis he was a scholar. While he did not equal that worthy as a scientific navigator (in fact Hudson's voyages are difficult to follow in detail from his observations), he exceeded Davis as a geographer. He evidently studied the voyages of his predecessors, and when in Holland he missed no opportunity to consult with geographers and cartographers while negotiations were going on with the merchants and financiers who controlled the Dutch East India Company. Among others, he became friendly with the greatest of all Dutch geographers of the period, the Reverend Peter Plancius, who had also had Barents and Heemskerk as his pupils.

Plancius favored the traditional Dutch theory of a Northeast Passage. He had somehow acquired, however, the journals and logbooks kept by George Weymouth on his attempt at the Northwest in 1602. These he lent to Hudson who was impressed and influenced by Weymouth's accounts of sailing one hundred leagues up Lumley's Inlet (Frobisher Bay) and his exploration of two other bays where he 'found there the water wide and mighty like an open sea, with very great tides.' This observation was eventually to aid Hudson. Besides the reassuring statements of Davis and Weymouth, Hudson was further influenced in his opinions by letters and maps which he received about the same time from his friend Captain John Smith in Virginia. These letters, written by Smith just before he had himself thoroughly explored Chesapeake Bay, informed Hudson that there was a sea leading into a Western Ocean just to the north of Virginia. These documents probably included a variation of the old Verazzano map showing the American continent with a very narrow isthmus in about the latitude of Chesapeake Bay, separating the Atlantic and Pacific Oceans. All of this evidence had no influence with the Dutch promoters. Moreover, Plancius did not agree that there was any possibility by the west, for he said he had 'the accounts of a man who had searched and explored the western shore of that sea, and had stated that it formed an unbroken line of coast.' [4]

After long discussion the Directors of the Amsterdam Chamber of the Dutch East India Company signed a contract with Henry Hudson to search for a Passage by the north of Novaya Zemlya — in effect, to continue where he left off the previous year. This contract was witnessed by Jadocus Hondius the noted sculptor and engraver, to whom Hudson had given geographical details of his Arctic explorations for a map of those regions.

Hudson cleared the Texel 6 April in the ship *Half Moon*. A second vessel named *Good Hope* is mentioned as ready for the voyage but it is uncertain whether or not she actually sailed; there is no mention of her afterward. Along with a mixed Dutch and English crew Hudson was accompanied by Robert Juet of Limehouse, his mate on the second voyage, and John Colman who was mate on his first. No other Englishman is mentioned, nor the exact number of the crew. It is not known in what capacity either of these veterans sailed, but Juet kept the only surviving journal.

Passing North Cape 1 May and approaching Novaya Zemlya, Hudson ran into trouble. Many of his Dutch sailors, fresh from the warm tropical waters of the East Indies, became depressed by bleak, cold seas and pitching ice. A mutiny broke out forcing the expedition to turn back. We learn this from historians who apparently received their information directly from Hudson. It is significant, however, in view of subsequent occurrences, that Juet makes no mention of the mutiny. He does make an important note in his journal for 19 May when he says, 'Then we observed the sunne having a slacke.' G. M. Asher considers this to be the first observation of a sun spot, more than eighteen months before that phenomenon was thought to have been first observed. Returning to the Faroe Islands where they stopped for water, Hudson obtained the crew's consent to seek for a

Passage to the westward in the latitude of 40°. It may be unjust
to suggest that Hudson did not resist the mutiny too strongly
because he wanted to explore the region recommended by Captain John Smith. The mutiny, while doubtless not so intended,
provided a convenient way to avoid pushing on to the Kara
Sea as his employers wished, and at the same time to seek a
Passage in a more promising region.

Crossing the Atlantic he searched fruitlessly for Buss Island;
spoke to several French fishermen on the Newfoundland Banks;
paused to cut a new foremast on the Nova Scotia coast; talked
with Indians who appeared in two French-built shallops and
wished to trade beaver skins for cloth; and cruised south along
the coast enjoying the fishing and lobstering. Within thirty
miles of his friend John Smith in Virginia, he turned north and
explored part of Delaware Bay. The month of September was
spent exploring New York Harbor and the Hudson River
about as far as the region of Albany. In a skirmish with the
Indians, John Colman the mate was slain. At a party aboard
ship their Indian guests got so drunk that the tradition of it
survived among the Delawares and Mohicans for two hundred
years. Hudson left the mouth of his River 4 October and after
some further trouble with the crew returned directly across
the Atlantic, arriving in Dartmouth Harbour on 7 November
1609.

Hudson immediately sent word of his arrival to his employers
and suggested that he search again to the northwest. But, by
January when he received orders to report in Amsterdam, the
English Government, doubtless informed of the discovery of
an important, navigable river, would not allow him or any
English members of his crew to go, maintaining that he had
made a voyage 'to the detriment of his own country.' Hudson
sent his logs and reports to Amsterdam through van Meteren,
who was thoroughly provoked by the action of the English.
Half Moon returned to her home port in July. This voyage of

Hudson was of course the basis for the Dutch claim to and eventual settlement of New Amsterdam.

Enthusiasm for a Northwest Passage in England had not abated. As one group of wealthy merchants became disillusioned, another formed ready to risk their money on the venture. Hudson, who still wanted to pursue Davis's 'furious overfall' and explore Weymouth's suggestion of a strait through Lumley's Inlet, had no difficulty in obtaining English backers. One of the most active and public spirited merchants in London at this time was Sir Thomas Smith, an original member of the East India Company and head of the Virginia Company. He was joined by the young, rich, and enthusiastic Sir Dudley Digges, and John Wolstenholm, the eminent Yorkshire promoter of expeditions who was knighted ten years later.

On 17 April 1610 Henry Hudson sailed down the Thames in confidence that he would confirm the theory of George Weymouth which he had argued so passionately but unsuccessfully with the Reverend Peter Plancius. If he had any sailorman's superstitions about commanding Weymouth's old ship *Discovery* on this voyage, they were probably of the auspicious sort.

Robert Juet, whom he must have trusted by this time, was again his mate. Several others, including Philip Staffe the carpenter, had served under Hudson before. Honest John King was quartermaster, Edward Wilson, a young man of twenty-two, was surgeon, and Robert Bylot, an able man and a navigator, sailed in an unspecified capacity but must have been one of the officers. Once more Hudson's son John was one of the ship's boys. Sir Dudley Digges had sent his servant Abacuck Pricket, a onetime haberdasher, along as an observer, and a young mathematician named Thomas Wydhouse (or Woodhouse) was also a passenger. On his way down river Hudson sent back a Master Coleburne, who had been put on board by the promoters as an advisor, and who may have been the same man who instigated the mutiny against Weymouth. At Graves-end Hudson picked up, apparently unbeknown to the backers of the voyage, Henry Greene a profligate protégé of his, taken along apparently for rehabilitation.

Sailing around by the north, *Discovery* passed the Orkneys and the Faroes, and on arriving off Iceland Hudson put in for refreshment. There trouble developed when Greene and the surgeon got into a fight. Hudson condoned Greene and con-demned Wilson's sharp tongue, which did not set well with the other members of the company. Juet, in a drunken tirade, commented that Hudson had taken Greene on board to act as a stool pigeon. Hudson heard of this after they left Iceland and very nearly turned back to put Juet on the beach.

From the ice-thick Greenland shore, Hudson pushed west-ward and by the end of June was off Resolution Island. Enter-ing the famous Strait which bears his name, Hudson's little ship was buffeted back and forth by strong currents and racing ice, making tedious headway. It was early in the season for the best passage of this water. Slowly he explored Ungava Bay and along the southern shore of Hudson Strait, always working westward. Whatever qualities Hudson may have lacked he was endowed with more than his share of the tenacity of all successful Arctic explorers. Overcoming currents, ice, storms, and more trouble with the crew, he arrived 1 August at two towering headlands which he named Cape Wolstenholm and Cape Digges — the gateway to the inland sea. After securing fresh meat from the flocks of nesting fowl, Hudson sailed into his broad blue bay. He was not the first man to do so for it is pretty certain that Sebastian Cabot entered it briefly nearly a century before, and there is good cartographical evidence that the keels of Portuguese navigators had sliced its waters. But if ever a man deserved to have a geographical feature bear his name, Hudson deserves his on this bay.

As he left the two capes towering thousands of feet into the

cold northern sky, Hudson turned south 'into a spacious sea
. . . confidently proud that he had won the passage,' and, keeping the eastern shore in sight, sailed until he found himself in
the shallow cul-de-sac of James Bay. The year was far advanced.
The ice closed in behind him; and there he lay with no way to
return, nearing the end of his stores which had been provided
for six months only. The officers became mutinous. On 10
September a trial was held with the result that Juet was de-
moted, Bylot replacing him as mate. The boatswain was also
stripped of rank, and William Wilson, an especially unruly
crew member, was given the position.

In preparation for wintering they worked down into the
southeast of James Bay and *Discovery* was grounded 1 November and frozen in ten days later. The winter itself was a nightmare. Provisions were scant although the men augmented them
with birds and fish. The crew apparently thought Hudson
was holding back food, while he believed they were hoarding
provisions. The men bickered among themselves; Hudson himself became increasingly irritable. He replaced his mate Bylot
with John King, a man totally unqualified for the job.

The ship was free 12 June, and the crew began preparing
for the voyage home. Hudson, on the other hand, intended to
continue the search. But in his plans he had failed to consider
the crew. On the morning of 22 June he was seized and bound
as he came out of his cabin. The shallop was hauled alongside
and Hudson, his son, and five sick men, including Thomas
Wydhouse, put off with neither spare clothing nor provisions.
They were, however, handed a musket and an iron kettle.

It must be remembered that from the time the ship entered
Hudson Bay we have only the account of Pricket to rely on.
Hudson's journal terminates abruptly after he passed the two
great capes, for Pricket saw to it that no contradictory account
returned. Pricket gives us the impression that there was great

confusion; apparently only Henry Greene, William Wilson, and perhaps Juet knew what was intended, although four of the crew had also been in on the plot. The mutineers threatened to send off the surgeon and Pricket in the shallop if they objected, and King, the only man who protested, was finally put in with Hudson. The carpenter Staffe, when he realized what was happening, took his tools and voluntarily cast his lot with his captain. Robert Bylot, who was below, said afterward that he thought they were only going to keep Hudson and the others in the boat until he consented to increase their food rations.

With Hudson and his son, Wydhouse the mathematician, John King, Philip Staffe, and the sick sailors in the shallop, the rest of the crew got the ship underway and stood out of the ice towing the boat behind. As they neared the edge of the ice the boat was cut adrift and 'then out with their top-sayles, and towards the east they stood in a cleere sea.' It is a scene of the deepest pathos, inspired by the most monumental skulduggery. There is irony too in the fact that Greene, the leader, had turned on the man who had befriended him, and Juet had forsaken his old shipmate and commander. For all this, of course, we have only one side of the story, for Pricket cast in the roles of chief villains only those who perished on the return voyage.

After sailing off from the shallop they hove to and ransacked the ship, finding some provisions that Hudson had been keeping in reserve. Then, with Greene as Captain, they headed for Hudson Strait. Without Bylot they would have been hopelessly lost. At last the two lofty headlands guarding the Strait came into view. In their joy they ran the ship on a rock, from which the flood tide eventually floated her. On the morning of 27 July they rowed ashore and killed about thirty birds. On the following day they went to Digges Island where they hoped to get more birds to help provision the ship for the ocean crossing. But as they were about to land several canoes with fifty or sixty

Eskimos appeared. Hostages were exchanged, and then each group demonstrated its method of hunting fowl. All seemed friendly.

The next day Greene intended to trade with the Eskimos for venison and went ashore with William Wilson, Pricket, and three sailors, John Thomas, Michael Perse, and Adrian Motter. On landing Pricket, who was lame, stayed with the boat. Perse and Motter climbed up the rocks to gather sorrel, and the other three began displaying knickknacks to the natives. Pricket, lying in the bottom of the boat, saw a leg swing over the gunwale and just in time warded off a blow from the invading Eskimo's knife. After a struggle, during which he was wounded, Pricket dispatched his assailant with his dirk. In the meantime the Eskimos had attacked those ashore and Thomas and Wilson had 'their bowels cut out.' Perse and Greene were wounded, but managed to drag the others into the boat and tumble in themselves. Motter, desperately trying to reach the boat, rushed into the sea and, wading and swimming, held on to the transom. The natives driven off, Motter hauled aboard, and the boat's head got around, they rowed off as hard as wounded men could. The Eskimos sent a parting shower of arrows after them, killing Greene instantly and wounding Perse and Pricket again. Bylot, Juet, and the others with the ship picked up the desperate men, but the disemboweled Thomas and Wilson, 'swearing and cursing in a most fearful manner,' died shortly; Perse died two days later.

Now there were only nine survivors to work the ship. Salting down three hundred birds for food, they began the dreadful passage home. Nearing the end of the crossing, buffeted by contrary winds and weak from hunger, they collected the bones of the birds they had eaten 'to fry them with candle greese till they were crisp, when with vinegar put to them they made a good dish.' The men were so feeble that except for Bylot none could stand at the helm, and Juet starved to death.

At last the coast of Ireland came into view and a Cornwall fisherman brought them into Bantry Bay 6 September and eventually into Plymouth from where they returned to Gravesend. One would have supposed that the eight survivors would have been slapped into prison immediately, but not at all. Bylot and Pricket hastened to report to Sir Thomas Smith, and apparently assured him that the Northwest Passage had been found. On 24 October the Masters of Trinity House examined the mutineers and agreed that they all deserved to hang. But they did not hang. Various hearings took place at widely separated intervals. There is no indication that Bylot was ever tried. Seven years after they returned to England, Pricket, Edward Wilson the surgeon, and two of the crew were tried and acquitted. Hudson's widow asked for and received help for her youngest son Richard from the Directors of the East India Company. Richard Hudson served them well in India for most of his life. As for Hudson himself, Captain Thomas James, who wintered on Charlton Island 1631-2, found evidence that Hudson and his companions had reached land, but then traces vanished in the stunted growth of the cold Canadian forest.

Hudson in retrospect appears to have lacked some of the important attributes of a successful leader. Throughout the accounts of his voyages flows the constant dissatisfaction of his officers and crews. Men did not follow him out of fear, as they did Frobisher, or out of love, as in the case of Davis. Hudson appears to have been something of a dreamer, albeit a courageous one, a student of geography, and a man of infinite perseverance and stubbornness. In four short years he attacked, as had no one else, the frozen Arctic by the north, the east, and the west, coasting the ice for thousands of miles and probing bays and inlets for the elusive Passage. His name is perpetuated on the three great waters — river, strait, and bay — which he explored. He had made large and notable additions to geographical knowledge; for Pricket fortunately brought back his 'card' and the information thereon was published in the famous map by Hessel Gerritz in 1612. Hudson's original chart was evidently sent to his old friend Peter Plancius, who gave it to Gerritz to engrave and probably supplied him with the information for the explanation of the chart. The publication of Gerritz's chart and the remarks by Samuel Purchas in the first edition of his *Pilgrimage* published in 1613 spread Hudson's fame quickly. Both Gerritz and Purchas firmly believed that Hudson had found the long-sought Northwest Passage, and, as we shall see, they were not alone.

11

In Hudson's Wake

*W*e do not know what story Robert Bylot told of his part in the abandonment of Hudson. It must have been sufficiently convincing to keep him from trial. After all, he was the only survivor with enough knowledge of navigation to pilot a ship back to that tragic bay which held such high promise of a passage to the South Sea. But, in fact, the return of the survivors of the Hudson expedition created enormous interest and enthusiasm. The sanguine tales, told by men desperate to save their own skins, diverted attention from their shocking crime. That they had sailed with Hudson through a broad strait into a wide sea was at the moment more important than their desertion of him. He had explored the eastern shore of that sea; no man knew the western shore, but it was reasonable to assume it led into the passage to China. It will be remembered that the mutineers had run *Discovery* on a rock at the western end of Hudson Strait and that they were set afloat again by a flood coming from the westward. This was presumed strong, if not conclusive, evidence that an opening to the ocean

HUDSON BAY

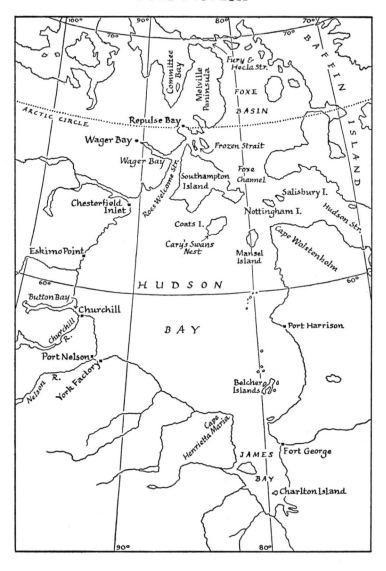

lay in that direction. The Northwest Passage was now considered to be a virtual certainty.

Sir Thomas Smith and his colleagues had no difficulty obtaining assistance for another expedition. The prospect of great riches reinforced humanitarian demands that there should be an attempt to find Hudson and his comrades. Wolstenholm commented that the idea and preparations for another voyage so possessed Sir Dudley Digges that he could think of nothing else. About 160 adventurers joined Smith, Digges, and Wolstenholm and there is little doubt that they were among the 288 individuals who, in July 1612, were granted a Royal Charter by James I as the 'Governor and Company of the Merchants of London, Discoverers of the North-West Passage,' commonly known as the Northwest Company. This imposing list of people included every eminent person who had shown curiosity in the Arctic, as well as many other distinguished individuals. Headed by the Archbishop of Canterbury and twenty-five peers of the realm and under the patronage of the brilliant young Prince of Wales, the Company included Sir James Lancaster who made the first English voyage to the East Indies; Richard Hakluyt the historian; Henry Briggs and Edward Wright the illustrious mathematicians; Robert Bylot, Abacuck Pricket and Edward Wilson all fresh from the Hudson voyage; and Captains Thomas Button and William Gibbons, of whom more presently. By this document Sir Thomas Smith became the first Governor of the Company, a position he also held in the East India and Muscovy Companies. Interlocking directorships were as practical a convenience then as nowadays. All previous charters or licenses for northwestern exploration and trade were revoked. The new company received a monopoly of any passage between Cape Desolation, Greenland, and about the fifty-eighth parallel in Labrador, extending north, northwestward, and west all the way to China, Japan, and the South Seas and all adjacent countries. This area took in both Davis Strait and Hudson

Strait, the only two possible openings for a Passage, and all waters in between. It was an all-inclusive, powerfully backed document.[1]

In mid-April of 1612, three months before the charter was granted, Smith and his colleagues had already dispatched an expedition which now came under the formerly organized Northwest Company. A Welshman, Captain Thomas Button, was in command of the large ship *Resolution*. He was accompanied by the veteran *Discovery* under Captain John Ingram. To insure his finding Hudson Strait and the desired landfalls, Button was accompanied by Robert Bylot and Abacuck Pricket, returning to the Bay of their ill fame. Two other Captains, William Gibbons, a relative of Button's, and William Hawkeridge, went along as volunteers, perhaps for the experience, for they made voyages to the same region within a few years.

The little we know of this important expedition we owe to Luke Foxe who obtained his information from Pricket, Hawkeridge, and Sir Thomas Roe, a member of the Northwest Company, who published what he learned in his book in 1635.[2] The expedition was well equipped. *Resolution* was probably a ship of the Royal Navy selected in January 1612, with the help of Phineas Pett, Master of the dockyard. Pett went to Gravesend 14 April, probably for a final inspection to meet Captain Button before he sailed. Curiously enough the two ships of Captain James Cook's third expedition were also named *Resolution* and *Discovery*. By another coincidence Button's direct descendant, Button Gwinnet, was one of the signers of the Declaration of Independence.

Button's instructions, dated 5 April 1612, were drawn up by the Prince of Wales who may have been inspired or advised by Sir Dudley Digges. Of all the backers of Hudson and members of the Northwest Company, Digges was one of the most enthusiastic. In 1610 he is supposed to have written a manuscript, found in a copy of John Davis's *The Worldes Hydrographicall*

Description in 1851, entitled *Motives Inducing a Project for the Discoverie of the North Pole Terrestrial*: *the Streights of Anian into the South Sea; and the Coasts thereof* and he was the author of a small tract published in 1611 entitled *Of the Circumference of the Earth; or a Treatise of the North-East* [misprint for *West*] *Passage*. In any event the Prince, who died before the expedition returned, specifically instructed Button to sail directly to Digges Island, and at the adjoining mainland to observe the direction from which the flood came and sail into it. He was to hold regular religious services, keep full journals, and to spend no time on anything except the Passage. If he found the Passage one ship was to return at once with the news, while he sailed on to Asia.

Entering the Strait, Button named the island, hitherto known as Queen Elizabeth's Foreland, Resolution Island for his ship. Then working his way against heavy ice to Digges Strait, he set up a pinnace and lost five men in a fight with the natives, at the same spot where four of Hudson's mutineers met their reward.

One of Button's instructions from the Northwest Company was to search for Hudson. There is no indication that any serious attempt was made to do so, for this would have involved turning south toward James Bay where the abandoned men might have survived. Instead, all eyes and thoughts were on the Passage and he bore westward passing the cape at the southeast end of Coat's Island and naming it Cary's Swans Nest. Sailing hopefully on to the westward they came to the other side of Hudson Bay in about latitude 60° 40′ and called it Hopes Checked. The unbroken western shore was explored southward as far as the mouth of Nelson River which Button named Port Nelson after his sailing master who died and was buried there. Here the ships were grounded for the winter. It was a trying season. Many men died and Button himself was ill. He spent much of his time helping his officers keep up morale by giving them navigational and geographical problems to while away the long winter.

So many men had been lost that in the early summer of 1613 *Resolution* was abandoned. Button continued in *Discovery*. By 15 July he was back at Hopes Checked and worked carefully northward along the coast up into Roes Welcome to about 65°. He believed himself in a bay, which for some years was known as Button's *Ne Ultra,* and, turning south, sailed along the western shore of Southampton Island. As he continued southeasterly, passing but not perceiving Fisher Strait, he made land again at Coats Island which he regarded as an extension of Southampton.

About 9 August he saw an island which he named Mansel for his near neighbor, kinsman, and fellow naval officer Vice Admiral Sir Robert Mansel. Landing on the island he found the ruins of two Eskimo houses and in them human skeletons, walrus tusks, images, toys, and other objects. For the next ten days he sailed about between Mansel and Coats Islands, sighting Cape Pembroke on the north end of the latter twice, and eventually working east to Cape Wolstenholm on 19 August.

All during his expedition Button was careful to observe the set of the tides for it was thought the direction of a strong tide would lead to a passage to open ocean. When he arrived at the western end of Hudson Strait on his return voyage, he spent some time observing the strong tides about Salisbury Island and Nottingham Island. These tides were flowing into and out of still undiscovered Foxe Channel, but Button felt that they indicated the true direction in which the Passage would be found. He hoped he would not be blamed for not first exploring to the north, but he had followed his orders precisely in sailing directly across Hudson Bay and searching its western shore.

One oversight nags at us, however. If one of the purposes of the expedition was to find Hudson, why was not a search made down the eastern shore and into James Bay? Perhaps it was because Bylot and Pricket, who must have acted as pilots to a certain extent, kept them away from that direction. Even so, why did not one ship search while the other surveyed the western shore? Pricket, whose journal so subtly protected the survivors, might well have been capable of preventing this, although Bylot, who appears to have been a competent if temporizing man, might have regretted his part in the crime.

Button returned directly home, leaving the Strait by sailing between Cape Chidley and the small islands which bear his name and making a very quick passage of sixteen days. He apparently arrived the third week of September for Phineas Pett wrote that on the twenty-seventh 'my noble worthy friend Sir Thomas Button (then Capt. Button) alighted at my house, newly being returned from the dangerous Voyage of the Northwest Passage, where he had wintered.' Immediately all journals and logs kept on the voyage were impounded, just why is not known. They were apparently in Button's possession for some years thereafter but never published. Were it not for the scraps included by Foxe in his book and a little in *Purchas,* we should know nothing of the expedition. And yet it was, from the evidence available, the best conducted expedition to the Northwest up to that time. Button was obviously a man of energy and good sense; his subordinates were able and experienced men, and they carried out their assignment to the letter. They explored the entire western shore of Hudson Bay, except for the region between Port Nelson and Cape Henrietta Maria, probably the westernmost point reached by Hudson. In fact, for many years thereafter the great inland sea was known as Button Bay, a name now reduced to a small indentation in the coast just west of Port Churchill, but his names for geographical features have lasted to our time.

While Button was away, increasingly hopeful statements were published in the several editions of Hessel Gerritz's work; when the ships did not return at the end of the first season, it was presumed that they had sailed to China or the East Indies. Although hopes were somewhat dampened after his return, the secrecy surrounding the voyage suggested that his information was encouraging. Button was knighted and became an Admiral.

Certainly his observations of the tides at the western end of Hudson Strait directly influenced the Northwest Company to send out another expedition the following year. Button's cousin and companion Captain William Gibbons, accompanied by Robert Bylot, sailed in March, once more in *Discovery*. Very little is known of this voyage. They evidently ran into a year of unusually heavy ice which forced them from the entrance to Hudson Strait down the Labrador Coast, where for ten weeks they remained icebound in an unidentified bay in about 58° which they called 'Gibbons his Hole.' When they got free, the season was so far gone that they sailed back to England, accomplishing nothing.

Yet the failure of Gibbons did not discourage the Northwest Company. On the contrary it stimulated its efforts. Thomas Smith was ever eager for explorations in this direction and his colleagues, Digges, Wolstenholm, and Alderman Francis Jones, onetime Lord Mayor of London, shared his enthusiasm. And there was good reason for the Company to be optimistic. After all, Hudson and Button had made important discoveries, pushing into a great inland sea; Gibbons had been unfortunate in his season. The record so far was very good.

Robert Bylot had been on all three of these voyages. He was a navigator now, with more experience in Hudson Bay than any other man at this time. It was therefore natural enough, indeed logical, that he be selected to command the reliable *Discovery* on her fifth Arctic voyage in 1615. William Baffin, who was to loom large in northern exploration, entered the Northwest Company's service for the first time as Bylot's mate and pilot. His previous service had been with the Muscovy Company which, since the days of Sebastian Cabot who first trained their navigators and inaugurated their excellent system of keeping log books and prepared charts, expected its officers to keep detailed journals and make frequent astronomical observations.

Baffin was well trained, and his log book, account, and map have survived.[3]

John Wolstenholm came aboard *Discovery* on 15 March 1615 at St. Katherine's Pool, leaving final orders and promising triple wages to the fourteen men and two boys on the crew if the Passage were found. Bylot and Baffin weighed anchor the next day and arrived at the Scilly Islands on the twenty-sixth. On 8 April they put in to Padstow, Cornwall, where they added provisions and finally sailed with a fair wind on the nineteenth. The twenty-sixth Baffin recorded that he took a longitude sight by observing an occultation of a star by the moon. From this observation he could obtain his time and figure his longitude — the first occasion on record that longitude had been figured at sea while under way. Cape Farewell was sighted 10 May and, after working through very heavy ice crossing the entrance to Davis Strait, at five o'clock in the afternoon of the twenty-seventh they saw Resolution Island. It was the purpose of this expedition to investigate the tides observed by Button at the entrance of Foxe Channel. Working along the north shore of Hudson Strait, Baffin mapped the coast and landed frequently to make observations.

While the ship was enclosed with ice 21 June, Baffin again experimented with longitude observations. This time he employed a different method. The day was clear with the sun and moon simultaneously visible. Using a quadrant with a two-foot radius, he took the altitude of the sun at the instant the moon crossed the meridian.[4] Figuring his variation, and by reference to an almanac, he calculated his position at 74° 05′ W. from London, within a degree of where Captain Parry figured it at the same spot in 1821. No further evidence is needed of Baffin's remarkable skill as an observer and mathematician.

They reached the western end of Hudson Strait the end of June and the next month was spent observing the tides around Salisbury and Nottingham Islands, the entrance to Foxe Chan-

nel, and the Bell Peninsula of Southampton Island. Mill Island
was given its name from the grinding noise of the ice. Coasting
the northeast shore of Southampton Island on 12 July, Bylot
named the point Cape Comfort because of the encouraging nature of the current. However, their hopes were dashed the next
day by shoaling water, slackened current, and thick ice. They
had reached the entrance of Frozen Strait and, deciding there
was no passage in that direction, they turned back. On the sixteenth they were at Sea Horse Point, which Baffin named for the
large and aggressive herd of walruses encountered there. By the
twenty-ninth they were at Digges Island, where the next day
they killed seventy fowl for meat and then set sail homeward.
They passed Resolution Island 5 August without sighting it and
anchored in Plymouth Sound 8 September, terminating the
voyage without the loss of a single man.

Baffin, at the end of this voyage, arrived at some very definite
and sensible conclusions. He writes:

> And now it may be that som expect I should give my opynion
> conserninge the passadge. To those my answere must be, that
> doubtles theare is a passadge. But within this strayte, whome is
> called Hudson's Straytes, I am doubtful, supposinge the con-
> trarye. But whether there be, or no, I will not affirme. But this I
> will affirme, that we have not beene in any tyde then that from
> Resolutyon Iland, and the greatest indraft of that commeth from
> Davis Straytes; and my judgment is, if [there is] any passadge
> within Resolution Iland, it is but some creeke or in lett, but the
> mayne [passage] will be upp fretum Davis; but if any be desirous
> to knowe my opynion in pertyculler, I will at any tyme be redy
> to showe the best resons I cann, eyther by word of mouth, or
> otherwise.[5]

Bylot and Baffin left the most accurate surveys thus far of
Hudson Strait and the waters between its western end and
Southampton Island. The names they bestowed on geograph-
ical features are still current. Besides making the first observa-

tions of longitude at sea, Baffin kept a longitude column in his log, as Davis had done, but he wrote that it was still 'Not usual in Jarnales.' He also made important observations on the variation of the needle, recording his observations in terms of deflection of the north end of the needle rather than the south end as had been the earlier custom.[6]

Bylot and Baffin carried out their orders to investigate the tides noticed by Button thoroughly and well. While we know that there was a passage by way of Foxe Channel and Foxe Basin through Fury and Hecla Strait, Baffin was substantially correct in advising searchers for the Northwest Passage to concentrate on Davis Strait. The Directors of the Northwest Company took his advice.

12

Beyond Hope Sanderson

*O*n 20 April 1612, a few days after Button dropped down the Thames, two ships — 140-ton *Patience* and sixty-ton *Heart's Ease* — sailed from Hull. James Hall commanded the larger vessel with William Gordon as his chief mate and Gatonbe as one of his quartermasters. *Heart's Ease* was commanded by an elderly Captain of high repute named Andrew Barker, accompanied by William Huntriss, probably as master. Huntriss, who had sailed with Hall previously, had been shot through both buttocks by an Eskimo arrow on the 1605 voyage. William Baffin probably sailed as pilot of the expedition on *Patience*. There seems to be some evidence that Hall gained his first experience on the west coast of Greenland on one of Davis's voyages.[1] If this is true, he makes an important link between Davis and Baffin, the two most successful navigators and explorers of their period in this direction.

Hall, who was never wholly convinced by the Copenhagen assayers that the ore which he brought back in 1605 was not silver, terminated his services as Greenland pilot for the Danes sometime after his return in 1607. Returning to England he secured the backing of 'the Merchant Adventurers of London': Sir James Lancaster, Sir Thomas Smith, Sir Richard Bell, and Mr. (later Sir) William Cockin, all members of the Northwest Company but acting as individuals. The object of the expedition is in some doubt and its origin obscure. Hall, who was himself a sponsor, probably convinced the merchants that his ore might be silver, for a metallurgist was provided to test the ore.

Of the voyage itself we have two accounts, one by John Gatonbe and the other by William Baffin.[2] Cape Farewell, which Gatonbe reported was named by Davis, was sighted and recognized by Hall 14 May, and three days later Cape Desolation was sighted. By the twenty-seventh the expedition anchored in Godthaab which they called 'Harbour of Hope.' Hall and his officers explored this region in their boats while the ship's carpenter set up a pinnace and a shallop. A musket was stolen by 'one of the wild men,' and a sailor was killed by a native dart. Working north, the ships were anchored at Sukkertoppen on 17 June. In July Hall took *Heart's Ease* and, leaving the larger ship, went north to try and reach the location of his supposed silver mine.

While lying in the anchorage where, in 1605, five Eskimos had been kidnapped to take to Denmark and another killed as a disciplinary measure, about 150 native boats came out to trade.[3] Hall had the misfortune to be recognized by an Eskimo, evidently a relative of one of those carried off seven years before. As Hall sat in a boat with Huntriss and two others, the savage deliberately sank his weapon into Hall's right side, piercing his liver. The others, who could have been easily killed, were not molested; Hall died the next day. Before dying he appointed Barker commander of the expedition. The day after burying Hall on one of the Knight Islands, the party found the spot where the ore had been dug. James Carlisle, the goldsmith, declared it worthless.

Heart's Ease rejoined *Patience* on the twenty-sixth and, after considerable argument by the mates, Barker assumed command on *Patience* and appointed Huntriss master of the other vessel. It was then agreed to return to England. Barker brought his ship into his home port of Hull on 17 September, while William Huntriss, two days later and with flags at half-mast, brought *Heart's Ease* up to St. Katherine's Pool.

Baffin, in the fragment of his journal that has been preserved, tells us that he was constantly taking sights and making observations on shore. Previous to this voyage with Hall nothing definite is known of Baffin's life. He was apparently a Londoner, with a wife and home in that city, who worked his way from a humble position by his ambition and talents. Purchas called him 'that learned-unlearned mariner and mathematician.'

Shortly after returning from Greenland, Baffin entered the service of the Muscovy Company which had sent Hudson on his voyages of 1607 and 1608. In 1609 and 1610 they had sent Captain Jonas Pool to explore Spitsbergen, and secured in the following year a charter granting them sole rights to the Spitsbergen whale fishery. In 1612 Thomas Smith, as head of the Company, sent a fleet to drive fifteen Dutch, French, and Biscayan ships from those waters. In 1613 another Muscovy fleet of seven ships was sent to Spitsbergen under Captain Benjamin Joseph in the 260-ton *Tiger,* with William Baffin as chief pilot. Seventeen foreign ships were allowed to fish along the Spitsbergen coast only by agreeing to give half of their catch to the English. The fleet returned with full holds in September. Baffin's narrative of this trip was published by Purchas; another account by Robert Fotherby remained in manuscript form until published by the American Antiquarian Society in 1860.[4]

Baffin and Fotherby were together again under Captain Joseph in the ship *Thomasine* as head of a fleet of thirteen vessels on a second Spitsbergen voyage in 1614. These two explored to the eastward as far as Hinlopen Strait in a most unfavorable season, and Baffin arrived back in London, 4 October. He then, as we have seen, took service with the Northwest Company for the expedition to Hudson Bay with Robert Bylot. Retained for a second voyage the following year, he again sailed as pilot, Bylot being master. *Discovery,* outfitted by the same group for her sixth and last recorded Arctic voyage, sailed with seventeen men on 26 March 1616, to attempt the Northwest Passage by Davis Strait.

The first land seen after leaving England was the west Greenland shore on 14 May, at Cockin Sound or Sukkertoppen as it is since known. They pushed on north to 70°20′ just north of Disko Island on what Davis had called London Coast, and anchored 20 May. Here they were visited by Eskimos and their dogs, took on fresh water, and observed the tides. Two days later, underway again, they came upon a dead whale and removed 160 plates of whalebone from its head before a rising wind and high sea broke the carcass loose from the ship. By 30 May they were at Hope Sanderson, the northernmost point Davis had reached, and came into heavy ice.

The first of June, clear of ice and working through Upernavik Islands, they named Women's Islands after two old women met there. On the tenth Baffin tried without success to push through the middle pack. He then worked inshore and spent several days trading with the natives, who brought seal skins and walrus and narwhal tusks to swap for beads and iron. Abundant narwhals disported amongst the dissipating ice as they continued on their way again by the eighteenth. On Midsummer Day sails and rigging were so iced up that the men could sarcely work the ship, although the cold was not extreme. Finally, on 1 July they came into an open sea, the 'North Water' of later whalers, in 75°40′. Next morning a fair headland was named Cape Dudley Digges (latitude 76°35′) and beyond that a fiord, where they attempted to anchor without success, was called Wolstenholm Sound. Continuing ever northerly, they named the next fiord Whale Sound for the enormous number of the creatures lying in the water, who paid no attention whatsoever to the ship. Between this sound and the next, which was named for Sir Thomas Smith, Hakluyt Island was given the geographer's name. Carrying onward about the head of Baffin Bay, they named a small group of islands for Mr. Alwyn Cary the ship's husband or, as we would say, agent. As they crossed the head of the Bay with a fresh wind and open sea, another vast inlet opened before them, and Baffin promptly called it Alderman Jones Sound.

On 12 July, in latitude 74°20′, they called a great strait Sir James Lancaster Sound and, says Baffin, 'here our hopes of passage began to be lesse every day then other, for from this sound to the southward wee had a ledge of ice betweene the shoare and us, but cleare to the seaward.' He did not know that here lay the only feasible entrance to the Northwest Passage. They worked southeasterly along heavy ice and sighted the shore in 68°. The season far gone and the men getting scurvy, they made for the coast of Greenland, anchoring in Cockin Sound 28 July. After the sick had been treated with scurvy grass boiled in beer and sorrel salad, they turned *Discovery*'s prow for England and anchored in Dover Road 30 August.

Baffin submitted his detailed journal and map to Purchas who published only the abbreviated narrative, saying that the detailed log and map were too expensive to reproduce. Because of this decision Baffin's discovery gradually came to be discredited and doubt cast on the very existence of Baffin Bay. In 1818 a book was published, entitled *The Possibility of approaching the North Pole, asserted by the Hon. Daines Barrington,* containing a circumpolar map showing a great bay and written across it 'Baffin's Bay, according to the relation of W. Baffin in 1616, but not now believed.' The eminent Arctic authority Sir John Barrow in his *Chronological History of the Voyages into the Arctic Regions,* which appeared the same year, entirely deleted Baffin Bay from his Polar map. But in the very year that Baffin Bay was entirely discredited, Sir John Ross rediscovered it and confirmed Baffin's discoveries and observations.

After returning, Baffin wrote a letter to Sir John Wolstenholm in which he flatly states that 'there is no passage nor hope of passage in the north of Davis Straights. We having coasted all, or neere all the circumference thereof, and finde it to be no other than a great bay, as the voyage doth truly show.' He adds that Davis should not be blamed for reporting high hopes of a Passage, for looking from Hope Sanderson 'the sea is open, and of an unsearchable depth, and of a good colour.' Baffin apparently considered the matter settled for he then took service with the East India Company and made a two-year voyage to the East Indies. Possibly he thought, as had Davis, that there might be an opportunity to try the Passage from the Pacific side. He continued taking observations and charting coasts wherever he went and he was commended by the Company for doing so.

Baffin last sailed as master of the ship *London* in the fleet assigned to drive the Portuguese from Ormuz in the Persian Gulf. He went on shore 25 January 1622 to observe the height and distance of the castle wall in order to find the range 'for the better levelling of his piece. But as he was about the same, he received a shot from the castle into his belly, wherewith he gave three leaps, and died immediately.' [5]

Following Baffin's death his widow, that 'troublesome impatient woman,' brought claims against the Company. The East India merchants were generous but Mrs. Baffin continued to be a nuisance even after remarriage when she 'had made an unequal choice of a man not of the best governed,' and until she was so old, deaf, and foolish that her temper lost its sting.

With Baffin's and Bylot's voyage of 1616, the unbroken series of annual expeditions in search of the Northwest Passage came to an end. The Northwest Company was satisfied to accept Baffin's negative conclusions and leave the field to others.

13

Three Came Back

Three years after Baffin concluded that a passage through Davis Strait did not exist, another attempt, little known in England at that time, was made.

We have already noted Christian IV's expeditions to Greenland in 1605 to 1607. A true lover of the sea, he desired not only to increase his country's commerce but also to participate in expeditions to extend geographical knowledge. On one occasion he had himself acted as his own Admiral under the name of Captain Christian Fredericksen, voyaging as far as Wardhouse. He was always ready to assist Danish merchants with ships and money and in 1610 sent two vessels to Novaya Zemlya for the combined purpose of trading and searching for the Northeast Passage.

One of these ships was commanded by an ambitious Captain named Jens Munk. Munk, who was born near Arendal, Norway, 3 June 1579, led an extraordinarily adventurous life. In 1591, at the age of twelve, he went to England, and from there journeyed to Oporto where he lived with a merchant named Duart Duez to learn Portuguese. After a year he sailed as cabin boy to Bahia to join Miguel Duez, a brother of his employer, but when he arrived in Brazil he found that Miguel had left for Europe. He then decided to stay with his skipper, a Dutchman named Albert Jansen, and continue voyaging. Unfortunately, a short distance out of Bahia the French attacked the fleet of thirteen Dutch and Portuguese vessels, of which his ship was one, and all were taken or destroyed. Jansen's ship was burned and Munk was one of seven survivors who clung to wreckage until picked up by the French and put down on a wild part of the Brazilian coast. Escaping from Indians, Munk found his way to Bahia where he lived fifteen months, part of the time as a shoemaker's apprentice and part with a portrait painter. Then Miguel Duez returned from Europe and installed him in his own home and employ. In 1598 two unlicensed Dutch vessels arrived in the port and were about to be confiscated by the Spanish authorities. Duez, a Portuguese with no love for Spaniards, decided to warn the Dutchmen, and the nineteen-year-old Munk swam out to the ships to tell them of their danger. The Spaniards were hard on his heels, and the Dutch barely had time to pull the young man over the side, cut their cables, and get to sea, taking Munk with them to Amsterdam.

Refusing lucrative offers from the grateful Dutch, Munk returned to Copenhagen and obtained employment as a supercargo on ships trading to Spain, about the Baltic, and other European ports. By 1605 he seems to have prospered sufficiently to be entering into commercial operations on his own account as a Captain and merchant. He made voyages to Iceland, Archangel, and Novaya Zemlya and, after returning from the latter in 1610, obtained a Captain's commission in the Danish Navy when war broke out with Sweden in 1611. He served with distinction in the Swedish war and carried out many special commissions in the King's service. In 1614, for example, he returned some Russian ambassadors to Archangel; in 1615 he was apprehending English and Irish pirates in the North Sea and about the Faroe Islands; and during the two following years he was instrumental in establishing the Danish and Norwegian whaling industry. As Denmark's most experienced and widely-traveled Captain, he was ordered to take an expedition of three ships for the newly founded Danish East India Company to the East in 1618, but not liking their terms he obtained the King's permission to decline.[1]

The recent discoveries made by the English explorers in Hudson Bay were well known in Europe and caused particular excitement in Denmark, doubtless because of the close relationship between the English and Danish sovereigns. Munk himself may have suggested that the Danes attempt the Northwest Passage. After his unpleasant relationship with the East India Company he may have hoped to find the Passage and arrive in the East ahead of their ships. But even if Munk did not propose the expedition, he was certainly qualified to command it, with his years of service as a navigator and his experience in the Arctic waters of Europe and Iceland.

On 9 May 1619, two naval vessels, the small frigate *Enhiörningen* (*Unicorn*) and the Swedish sloop *Lamprenen* (*Lamprey*), which had been captured seven years earlier, were equipped and sailed from Copenhagen, with sixty-five men aboard. Munk's chief mate was William Gordon, an Englishman who had sailed with Bylot and Baffin in 1616 and who was otherwise experienced in Northern waters. Another Englishman, a John Watson, served as mate on the sloop. While the Danes had plenty of seamen seasoned in Northern European navigation, they needed these Englishmen with their experience in the Northwest just as they needed Hall, Knight, and Cunningham for the Greenland voyages.

The story of Jens Munk's voyage is known from his own account published in Copenhagen in 1624.[2] Putting into the Sound on 9 May, they were held up by head winds and did not actually sail from Denmark until 16 May 1619. They stopped at Karmsund, Norway, for a few days to sign on three new hands.

One month after their departure from Norway on 30 May, they sighted Cape Farewell. By 8 July they had crossed Davis Strait. First entering Frobisher Bay, Munk discovered his error and worked out around Resolution Island into Hudson Strait, which he usually refers to as *Fretum Christian*. He was nearly killed on the twelfth when, while shooting birds, his 'gun burst into pieces, and took the brim clean off the front of my hat.'

Munk's passage of the Strait was very difficult. He worked along the north shore for some distance, then crossed over and made a circle in Ungava Bay, and continued westward along the southern and middle part of the Strait, eventually reaching the vicinity of Digges Island on 20 August. Throughout this appallingly slow passage of Hudson Strait, he was greatly hampered by strong gales and ice. For days on end the two ships, lashed together, were taken wherever the floes wandered. The severe pressure of the ice damaged the ships, and when an enormous iceberg split in two, causing high waves, the sloop was in great danger of grounding. At times, however, they were able to trade with the natives, to wash their salty clothes, and to hunt caribou. On 8 August one of the seamen died — the first of many. Passing close aboard the northern end and then encircling Mansel Island, Munk sailed directly across Hudson Bay to Port Churchill, as it is now called, on the western shore. Arriving in foul weather on 7 September at this harbor, which he called Jens Munk's Vinterhaffn, he lit a beacon fire to guide in *Lamprey* which had been separated from him. The sloop arrived two days later. Many of the crew were ill, but after getting on shore where they made a good fire and gathered berries to eat, they recovered. A polar bear was shot for fresh meat, and the harbor and nearby shoreline were explored in the ship's boat and a shallop they had assembled from six sections brought along for that purpose.

The weather, however, was stormy with strong winds. On 18 September, after consultation, the officers decided to winter. The ships, deeply cut by the ice, were brought up the river. *Uni-*

corn was so sharp bottomed that she could not be beached and still remain upright, so Munk 'caused the ship's keel to be dug down into the ground, and branches of trees to be spread under the bilge, packed together with clay and sand, in order that the ship might rest evenly on the bilge on both sides, and thus suffer less damage.' Still the ice moved her, and at high tide she leaked badly. Finally she was berthed again, moored by six hawsers and further secured and protected by timbers and stone pilings. By 1 October the ships were all in winter quarters. Extra clothing was issued, fireplaces built on *Unicorn* where the crews of both vessels ate and kept warm, and additional timbers and stone breakwaters built to protect the vessels against the ice. Wine was rationed but beer could be drunk in any quantity. Watches were established and men assigned to get wood, burn charcoal, and melt snow for water. On the seventh, Munk took his boat upriver as far as he could go, about four and a half miles, and on his return came to a point on which he found 'a picture on a stone, drawn with charcoal, fashioned like the half of a devil, wherefore I called the same promontory Devil's Cape.' In many other places he saw the signs of summer encampments of the Indians.

In late October there was a hard freeze and a black fox was caught. Thereafter groups of men went into the forest hunting and setting traps, and until the snow got too deep (Munk regretted that they had no snowshoes) they had plenty of fresh meat — hares, ptarmigan and other birds. On St. Martin's Eve (10 November), when goose is as traditional in Denmark as Thanksgiving turkey in New England, they dined on ptarmigan and were issued extra wine. Indians must have been hanging about unseen for in mid-November a large, muzzled, black dog came to the ship and the man on watch, thinking it was a fox, shot it. All continued well through December; the weather often sunny and mild although the snow was deep. Long hours were spent in the forest tending traps and occasionally shooting, so there was no lack of fresh meat and the ships' stores were plentiful. In general the men were healthy, active, and in good spirits, although one sailor and the sloop's surgeon died of scurvy. Ample wine and beer, which had to be boiled because it had frozen, was issued Christmas Eve 'so they had quite as much as they could stand, and were very jolly, but no one offended another with as much as a word.' Christmas was solemnly observed with a sermon and Mass celebrated by the priest for the expedition.

Almost immediately after the new year arrived, a change took place. Ominously, New Year's Day, 1620, gave them the coldest weather they had yet experienced, and it continued. While food was plentiful it was restricted to salt meat, some fresh meat, beer and wine. Soon the first symptoms of scurvy were painfully evident. One by one the men became fearfully sick. On 21 January thirteen were in bed and the cook and another sailor died. The situation rapidly deteriorated. The remaining surgeon and priest were desperately ill and one of the Danish mates, Hans Brock, died on the twenty-third.

Munk, in desperation, asked the mortally stricken Casper Caspersen if he could not recommend some remedy from his medicine chest, but the poor surgeon could only answer 'that, if God would not help, he could not render any advice or assistance at all.' By 16 February only seven men could 'fetch wood and water' and do the necessary work. That same day a sailor who had been ill the entire voyage died, and three days later the priest. During March a man died every day or two, among them the surgeon and the Captain of *Lamprey*. The twenty-sixth, Munk got ashore and gathered some berries and distributed them among the men. That seemed to help. On the thirtieth, after the death of a carpenter, the distracted commander wrote:

> . . . at this time commenced my greatest sorrow and misery, and I was then like a wild and lonely bird. I was now obliged

> myself to run about the ship, to give drink to the sick, to boil drink for them, and get for them what I thought might be good for them, to which I was not accustomed, and of which I had but little knowledge.

On 1 April his nephew Erick Munk died, as did the English mate Gordon a few days later. The survivors were now so weak that they could no longer fetch wood from the forest; their shallop had to be burned for warmth. During most of this time, through March and April, the weather was mild and not uncomfortable. It was warm enough in mid-April to fix a wine case so that those not too weak could bathe. But on 14 April only four men besides Munk had strength enough to sit up in their bunks. Day after day the dreadful toll continued and with increasing difficulty the bodies were buried. The twenty-first was so warm that as many of the sick as possible crawled forth from their berths to the deck, but some fainted and Munk struggled to get them back to bed.

Then on 25 April a wild glad cry was heard as the geese began to arrive

> at which we were delighted, hoping that the summer would now soon come; but, in this expectation, we were disappointed, for the cold lasted on much longer.

In early May, John Watson, the remaining Englishman, died, and on the seventh the men able to move buried the dead

> but, on account of our extreme weakness, it was so difficult for us that we could not carry the dead bodies to their burial in any other way than by dragging them on a little sledge which had been used in the winter for the transport of wood.

Three days later they managed to get a goose from the rapidly increasing numbers of those birds. There were now only eleven men alive. But the deaths continued and it was no longer possible to bury them. Munk grieves:

On the 19th of May, died Erich Hansen Li, who throughout the voyage, had been very industrious and willing and had neither offended anyone nor deserved any punishment. He had dug many graves for others, but now there was nobody that could dig his, and his body had to remain unburied.

Two days later Munk and three others managed, with the greatest difficulty to get on shore, build a fire, and anoint their joints with some bear grease they had saved. Two of them stayed on shore but Munk and one other returned to the ship. They caught another goose, but by 4 June only Munk and three others were alive, 'all lying down, unable to help one another.' The ship was a charnel house and Munk in despair writes:

Inasmuch as I have now no more hope of life in this world, I request, for the sake of God, if any Christian men should happen to come here, that they will bury in the earth my poor body, together with the others which are found here, expecting their reward from God in Heaven; and, furthermore, that this my journal may be forwarded to my most gracious Lord and King (for every word that is found herein is altogether truthful) in order that my poor wife and children may obtain some benefit from my great distress and miserable death. Herewith, good-night to all the world; and my soul into the hand of God, etc.

Munk alone on board was alive 8 June and says

As I could not now any more stand the bad smell and stench from the dead bodies . . . I managed, as best I could, to get out of the berth. . . . When, by the assistance of God, I had come out of the cabin, I spent that night on the deck, using the clothes of the dead. But, next day, when the two men who were on shore saw me and perceived that I was still alive . . . they came out on the ice to the ship, and assisted me in getting down from the ship to the land, together with the clothes which I threw to them; for the ship was not farther from the shore than about twelve or fourteen fathoms. For some time, we had our dwelling on shore under a bush . . . and there we made a fire in the day time. Later on, we crawled about everywhere near, wherever we saw the least green growing out of the ground, which we dug up and sucked the main root thereof. This bene-fited us, and, as the warmth now commenced to increase nicely, we began to recover.

Three men recovered. In ten days' time they caught fish and made broth, for their mouths were so sore they could not eat. Wine was brought from *Lamprey* and at last they obtained a gun and shot birds. Each day they grew stronger, and by the end of June they started clearing up *Unicorn,* throwing bodies overboard and transferring supplies to the smaller vessel. Even *Lamprey* was a large craft for three hands to handle, but they got her out and ready, and on Sunday, 16 July, on a warm after-noon with clouds of blackflies in the air, Munk and his two companions set sail on their homeward voyage. After their har-rowing experiences, the trials of the homeward passage were taken in stride. They were beset by the usual ice and smashed the rudder before they got out of Hudson Bay. On 11 August Cary's Swans Nest, and two days later Mansel Island, were passed. The next day they reached the western entrance of Hud-son Strait and the fourteenth 'Much snow fell, and the wild geese commenced briskly to fly south again.' From there, surviving icebergs, gales, and wild storms, they pushed steadily on. On 4 September, in tremendous rain and wind, they could not leave the pumps until toward evening and, 'as we were quite ex-hausted with pumping, we drifted the whole night without sails, in order to get some rest, as far as the pump would allow of it.' A week later, with the ship half full of water, the foresail was torn from the bolt rope. On 13 September near the Shet-lands they spoke a ship, but the seas were so high they could get no assistance. Two days later the Orkneys were passed, and on 20 September they raised the coast of Norway. The next day they dropped anchor in a deserted harbor but, lacking a boat, could not get ashore. Finally a peasant who happened by was forced at gun point to assist them, and Munk managed to get ashore to Söndfjord and obtain assistance to take the ship to Bergen. The nightmare voyage was over. Of the sixty-five men who had sailed, three came home, including Jens Munk.

When the Hudson Bay Company established themselves at Port Churchill in 1688 they found cannon from Munk's ship and the tradition of it lasted among the Indians for many years. Thomas Hutchins, a Hudson Bay Company factor, wrote about 1770:

> Munk wintered in Churchill River. I have seen the bricks and other marks where he had his house, & two of his cannon has been found, one of which in my time at Churchill, about the size of a three-pounder, and marked Christian the IVth of Denmark, etc.[3]

So far as is known none of these relics survives today.

Munk's rather crude, small-scale map of the Strait and Bay is the first published map of the entire Bay and the second of the Strait. Many geographical features are shown for the first time and for some years Churchill River was called Munk's River on many maps.[4]

Munk planned to return to the Northwest the following year but never sailed, although preparations were apparently far advanced. Jens Munk continued his service in the navy and died serving in the Thirty Years War, 23 June 1628. He was buried in the church of St. Nicholas in Copenhagen which, except for its tower, was destroyed by fire in 1795.

For many years, largely due to an assumption of T. Rundall's,[5] it was thought that an English expedition to Hudson Bay under Captain William Hawkeridge had sailed simultaneously with Munk in 1619. But Gosch suspected what Miller Christy proved — that Captain William Hawkeridge, about whom we know little before that time (except for the brief account of his voyage in Foxe), actually sailed in 1625.[6]

Sir John Wolstenholm and some of his friends planned an expedition under a certain Captain Bullock for the 1619 season, but there is no indication that their intended expedition ever sailed. Of all the Northwest Company members, Wolstenholm evidently was still hopeful that the Passage might be found in spite of Baffin's negative opinion — an opinion officially accepted by the Company. Preparations for an expedition to leave in the spring were begun in January 1625. The King contributed his pinnace *Lion's Whelp* by giving her to George Villiers, Duke of Buckingham and Lord High Admiral of England. He handed her over to the Merchant Adventurers of London, receiving in return a proportionate capital share in the enterprise. James I died 27 March 1625 before the legal documents could be signed, so they again had to be processed. They were rushed through and signed by Charles I on 31 March.

Wolstenholm was joined, not only by George Villiers, but also by his friends and colleagues — Sir Thomas Smith, Sir Dudley Digges, Sir William Curten, and others. Besides the King's pinnace *Lion's Whelp,* a small ship of unknown name was provided. Captain William Hawkeridge was engaged to conduct the expedition. Wolstenholm obtained permission from the East India Company for the ships to go to the Indies should they find the Passage. The East India Company not only agreed to receive the ships in the East and treat them kindly, but also to provide them with cargoes for the return voyage. The only exception they made was that if there were already ships of the Company ready to sail with pepper, no cargoes of that commodity would be allowed to go on the Northwest Passage ships.

It will be remembered that Captain Hawkeridge was a friend and companion of Button on his expedition to Hudson Bay where they wintered in 1612–13. A cousin of Phineas Pett, master shipwright of the Deptford Dockyard, he came from Devon, the home of many great mariners. As a young man he had sailed to Newfoundland as a servant to Captain (later Sir) Richard Whitbourne, of Exmouth. Christy writes

This first reference to him occurs in a curious connection. Whitbourne says that, in the year 1610, one morning early, as he was standing by the water's side, in the Harbour of St. John's, a strange and beautiful creature with a head and face resembling those of a woman, shoulders square and white like those of a man, and a fluked tail, swam towards him and approached so close to him that he retreated from the water's edge; but, he adds, 'the same came shortly after unto a boate, wherein one William Hawkridge, then my servant, was, that hath bin since in a ship to the East Indies, and is lately there imployed againe by Sir Thomas Smith in the like voyage; and the same creature did strive to come in to him and others then in the said boate; whereat they were afraide, and one of them strooke it a full blow on the head, whereby it fell off from them. . . . This (I suppose) was a maremaide.' [7]

Thus he has the rare distinction of joining Hudson's men as an observer of the elusive siren of the deep.

After Button's expedition, Hawkeridge made several voyages for the East India Company, but became involved in a drawn-out court action with them for bringing home goods on his own account in defiance of Company practice and he was released from Company service just in time to undertake the new Northwest venture.

Hawkeridge's expedition sailed in June and, like Munk's, entered Frobisher Bay in error on the twenty-ninth and barely escaped being wrecked in the fog. The two vessels were separated but met about 16 July and entered Hudson Strait. Keeping along the northern shore, Hawkeridge reached its western end 16 July. It is impossible to follow his course, but he kept to the western end of the Strait, the entrance of Foxe Channel, and the islands in the northern part of Hudson Bay the entire time, accomplishing nothing.

The Northwest voyage of this able but unfortunate man was nearly the last of a long series. The promoters who had spent so lavishly to find the Passage were now quite discouraged and interest lapsed for several years.

14

'North-West Fox'

When Captain James Knight made his voyage of no return in 1606, Luke Foxe, a lusty and hopeful young man of twenty, 'presuming upon some parts . . . [he having] had, as the use of globes and other Mathematicke Instruments,' pleaded to go with him as mate. Even at that age Foxe was an experienced, competent sailorman. Later, in more mature years, he recognized the justice of Knight's decision not to accept his application, for he wrote: 'my ambition soared a pitch higher than my abilitie . . . [and I] thought myself to bee fit for the best imployment, and desired to be pluckt before I was ripe.'

Like Frobisher, Luke Foxe was a Yorkshireman. He also, like his more famous predecessor, went to sea very young. Little is known of his early life beyond what he tells us in *North-West Fox,*[1] but he was not a deep-water sailor. 'I am but a North-country coaster, and hath but been brought up in small Vessels.' In such craft he sailed out of Hull to Whitby, Newcastle, Yarmouth, and London; and more distantly to the Baltic and the Scandinavian countries, to Holland, France, Spain, and the Mediterranean. Of one thing we are certain. For the next twenty-five years he devoted his spare time to learning all that he could about the Northwest Passage. He passed up no opportunity to make the acquaintance of and to interview as many as possible who had sailed to the Northwest — among them Pricket, Bylot, Baffin, and Button. He borrowed their logs and journals so that he would be better prepared when the right opportunity arrived. Nor did he neglect to try and bring that opportunity about. Indeed, when the time came he was, he tells us, 'neither importuned nor intreated to his undertaking by any, eyther noble or gentle,' and 'the truth is that I had beene itching after it ever since 1606, when I should have gone Mate to John Knight.' But, continues Foxe, 'he durst not depend upon me in that place [mate] for the voyage, so as I did not proceed with him.'

Foxe, who had a lively and inquiring mind as well as a whimsical sense of humor, furthered his education in navigation and geography with John Tapp, an author, publisher, and seller of books, especially for mariners. Through Tapp he met Thomas Sterne a globe maker who had, says Foxe, 'engrossed all those former voyages by relation, manuscripts, and maps.'

Foxe's most eminent friend and supporter was his fellow Yorkshireman, Henry Briggs, for twenty-three years a professor of astronomy at Oxford, who introduced the use of logarithms — first explained in 1614 by Lord Napier — for navigational and other purposes. It had been said that 'no greater service has ever been done by one man to navigation, and Luke Foxe . . . was among the first explorers who reaped the benefit of it . . .' [2] Briggs, moreover, shared Foxe's interest in the Northwest. In 1622 he published his *Treatise on the North-West Passage to the South Sea, through the Continent of Virginia, and by Fretum Hudson,* which was reprinted by Purchas three years later with the addition of a map of North America.[3] Briggs's *Treatise,* while showing him to be better mathematician than geographer, summed up much of the latest opinion of the day, including such notions as the South Sea's lying on the western side of the Virginia mountains, and perpetuated the confusion about the rivers emptying into Chesapeake Bay and Hudson Bay, about the actual western extension of Hudson Bay, and about the insularity of California, a popular seventeenth-century belief. His map is better than his theories and interprets reasonably well the available geographical knowledge. His principal theory was that contact with the South Sea might be more practical by going up rivers to the mountains and down other rivers to the ocean, but he did not overlook the possibility of finding a Passage where Button had explored the tides in Hudson Bay.

However speculative his ideas regarding the Passage, it was the active interest and encouragement of Henry Briggs that was largely instrumental in getting Foxe launched on his expedition. Briggs introduced Foxe to Sir John Brooke, who must have been a man of wealth and influence, but of whom we know little.

In any event, Foxe, Briggs, and Brooke, in December 1629, petitioned Charles I for the loan of a ship and for his 'countenance to the Action.' The King, through one of the Lords of the Admiralty, wrote for the opinion of Sir Thomas Button. Button replied that his journal, notes, and papers, which he had not looked over for many years and had not expected to use again, reaffirmed his belief that a Northwest Passage existed and that its discovery would not be difficult. He generously offered the use of his material and made himself available for consultation. He advised future expeditions against wintering or spending time in Hudson Bay as he and Hudson had,

> but as soone as he comes to the west parte or Cape of Noting-ham Iland where he is to anchor, and, according to the sett of that tyde which he shall finde there, to direct his course; w'ch must be and is the only way to fynde that passadge, w'ch I doe as confidently beleave to be a passadge as I doe there is on[e]

either between Calis and Dover or between Holy Head and Ireland.[4]

Button also suggested that Sir John Wolstenholm and Sir Dudley Digges, who had been among those granted a charter by James I in 1612, should be consulted before a new charter was granted. He also took the opportunity to appeal his own distressing condition. After thirty-seven years in the King's service there was considerable money due him; he had been forced to sell and mortgage some of his property and was facing ruin because of outstanding debts. The money was never paid, but the injustice was not unusual for public servants in those days.

The Admiralty lent the Company Adventurers the *Charles,* a pinnace of seventy or eighty tons for the expedition. Foxe boasts that she was of his 'own Chusing, and the best for condition and quality, especially for this voyage, that the world could afford' — a statement for public consumption, apparently, as she was an old tub, half-rotten, and about to be sold out of the service anyway. Foxe originally hoped to sail in 1630, but by the time his petition was granted it was too late in the season. The Company Adventurers, having spent considerable sums of money to recondition the old vessel, gave Foxe permission to trade in her under letters of marque * for the rest of the year. Meanwhile Sir Thomas Roe, Ambassador to Sweden, returned to England and lent his support to the enterprise. He, with Sir John Wolstenholm and the Master and Wardens of Trinity House, was asked by the King to assist the venture. Wolstenholm the younger was appointed treasurer for the Adventurers.

Foxe was unsuccessful in signing on a single man who had previously sailed in northern seas. Then the officials of Trinity House selected his crew and officers. Although he was satisfied with their choice of crew he blamed Wolstenholm for not hav-

* A letter of marque licensed a private vessel to cruise as a privateer.

ing consulted him. He felt, quite justifiably, that he should have had a hand in picking his men, and particularly the officers. Indeed, the constant laziness and timidity of his master and master's mate made the voyage more difficult for Foxe, and his manuscript journal contains continued reference (deleted from the printed book) to the incessant friction between them. The master's journal does not give as much evidence of this unpleasantness.

The ship was put in as good condition as possible, and she was bountifully supplied.

> I was Vitualed compleatly for 18 Moneths; but, whether the Baker, Brewer, Butcher, and others, were Mr. of their Arts or professions, or no, I know not; but this I am sure Bread, good Iseland Ling, Butter and Cheese of the best, admirable Sacke and Aqua vitae, Pease, Oat-meale, Wheat-meale, Oyle, Spice, Sugar, Fruit, and Rice; with Chyrurgerie, as Sirrups, Julips, condits, trechissis, oyles, potions, suppositors, and purging Pils; and, if I had wanted Instruments, my Chyrurgion had enough.
>
> My Carpenter was fitted from the thickest bolt to the pump-nayle or tacket.
>
> The Gunner, from the Sacor to the Pistoll.
>
> The Boatswaine, from the Cable to the Sayle-twine.
>
> The Steward and Cooke, from the Caldron to the Spoone.

Foxe himself was equipped with a map of all his predecessors' discoveries, and a letter from the King to the Emperor of Japan.

During the preparations Foxe came into contact with Captain Thomas James, who was being backed by the merchants of Bristol for a similar voyage. James requested of Henry Briggs, before his death 26 January 1631, that the two expeditions be combined under his command — an idea that doubtless endeared him to Foxe. His further suggestion was more acceptable: that, regardless of who first discovered the Passage, he and Foxe should be accorded equal honors.

Foxe sailed from Deptford 5 May 1631 and, going around by

the Orkneys, crossed the Atlantic and entered Hudson Strait on 22 May. The next day off the south end of Resolution Island he sighted smoke which, unknown to Foxe, came from James's fire. Passage of the Strait was slowed by driving ice. But if the sea was encumbered, the sky was blue and often hot. On the twenty-third Foxe wrote, 'This evening the Sun set cleare; the Ayre breathed gently from the East; and we lay quietly all night amongst the Ice.' He described and distinguished between icebergs and floe ice so well that Captain Markham, who passed through the Strait 250 years later, thought that: 'It would not be possible to give a more accurate account of the conditions of the ice in Hudson's Strait at the present day . . .'

Solid ice frustrated the execution of his instructions: to explore first the channel to the northwest of Nottingham and Salisbury Islands. Foxe accordingly decided to carry out the second part of his orders first: to explore the coast of Hudson Bay southward along its western shore to Port Nelson and eastward to the vicinity of Cape Henrietta Maria, Hudson's most westerly point. Sailing past Mansel Island and around Cary's Swans Nest, he crossed Hudson Bay and turned northward along the shore of Southampton Island. A little island off Cape Fullerton on 27 July was named Roes Welcome, a name that has since been transferred to the Strait between Southampton Island and the mainland. As he worked down the western shore he charted and named White Marble Island, Brooke Cobham, and also took the opportunity to honor an old friend by naming a small cluster of islands 'Briggs his Mathematicks.' The weather continued mild and he stayed near the mainland, looking always for an opening he knew was not there; for he wrote that he was 'out of the road for finding a passage.' He was at Churchill Bay (Button's Hubbart's Hope) on 5 August and reached Port Nelson three days later, where he stayed until the twentieth. While setting up a pinnace and trying to find a spar suitable for a new main yard, he found many remains of Sir

Thomas Button's wintering, including an inscribed board telling of the *Resolution*'s abandonment. He turned eastward and explored the southern shore of Hudson Bay between Port Nelson and Cape Henrietta Maria, linking the explorations of Hudson and Button. It is to Foxe's great credit that he completed this important piece of new exploration, even though he knew there was no chance of finding a Passage in that direction.

While on this section of unexplored coast he met, on 29 August, Captain Thomas James, who invited him on board his ship for dinner. The two explorers had a pleasant evening together, although Foxe in commenting on the occasion makes some rather ill-mannered remarks about both his host and his ship:

> I was well entertained and feasted by Captain James, with varietie of such cheere as his sea provisions could aford, with some Partridges; wee dined betwixt decks, for the great cabin was not bigg enough to receive our selves and followers; during which time the ship . . . threw in so much water as we could not have wanted sause if wee had had roast Mutton.
> . . . they were to be pittied; the ship taking her liquor as kindly as our selves, for her nose was no sooner out of the pitcher, but here nede, like the Ducks, was in't againe. The Gentleman [James] could discourse of Arte (as observations, calculations, and the like), and shewed me many Instruments, so that I did perceive him to bee a practitioner in the Mathematicks; but, when I found that hee was no Seaman, I did blame those very much who had councelled him to make choyce of that shippe for a voyage of such importance . . . Our discourse had beene to small purpose, if wee had not pried into the errours of our predecessors. And (being demanded), I did not thinke much for his keeping out his flagg . . . To this was replide, that hee was going to the Emperour of Japon, with letters from his Maiestie, and that, if it were a ship of his Maiesties of 40 Peeces of Ordnance, hee could not strike his flag. 'Keepe it up then,' quoth I, 'but you are out of the way to Japon, for this is not it.'

Having completed his survey of the western and southern shores of the Bay, Foxe writes:

> and now the further search of a passage this way was hopelesse, and there needed no more search in all the side of this Bay, from 64 deg. 30 m. circularly to 55 deg. 10 m.; and, seeing that we could not attempt the N.W. from *Notinghams* Ile (as I was instructed), for the heavie quantitys of Ice which choaked all the 3 channels at our entering in the midle of *July,* now I did hope were disolved, or els never, and it was best to make tryall thereof whilest this good wind lasted . . .

Heading north to attempt the exploration of the channel, which was his first objective, and finding the ice gone, he proceeded up it, around the peninsula of Baffin Island, and into the Basin, both of which now bear his name. Although this was a well-conducted piece of original exploration, Roe later criticized him for staying on the Baffin Island side. To the Merchant Adventurers of Bristol, he wrote: 'But I never knew men seeke a North-west passage on a North-east shore.'[5] Foxe penetrated his Basin to 66° 47' N., but on 22 September, as scurvy was beginning to weaken his men, he turned back. Returning directly through Hudson Strait he passed Cape Chidley on the fifteenth, and on 31 October 'I came into the Downes with all my men recovered and sound, not having lost one Man, nor Boy, nor any manner of Tackling, having beene forth neere 6 monleths, all glory be to God.'

This was an achievement of which few of his predecessors could boast. Yet Foxe was very severely criticized for not wintering and continuing his explorations. He did not receive in his lifetime the credit he deserved for his considerable contributions to geographical knowledge. Many of the names which he gave to geographical features are still used, although others, which were overly cumbersome or facetious, have been superseded. His book was not published until 1635, four years after his return and two years after Captain James published his account. The *North-West Fox* shows the author as a self-made man — ill-educated, competent, and humorous, with the self-reliant conceit of one who has come up the hard way. The book, strained, verbose, and at times incomprehensible, has merit not only for the account of his own voyage but also for preserving nearly all that we know of those of Gibbons, Button, and Hawkeridge. It badly needed a good editor, as Foxe realized. He says he attempted to correct the errors in the book for

> . . . being no Scholler, and having had no helpe, which I did know was very needfull, but [I] was not able to buy it, and I was told it would not be had for naught, especially by the Scholler that was acquainted with the language of the Sea. Therefore, now I feels the want of Mr. Hackluit. . . .
>
> Whereupon, not knowing otherwise how to proceede, I was enforced, with such Tackling, Cordage, and Raftage as I had, to Rigge and Tackle this ship my selfe.

Like Button, he was treated shabbily after doing a good job. For six months after his return Foxe stayed in charge of the pinnace *Charles,* paying for her upkeep at his own expense, while the Lords of the Admiralty deliberated whether or not to take her back into the King's service. In March 1632 she was given outright by the King with all her guns and equipment to Sir John Wolstenholm in compensation for the heavy expenses he had undergone for the voyage. Foxe petitioned both Wolstenholm and the Admiralty for reimbursement for maintenance of the vessel up to the time she was bestowed on Sir John, but it seems he never received any satisfaction.

It must have rankled the exuberant Yorkshireman to see James, who accomplished far less than he, received with honor while his own work was little thought of for many years. Luke Foxe lived to see his book published, but died at Whitby a few months later, in July 1635.

15

The Strange and Dangerous Voyage

*D*irect rivalry between Bristol merchants and the London adventurers resulted for the first time in two curiously related and yet strangely different voyages. Nearly simultaneously with Luke Foxe's departure from London in 1631, Captain Thomas James sailed from Bristol. In fact, the news of Foxe's preparation directly inspired the Bristol company to back a competitive venture. The race was on, an almost ludicrous race: two ships, one named for the King, the other, *Henrietta Maria,* for the Queen; the captains both carrying identical letters to the Emperor of Japan, both hoping to be the first to deliver his. As we have already followed Foxe to Hudson Bay, we shall now follow James on his 'strange and dangerous voyage.'

The Company of Merchant Venturers of Bristol, a venerable and responsible body, furnished Thomas James with his ship. James was a well-educated man of good Welsh family origin, but like most of the old Arctic explorers, his early life is obscure. Born in 1593 somewhere in the Bristol region, his background was very different from that of the self-educated, practical seaman, Foxe. And yet James had seagoing experience, for in 1628 he was commanding his own 200-ton letter of marque ship *Dragon*. Like Foxe, James journeyed to London to seek the King's support. He also carried a letter to Sir Thomas Roe, who was a brother-in-law of John Tomlinson, Mayor of Bristol. Already busy with preparations for the Foxe expedition, Roe wrote Tomlinson that he was delighted to hear that the Bristol merchants were planning such an expedition, and expressed the opinion that His Majesty would grant the same privileges to them as to the London group. Sir John Wolstenholm, probably because of previous commitments to Foxe, was in no position to aid James financially. Nevertheless through the Earl of Danby he did arrange an interview for James with the King. James returned to Bristol with the same privileges as the London group. Thus, while the financial backing came from Bristol, James had, like Foxe, the moral support of Roe, Wolstenholm, and the Earl of Danby, as well as the King himself.

James decided that one ship was better than two and selected a small vessel for he says: 'A great Ship . . . was unfit to be forc'd thorow the Ice, wherefore I made choice of a well-conditioned, strong Ship, of the burthen of seventie Tunne; and in God and that only Ship to put the hope of my future fortunes.' [1] *Henrietta Maria* was about the same size as Foxe's *Charles* and the size of her crew, twenty-two men, was identical. The ship was well found and victualed. James says: 'The Baker, Brewer, Butcher, and others . . . truly they prooved themselves Masters in their Arts,' a phrase which Foxe poked fun at in his book.

About the wisdom of having a crew experienced in the Arctic, the two explorers differed. Whereas Foxe endeavored, unsuccessfully, to obtain experienced men, James writes:

> I was sought to by divers that had bin in places of the chiefest command in this action formerly, and others also that had

used the Northerly Icie Seas; but I utterly refused them all, and would by no meanes have any with mee that had bin in the like voyage or adventures, for some private reasons unnecessary here to be related.

What those private reasons were we do not know, but they could not have been very convincing. One suspects he did not want his own inexperience shown up. Both explorers sailed, therefore, without a single man with Arctic experience.

Like his rival, James prepared himself by studying all journals, charts, and other information he could find of previous voyages. But he apparently did not have Foxe's personal acquaintance with navigators who had been there and, whereas Foxe had been studying these things for twenty years, James evidently 'boned up' in a like number of months. On the other hand, James was a mathematical navigator of great skill, which even Foxe admits, and took with him a remarkable number of nautical instruments and a considerable library of useful books.

Everything was ready by 1 April 1631, and after a final trip to London, where he received the King's instructions from Sir Thomas Roe, James was aboard *Henrietta Maria* waiting for a fair wind. The wind came 3 May, and Captain James stood down the Severn Channel two days before Foxe commenced his voyage. He made Greenland a month later and immediately, 6 June, encountered heavy ice which crushed his shallop. James's honest fear of the ice is quickly sensed from reading his book. Certainly he had little luck or skill in avoiding it. This very day he wrote:

> In the evening, wee were inclosed amongst great pieces, as high as our Poope, and some of the sharpe blue corners of them did reach quite under us. All these great pieces (by reason it was the out-side of the Ice) did heave and set, and so beat us that it was wonderful how the Ship could indure one blow of it . . .

It took him several days to round Cape Farewell and cross Davis Strait, being, so he says, 'much tormented, pestered, and beaten with Ice, many pieces being higher than our Topmasthead . . . The weather, for the most part, a stinking fogge, and the Sea very blacke . . .'

The seventeenth 'we heard the rut of the shoare . . .* It made a hollow and a hideous noyse . . .' and in the morning they saw they were off Resolution Island near the entrance to Hudson Strait. James's passage through the Strait, like his entire voyage, is one hair-raising escape after another from disaster. If he was not running aground he was being gripped by icebergs. The twenty-first saw *Henrietta Maria* fast on a sharp rock and settling over so far with the ebb that her gunnel was in the water, but luckily she was freed with the flood. By 15 July James reached the western end of the Strait. Having the same instructions as Foxe, he too attempted first to explore to the northwest of Nottingham Island, and he met the same impenetrable ice. He made the same decision to sail across to the western shore of Hudson Bay. His ice-impeded way was slow, and for two days the ship stuck fast with all sails set. The entire crew left the ship and "wee drank a health to his Majestie on the ice — not one man in the Ship, and shee still under all her sayles.' The western shore near Churchill Bay was sighted 11 August, and James turned southward, banging along the shoal bottom and losing anchors, until he reached Port Nelson.

James shares with Foxe the honor of exploring the coast between Port Nelson and Cape Henrietta Maria. He kept the lead going, and the morning of the nineteenth 'being fine cleere Sun-shine weather, we stood . . . into thicke puddelish water . . .' and anchored, but by afternoon 'it began to snuffle and blow,' the anchor was raised with difficulty, and progress was slow. The following day a small rope fouled the cable as

---

* The word 'rut' is still commonly used in Maine for the noise made by the ocean.

the men were walking the capstan and several of them were hurt.

> But our Gunner (an honest and a diligent man) had his legge taken betwixt the Cable and the Capstang, which wrung off his foote, and tare all the flesh off his legge, and crushed the bone to pieces, and sorely withall bruised all his whole body; in which miserable manner hee remained crying till we had recovered ourselves, our memory, and strengths to cleare him.

The surgeon amputated the gunner's leg; the unlucky man died in November.

Falling in with Captain Foxe on the twenty-ninth, James gives his modest account of the visit we have already had described by Foxe.

> In the morning, Captaine Foxe and his friends came aboord of mee, where I entertained them in the best manner I could, and with such fresh meat as I had gotton from the shoare. I told him how I had named the land The South Principality of Wales [Foxe had called it New Yorkshire]. I shewed him how farre I had beene to the Eastward, where I had landed; and, in briefe, I made knowne to him all the dangers of this Coast, as farre as I had beene. He told mee how himselfe had beene in Port Nelson, and had made but a Cursory discovery hitherto, and that he had not beene aland, nor had not many times seene the land. In the evening, after I had given his men some necessaries, with Tobacco and other things which they wanted, hee departed aboord his Ship, and, the next morning, stood away South-South-west, since which time I never saw him.

Nothing shows the contrasting character of these two old sea dogs better than their separate accounts of this meeting.

Leaving Foxe, Captain James continued along shore and on 2 September reached and named Cape Henrietta Maria; and it is his name, rather than 'Wolstenholm's Ultimum Vale' given it by Foxe on the very same day, that has survived. A few days later he was working down the western shore of the Bay which ever since has borne his name. This might almost be called an original discovery, for it is not known precisely how much of the Bay Hudson explored. As a matter of fact, it was thought at this time — and James did nothing to dispel it — that this Bay was divided by a long finger of land into a western and eastern half. Hudson was considered to have wintered in the eastern part and James, thinking himself in the western half, spent much time planning to round the dividing peninsula to the place of Hudson's wintering. Of course no such point of land exists, but James showed it on his map.

In the shoal waters of James Bay he ran aground again — nearly, so he says on one occasion, losing his temper — and in a great storm lost his shallop. He discovered several islands, but the season was getting late, snow was frequent, and ice was beginning to form. For several days they were caught in ice, snow, and shoal water at Charlton. The ship was pounding her bottom at times, and they were unable to get off or find a suitable harbor. Finally, after consultation with his officers, James decided to sink the ship in shoal water to prevent her breaking up. On 29 November holes were bored in her sides and she settled to the bottom. Her rudder was lost and there was no ironwork to hang another. It was the carpenter's opinion that the ship would never sail again.

The deep snows and severe cold of a Hudson Bay winter descended upon them, but there was time to construct two houses and a store shed in the lee of a southern facing bank. There was a good spring of water nearby and supplies were ample. The carpenter was put to work building a pinnace — 27-foot keel, 10-foot beam, and 5-foot hold — to be used for the return voyage to England the following summer should it prove impossible to raise the ship. The men suffered greatly from the extreme cold, and fuel was a constant problem made more difficult by deep snow and a shortage of axes.

By February the dread scurvy was becoming serious:

The cold was as extreme this moneth as at any time we had felt it this yeere, and many of our men complained of infirmities; some of sore mouthes, all the teeth in their heads being loose, their gums swolne, with black rotton flesh, which must every day be cut away. The paine was so sore on them that they could not eate their ordinary meat. Others complained of paine in their heads and their brests; some of weaknesse in their backs; others of aches in their thighs and knees; and others of swellings in their legges. Thus were two thirds of the company under the Chirurgions hands. And yet, neverthelesse, they must worke daily, and goe abroad to fetch wood and timber, notwithstanding the most of them had no shooes to put on. Their shooes, upon comming to the fire, out of the snow, were burnt and scorcht upon their feete, and our store-shooes were all sunke in the Ship. In this necessitie, they would make this shift: To bind clouts about their feet; and endeavored, by that poore helpe, the best they could, to performe their duties.

The first of April five men were incapacitated, and 18 May, James wrote:

our Carpenter, William Cole, dyed, a men generally bemoaned of us all, as much for his inate goodnesse as for the present necessity we had of a man of his quality. He had indured a long sicknesse with much patience, and made a very godly end. In the Evening, we buried him by Master Wardon, accompanied with as many as could goe, for 3 more of our principall men lay then expecting a good houre. And now were we in the most miserable estate that we were in all the voyage.

During May, by great exertions, they managed to patch the holes in the ship, pump her out, and secure provisions that had been in solid ice all winter and were still edible. Luck was with them when the rudder was found by 'a happy fellow, one David Hammon, pecking betwixt the Ice, strooke upon it, and it came up with his lance, who, crying that he had found it, the rest came and got it up on the Ice and so into the Ship.'

> The nine and twentieth, being *Prince Charles his birthday,* we
> kept Holy-day, and display'd his Majesties colours, both aland
> and aboord, and named our habitation *Charles Towne,* by con-
> traction *Charlton;* and the Iland *Charlton Iland.*

The last day of May they found some vetches growing, the
first green thing they had seen, and soon after, sorrel. The
scurvy symptoms began to disappear and the men went about
their work with more vigor. Without success they tried to hang
the rudder:

> The sixth, we went about to hang it; and our young lustiest
> men tooke turnes to goe into the water, and to rake away the
> sand; but they were not able to indure the cold of it halfe a quar-
> ter of an houre, it was so mortifying; yea, use what comforts we
> could, it would make them swound and dye away. We brought
> it to the Sternepost, but were faine to give it over, being able to
> worke at it no longer. Then we plugg'd up the upper holes
> within boord, and fell to pumping the water againe out of her.

Finally a warm June day came, and the rudder was hung.
The ballast was thrown overboard, and the ship was lightened
as much as possible in an effort to get her off. After several
attempts she was kedged off eighteen inches at a time. The
astonishing vagaries of the climate became more evident when:

> The sixteenth was wondrous hot, with some thunder and
> lightning, so that our men did goe into the ponds ashoare, to
> swimme and coole themselves; yet was the water very cold
> still. Here had lately appeared divers sorts of flyes, as Butter-
> flyes, Butchers-flyes, Horse-flyes, and such an infinit abundance
> of bloud-thirsty muskitoes, that we were more tormented with
> them then ever we were with the cold weather.

Although *Henrietta Maria* had received treatment harsh
enough to demolish most vessels she was, in spite of Foxe's un-
charitable remarks, a staunch old craft. It was found that, after

such repairs as it was possible to make, she did not leak badly. Provisions were put aboard, and as the half-completed pinnace was of no more use she was burned for firewood. On Midsummer Day, Captain James raised a high cross on Brandon Hill, where those who had died were buried. On it he fixed pictures of the King and Queen, a shilling and a sixpence, the King's arms, and the arms of the city of Bristol, 'formerly [sic], by this ceremony, taking posession of these Territories to his Majesties use.'

The following day James very nearly brought an end to his adventures. He decided to make a fire to see if it would be answered by the savages. Climbing a tall tree after dark to watch for the answering flames, he ordered a small evergreen set on fire. The forest was tinder dry and the foolishness of the order was compounded by the sailor who touched off a tree to windward of the one his Captain was perched in. Trees and ground moss virtually exploded, and the flames, racing before the wind, caught the tree in which the Captain clung. He got halfway down and then leaped through the flames for his life, landing, fortunately, without breaking any bones. It was truly a narrow escape. The forest fire raged all night and about noon the next day when the wind changed

> our Sentinell came running home, bringing us word that the fire did follow him at hard heeles, like a traine of powder. It was no neede to bid us take downe and carry all away to the sea-side. The fire came towards us with a most terrible rattling noyse, bearing a full mile in breadth; and, by that time we had uncouvered our houses, and laid hand on to carry away our last things, the fire was come to our Towne and seazed on it, and (in a trice) burnt it downe to the ground. We lost nothing of any value in it, for we had brought it all away into a place of security. Our dogges, in this combustion, would sit downe on their tayles and howle, and then runne into the Sea, on the shoalds, and there stay. The winde shifted Easterly, and the

fire ranged to the Westward, seeking what it might devoure. This night, we lay all together aboord the Ship, and gave God thankes that had Shipt us in her againe.

After one last ceremony ashore, 1 July, during which James recited some poetry he had written and fastened a letter describing their condition and their intentions to the cross, 'we presently tooke Boat and departed, and never put foote more on that Iland.' On nearby Danby Island James found stakes obviously sharpened with an iron hatchet and driven into the ground. These may have been relics of Hudson and his companions.

It was Captain James's intention to continue searching for the Passage in the northwest part of the Bay, but again he was almost constantly in ice and little progress could be made. The season wore on and the leaks in the ship grew worse. On 24 August, back at Nottingham Island, James with the unanimous assent of his officers decided to return to England. By 8 September he was clear of Hudson Strait and, after bucking headwinds and high seas, arrived 22 October in Bristol Road.

> The Ship being brought into Harbour, and halde dry aground to looke to her, it was there found that all her Cut-water and Sterne were torne and beaten away, together with fourteene foote of her Keele, much of her sheathing cut away, her bowes broken and bruised, and many timbers crackt within boord; and, under the Star-boord bulge, a sharpe Rocke had cut thorow the sheathing, the planke, and an inch and a halfe into a timber that it met withall. Many other defects there were besides, so that it was miraculous how this vessel could bring us home againe.

It is not to be wondered that Captain Thomas James came to the conclusion that there was no Northwest Passage — he blamed the Portuguese for promoting the idea.

> What hath beene long agoe fabled by some Portingales, that should have comne this way out of the South Sea, the meere

shaddowes of whose mistaken Relations have comne to us, I leave to be confuted by their owne vanitie. These hopes have stirred up, from time to time, the more active spirits of this our Kingdome to research that meerely imaginary passage. For mine owne part, I give no credit to them at all, and as little to the vicious and abusive wits of later Portingals and Spaniards, who never speake of any difficulties, as shoald water, ice, nor sight of land, but write as if they had beene brought home in a dreame or engine. And, indeed, their discourses are found absurd, and the *plots* (by which some of them have practised to deceive the world) meere falsities, making Sea where there is knowne to be maine land, and land where is nothing but Sea.

James was disillusioned. He did not intend to try his luck again in Hudson Bay. Within six months of his return he was appointed to the command of the pinnace *Ninth Whelp of the Lion,* the vessel commanded for eighteen months by his illustrious predecessor in the Northwest, Sir Thomas Button. In *Ninth Whelp* he guarded the Irish Channel and the mouth of the Severn until his last illness.

While James shares with Foxe the first exploration of the coast between Port Nelson and Cape Henrietta Maria, and a few of his names have survived, his wintering and sailing in James Bay added little to the knowledge brought back by the Hudson mutineers. He followed his contemporary up Foxe Channel a year later, but whereas Foxe charted miles of coast and named many geographical features, James did neither, although he kept nearer the western shore of the Channel. Nor did he go into the Basin nearly as far as Foxe.

In the inevitable contrast between these two brave seventeenth-century explorers one cannot escape certain conclusions. Two more unlike men could not have been found — Foxe, the self-educated, rough, but extremely competent sailor; James, the gentle, though experienced intellectual. James's book is one continual series of hardships, trials, narrow escapes, and disasters. He was constantly beset by ice and his ship seems to have been aground almost as often as afloat. Damage was heavy, men were lost. Sailing over the almost identical course the same year, Foxe experienced little difficulty from the ice, never ran aground, and the only damage to his ship, he says, was the cracking of his cutwater. It is obvious that much of James's constant trouble was due to his own incompetence in navigating in the ice and along uncharted coasts. One has the feeling that he hugged the ice and shore too closely. His decision to winter was a grave error, as Foxe pointed out. He could have returned to England and been back in Hudson Bay with a fresh crew and sound ship much earlier than he was free of the ice at Charlton Island. And yet, after his return and in spite of the evidence of the printed works of both men, James was received everywhere with honor, praised for his accomplishments, commiserated with for the hardships he had undergone. All this while Foxe, who had returned without the loss of a man and added considerably to the knowledge of Hudson Bay, was especially blamed for not wintering and otherwise criticized and neglected. Foxe was right, but being outspoken and conceited, he probably irritated people. James was more modest and tactful. The personalities of the two men undoubtedly had much to do with the respect in which their work was held during their lifetimes and for a considerable period thereafter.

Then, too, James had no small literary talent, and his book, *The Strange and Dangerous Voyage of Captain Thomas James,* is clearly and dramatically written. First published in 1633, while Foxe was still chewing his pencil, it was reprinted numerous times and remained popular for many years. Yet as far as geography is concerned, Foxe's book is of far greater consequence.

The most important result of James's voyage perhaps was the effect of his book, a century and a half later, on his fellow townsman of Bristol, Samuel Taylor Coleridge. John Livingston Lowes has ingeniously worked out in his book *The Road to Xanadu* the influence of several such Arctic voyages on Coleridge's imagination. James's account, along with de Veer's of the Barents voyages, was the source of many telling phrases in *The Rime of the Ancient Mariner.*

> *And now there came both mist and snow,*
> *And it grew wondrous cold:*
> *And ice, mast-high, came floating by,*
> *As green as emerald.*
>
> *The ice was here, the ice was there,*
> *The ice was all around:*
> *It cracked and growled, and roared and howled,*
> *Like noises in a swound! . . .*

Captain Thomas James and Captain Luke Foxe are inseparably paired. By plan they began their voyages within a few days of each other in 1631; by coincidence they died within a few weeks of each other in the spring of 1635. They settled once and for all the question of the existence of a navigable passage from Hudson Bay into the Pacific. There was none. The hopes that had soared so high after Hudson's discovery evaporated with the realization that here was only a great inland sea.

The return of Captain Thomas James brings to a close the first great period of Arctic explorations, a period distinguished by the failure of its primary purpose, to find a commercially practical Passage to the Far East, by the North, the Northeast, or the Northwest. In this regard, every expedition from Sebastian Cabot's to Thomas James's was a failure. Yet great benefits accrued from the search, especially to the English who were so tenacious in its pursuit: the Newfoundland cod fishery, the Russian trade, the Northern whale fishery, all of which brought vast wealth to England; Newfoundland and the lands bordering Hudson Bay were added to the King's dominions; the geography of the world was expanded and profound knowledge was accumulated on weather, meteorology, navigation, ice, glaciers, refraction, plants, animals, and new races of men. Not the least important was the experience gained by hundreds of English seamen in some of the roughest waters and most difficult conditions to be found anywhere; men learned to live in the cold wilderness and to survive long Arctic winters.

One can readily see the extent of these voyages by looking at a map of the American Arctic. Wherever they went, from the northern end of Baffin Bay to the southern tip of James Bay, their names and those of their friends, backers, and ships identify most of the geographical features. With few exceptions, each navigator added something to the accumulation of learning. But those who added the most and whose names shine with ever increasing brightness down through the years are Barents in the Northeast, and Frobisher, Davis, Hudson, and Baffin in the Northwest.

Part Two

Solving the Puzzle

16

Fiction and Fact

€ven though the English could at last sail to the Indies without Portuguese or Spanish interference, the advantages of a shorter route through a Northwest Passage could not be forgotten easily. When the trade of the Hudson's Bay Company, established after the Restoration of Charles II, proved so lucrative, it focused new attention on the area. Interest in a navigable passage quickened, especially as the old legend of the Strait of Anian seemed to promise certain passage from the Atlantic to the Pacific.

The origins of this mythical strait lie shrouded in a sixteenth-century mist. A misplacing of Marco Polo's Ania or Amien may have created it, or its name may have derived from Anus Cortereal, a Portuguese explorer of the Newfoundland and Labrador coasts in 1500–1502. In 1562 an Italian geographer described the Strait of Anian for the first time as a geographical formation separating Asia and America. At that time people believed that Asia extended farther to the eastward and that North America was narrower in its northern breadth than is the case. Later, as the true outline of the continents began to emerge, the strait

was thought to divide North America and to connect, somewhere in mid-continent, with the Northwest Passage.[1]

Michael Lok, already badly ice burned, was one of the first
explorers to believe in this possibility. Recuperating in Venice
from the financial disasters of the Frobisher voyages, he was
completely taken in by the convincing yarn of an old Greek
sailor called Juan de Fuca, who guaranteed he could sail through
the Northwest Passage to the South Seas in thirty days. Apparently disgruntled by his unfair treatment at the hand of the
Spaniards, de Fuca was offering his services to the English
Queen. She was simply to furnish him with one forty-ton ship
and a pinnace. Lok corresponded with de Fuca for several years,
and twice the Greek promised to make the expedition if Lok
would send him money. Fortunately, Lok did not have it to
send, and by 1602, when he did, the old sailor was dead.

Though it is probable that de Fuca had, as he claimed, served
the Viceroy of Mexico as a pilot on the west coast of America,
the truth of his other statements is less certain. He told Lok
that he had been sent to pilot three small ships in search of the
Strait of Anian along the California coast; a mutiny had caused
the premature return of this expedition. Sent out again in 1592
with a caravel and a pinnace, he had sailed into a broad inlet
between 47° and 48° latitude. He had continued in a northeasterly direction until he reached the 'North Sea' (Arctic Ocean);
then he had turned around and returned home. When the
Spaniards failed to pay him the promised reward, he then approached Lok. Yet in the end his mendacity received a more
lasting reward, for the strait between Vancouver Island and
the mainland bears his name.[2]

A no less influential figure was the fictional explorer Bartholomew de Fonte. The account of his voyage first appeared in
the form of a letter in a London magazine, *Monthly Miscellany
or Memoirs for the Curious,* in April and June 1708. James
Petiver, the owner and editor of the journal, is now generally

believed to have been its author. The letter tells of a voyage to
the northwest coast in 1640 and describes in great detail the
discovery of a passage from the Pacific to the Atlantic. While
de Fonte did not sail all the way through, he went far enough
to meet two Boston ships, to exchange courtesies with their
commander and obtain charts from him. At the time the letter
was printed it caused no stir in geographical circles. But in 1749
Arthur Dobbs seized on the tale and used it to support his
argument in his own book on Hudson Bay.[3] It was next printed
in full by Theodore Swaine Drage, together with a handsome
map by Thomas Jefferys showing the passage beginning at the
Strait of Juan de Fuca on the northwest coast, winding its way
northeasterly across North America, and emerging among the
islands north of Hudson Bay in the vicinity of Foxe Basin.[4]
Most of the individuals mentioned in the account, except Admiral de Fonte himself, were historical personages, and many
of the geographical places on the west coast were genuine. Consequently the story caused infinite confusion. The imaginary
passage on the Jeffreys map was incorporated in other eighteenth-century maps, and it took some years to rectify this erroneous geography.[5]

The third hoax is that of Lorenzo Ferrer Maldonado, who
flourished in the late sixteenth century. The earliest of the three,
his was the last to be published. Maldonado claimed in 1588 to
have made a voyage from Spain via Iceland to Davis Strait,
then northwest through various straits in the Arctic to as high
as 75°, along the Polar Ocean, and out the Strait of Anian into
the Pacific. He then turned around and sailed back the same
way. Published in 1788, the yarn was, in November 1790, the
subject of a paper read before the Academy of Sciences in Paris
by Philippe Buache de la Neuville. A reputable geographer, he
had been a strong supporter of the de Fonte account. This
learned attention inspired the Spanish Government to investigate the entrance to the strait. Orders were immediately sent

to Alejandro Malaspina, commander of the two ships *Descubierta* and *Atrevida* on a general scientific expedition to the South Seas. Malaspina proceeded at once, 1 May 1791, for the northwest coast. He examined the Alaskan shoreline quite thoroughly from Baranof Island to Prince William Sound, the vicinity of 60°, where Maldonado claimed his Strait of Anian entered the Pacific. He of course found nothing. He then wrote an exhaustive criticism of the story, pointing out its errors and inconsistencies and proving it a fake.

These stories of Maldonado, de Fuca, and de Fonte cropped up repeatedly and obscured the problem of a Northwest Passage. But none was taken seriously until the discovery of Bering Strait by Vitus Bering in 1728. Then geographers, who for years had enjoyed speculating about the location of the Strait of Anian, found it tempting to identify the fictitious Strait with Bering's discovery.

The hard facts of trade added to these intriguing geographical speculations did much to stimulate interest in the Northwest Passage. Two French Canadian fur traders, Médard Chouart, better known in history as Sieur des Groseilliers, and his brother-in-law Pierre Esprit Radisson, had sometime before 1658 learned from Cree Indian trappers of the existence of the 'Bay of the North' and of the abundance of furs in the forests stretching back from its shores. Keeping this knowledge to themselves, they planned to travel overland to the Bay and survey its possibilities. Unfortunately one of them had a talkative wife. In no time every *voyageur* and trapper along the St. Lawrence began to see in his mind's eye endless fur riches to the north. Fur prices were high, intrigue, influence, and jealousy rampant. Radisson and Groseilliers had brought back a fortune in furs to Montreal. Most of the proceeds went in fines for illegal trading, and when they applied for a license to undertake another trading journey, the Governor of Canada refused to grant them one. Not deterred, they left for the interior in August 1661. Although it has been claimed that they reached the shores of Hudson Bay on this trip, they could not have done so since they were north of Lake Superior. They were, however, more than ever convinced that the proper approach to the northern fur country was by sea through the Bay of the North. On their return to Montreal the Govenor again fined them heavily for proceeding without his license.

The incensed Groseilliers, after going to France to demand justice and obtaining no satisfaction, rejoined Radisson in Canada. Here the two *coureurs de bois* tried unsuccessfully to obtain a ship for a voyage to Hudson Bay. Groseilliers then traveled the coast of Nova Scotia and New England searching for support. At last, in 1663 in Boston, he met merchants who provided a vessel. Ice and the captain's inexperience forced them to turn back at the entrance to Hudson Strait. Plans for a second try the following year fell through when the vessels were sent instead on fishing trips to Sable Island and the Gulf of St. Lawrence. Back in Boston the frustrated Frenchmen met the King's Commissioners to New England, who had then completed their work attempting to adjudicate the boundary disputes between the British Colonies. One of these officials, Colonel George Cartwright, impressed with the story of a bay with shores teeming with beaver, persuaded Groseilliers and Radisson to come to England. On the way their ship was captured by a Dutch vessel; the party landed in Spain from where they made their way to England, arriving in 1665. Cartwright, ending his report of the Commission's achievements, wrote:

> Hearing also some Frenchmen discourse in New England of a passage from the West Sea to the South Sea, and of a great trade of beaver in that passage, and afterwards meeting with sufficient proof of the truth of what they had said, and knowing what great endeavours have been made for the finding out of a

north-west passage, he thought them the best present he could
possibly make His Majesty, and persuaded them to come to
England.

Colonel Cartwright's present caught the imagination of the
King. A ship was promised the Canadians, but in 1667 the
Dutch fleet arrived in the Thames and prevented their departure. The next summer the season for sailing was too far advanced by the time the ketch *Discovery,* purchased for the undertaking, was ready. In the face of this series of disappoint-
ments, Mr. Gooseberry, as the English called him, and Radisson
persevered. Not without reason, for their scheme fascinated the
courtiers and interested London financiers — a combination
which brought concrete results.

Charles II lent the ketch *Eaglet* from the Royal Navy, a
forty-foot vessel of fifty-four tons commanded by Captain William Stannard. *Nonsuch,* a somewhat smaller ketch which had
been sold out of the Navy the previous year, was contributed
by her purchaser, Sir William Warren. On 5 June 1668 the two
small craft sailed down the Thames. Radisson was assigned to
Eaglet while Groseilliers was aboard *Nonsuch,* which was commanded by Zachariah Gillam, the Boston Captain who had
taken the two Canadians as far as Hudson Strait in 1663. Both
Captains were instructed to winter in Hudson Bay and to give
precedence to trading for furs. Should evidence of a passage
to the South Seas be apparent, they were to conduct preliminary
investigations without hazarding the primary purpose of their
voyage; if it seemed warranted, a separate ship for discovery
would be dispatched later.

During the crossing the Atlantic was stormy. The ships were
separated and *Eaglet,* with some losses, staggered back into
Plymouth. But Captain Gillam with Groseilliers in *Nonsuch*
sailed on through Hudson Strait and wintered at the mouth of
Rupert River. There in the southeastern tip of James Bay, near

the spot where Hudson had vanished and Captain James had endured his hardships, they built Fort Charles, the first trading
post on the shores of Hudson Bay. An old and interesting ghost
again raised its head on this voyage when it was reported that
Captain Zachariah Gillam on his outward passage 'made the
land of Busse.' [6]

During the absence of *Nonsuch* the men backing the venture
decided to form a company, and when she returned 21 October
1669 with a cargo of prime furs their faith was vindicated. The
King granted a Royal Charter on 2 May 1670 to eighteen nobles
and gentlemen as the 'Governor and Company of Adventurers
of England Trading into Hudson's Bay,' with Prince Rupert
as Governor. By this charter the Company was given the exclusive right to trade within the entrance to Hudson Strait, with
territorial rights and jurisdiction over an enormous area thereafter called Rupert's Land. [7] The preamble to the charter states
that:

> Whereas our entirely beloved cousin, Prince Rupert and others
> . . . have, at their own great cost, and charges, undertaken an
> expedition for Hudson's Bay in the northwest part of America,
> for the discovery of a new passage into the South Sea, and for
> the finding of some trade for furs, minerals, and other con-
> siderable commodities, and by such their undertaking have al-
> ready made such discoveries as to encourage them to proceed
> further in pursuance of their said design, by means whereof
> there may probably arise very great advantages to us and our
> kingdom.

While the Company was not specifically obligated to search
for the Northwest Passage, this purpose was implied although
no attempt was made for nearly fifty years. The fur trade was
lucrative, competition with the French keen. Trading posts were
established at the mouths of each of the principal rivers emptying into the Bay. The Indians came down the rivers to trade,

and the Hudson Bay men rarely ventured any distance into the interior. The Adventurers were content: their profits were substantial. Why search for elusive icy passages which, if found, would probably interfere with their monopoly anyhow?

The Company paid its employees well, and captains and factors spent lives in its service. Governor James Knight, first employed by the Company as a shipwright, was about seventy-seven years old when he established the first settlement at Churchill Bay in 1717. Two years earlier northern Indians brought pieces of copper to the mouth of the Churchill and told tales of vast quantities of ore along a great river. Other Indians told of a yellow metal at the mouth of a river by the Western Sea. Knight returned to London, exhibited his specimens, and pointed out that the river mouths where the valuable metals were said to be could probably be reached by a Northwest Passage. He insisted that it was a Company obligation to continue this search. Knight was held in great respect as the only member of the Company's Committee with personal experience in the Bay.

In 1719 Knight was issued orders to sail from Gravesend with the frigate *Albany* under Captain George Berley and the sloop *Discovery* under Captain David Vaughan. His instructions were specific: 'You are, with the first opportunity of wind and weather, to depart from Gravesend on your intended voyage, and by God's permission, to find out the Straits of Anian, in order to discover gold and other valuable commodities to the Northward.' [8] Knight sailed, 5 June, carrying iron-bound chests in which to stow the gold, and apparently headed for Roes Welcome. But, like his earlier namesake on the coast of Labrador, he never returned. Both ships were lost and every member of the expedition perished.

When Knight failed to return the year he sailed, many thought he had found the Passage. But when there was no sign of him in 1721 the Company sent the sloop *Whalebone* under

Captain John Scroggs, who wintered at Churchill and sailed north in the summer of 1722. He sailed up Roes Welcome as far as Whalebone Point, which he named for his vessel, and returned to Churchill 25 July, being gone less than a month. It has been generally assumed that Scroggs found no evidence of Knight's expedition, but E. E. Rich's recent work states that Scroggs reported he had been where the two ships were wrecked 'and he doth affirm that Every Man was killed by the Eskemoes.' [9]

In any event, in 1767, one of the Company whaling sloops discovered, in an obscure harbor on Marble Island, the hulls of both ship and sloop lying on the bottom in five fathoms of water and the remains of a house on the shore. *Albany*'s figurehead and some guns were salvaged and sent home to the Company. Two years later Samuel Hearne, on a whaling voyage for the Hudson's Bay Company, saw the Marble Island remains and obtained accounts of the fate of the expedition from the Eskimos.

> When the vessels arrived at this place (Marble Island) it was very late in the Fall, and in getting them into the harbour, the largest received much damage; but on being fairly in, the English began to build the house, their number at that time seeming to be about fifty. As soon as the ice permitted, in the following Summer, (one thousand seven hundred and twenty,) the Esquimaux paid them another visit, by which time the number of the English was greatly reduced, and those that were living seemed very unhealthy. According to the account given by the Esquimaux they were then very busily employed but about what they could not easily describe, probably in lengthening the long-boat; for at a little distance from the house there is now lying a great quantity of oak chips, which have been most assuredly made by carpenters.

And when the Eskimos returned in the summer of 1721 only five men were alive and the number was soon reduced to two.

Those two survived many days after the rest, and frequently
went to the top of an adjacent rock, and earnestly looked to the
South and East, as if in expectation of some vessels coming to
their relief. After continuing there a considerable time together,
and nothing appearing in sight, they sat down close together,
and wept bitterly. At length one of the two died, and the other's
strength was so far exhausted, that he fell down and died also,
in attempting to dig a grave for his companion. The sculls and
other large bones of those two men are now lying above-ground
close to the house. The longest liver was, according to the Esquimaux account, always employed in working of iron implements
for them; probably he was the armourer, or smith.[10]

The same year the aged Knight was sailing to his doom, another prominent Hudson's Bay Company employee, Henry
Kelsey, sailed from York factory in the sloop *Prosperous* accompanied by the sloop *Success,* an ill-built vessel, under Captain
John Hancock. According to a report to the House of Com-
mons, this expedition was to discover 'a North-West Passage.'
Actually it was undertaken for trading and for exploring for
copper. Both vessels returned in a few weeks. The following
summer, Kelsey again sent out Captain Hancock in *Prosperous.*
Success under Captain James Napper also apparently sailed at
the same time but was wrecked four days later.

The Company, never enthusiastic about the Northwest Passage, had even less interest after the Knight disaster. Its experienced members and employees doubted the existence of a
Passage and suggested for all practical purposes, it would be
useless even if it became a reality. They would explore for metal
deposits but they did not intend to send ships on expensive and
fruitless searches. They were practical men who wished, above
all, to earn a proper return on their investments.

17

The Wild Irishman

Arthur Dobbs, high sheriff of the county of Antrim, Ireland, brought with him to England in 1733 an abstract of the accounts of all the explorers who had been to Hudson Bay. Having studied these journals and the de Fonte account, the wealthy Irishman concluded that there was a practical Northwest Passage, that it should be located and used, and that the South Sea Company was the proper organization to conduct the search. He presented his document to the Commissioners for Trade and Plantations. Since the Commissioners exhibited polite indifference, Dobbs took his case to higher authority and called on Sir Charles Wager, First Lord of the Admiralty. Besides holding the office of sheriff, Dobbs was also Engineer-in-Chief and Surveyor-General in Ireland, and Mayor of Carrickfergus, where his family seat, Dobbs Castle, had been founded four generations before.[1] He was, in short, an eminent and influential man.

Sir Charles, after listening to his guest's theory, introduced him to the officials of the Hudson's Bay Company. These men told Dobbs about their disastrous Knight expedition, explained the difficulties of navigation in northern waters, and expressed their belief that Company men would have discovered the Passage if it existed. Dobbs was unimpressed. He knew that several of the seventeenth-century explorers had maintained their belief in the Passage even as they were being repulsed by bleak northern shores and endless ice; and his inquiring mind was further whetted by French gossip of a 'Sea of the West.' Continuing his enthusiastic investigations he read, in 1735, a copy of the Hudson's Bay Company's Charter in the Plantation Office. The exact contents of this document, very little known in the early eighteenth century, had been jealously guarded by the Company. The exclusive and monopolistic nature of the Charter convinced Dobbs that, as only the Company could benefit from the Passage's discovery, it was in its interest to do something about it. Pressing the matter with the Company's Governor, Sir Bibye Lake, he met with notable lack of enthusiasm. But Dobbs was persistent. Sir Bibye, with great reluctance, was persuaded to use two of the Company's sloops already in Hudson Bay for a preliminary voyage especially to investigate the tides in Roes Welcome. The Governor hoped he could pacify Dobbs, who was creating too much publicity and public interest in the Company's affairs, by sending out an expedition of this sort. The traditional interests of the Company were also to be served by trading and establishing a new settlement for dealing with the Eskimos.

Thus on 7 July 1737, because of the pressure created in London by Dobbs, the sloops *Churchill* and *Musquash* under Captains James Napper and Robert Crow were sent north from Churchill to measure the tides, make borings in the earth, and establish a new trading post. It was a short voyage. Napper died at Whale Cove, 7 August, and the two sloops returned to the fort. Trade had been negligible and the coast inhospitable. The opinions of the Company were confirmed. Sir Bibye Lake told Arthur

Dobbs that the sloops had not found 'any the least Appearance of a Passage.'

About the time (1735) that Dobbs read the Company's Charter he had made the acquaintance of Captain Christopher Middleton, one of the Company's most experienced and able shipmasters. Middleton had seen a score of years in its service, taking a ship through the Strait to Hudson Bay nearly every year. He had also presented a paper on the variation of the magnetic needle to the Royal Society in 1736. Regard for his scientific abilities is indicated by his election as a Fellow of that distinguished organization. With their mutual interests and beliefs the two men became very good friends. From information supplied by Captain Middleton, including journals and accounts of the Hudson's Bay Company's voyages—especially as related to parts of Hudson Bay where a Passage might be found—Dobbs concluded that the Company was not acting in good faith. He was further disturbed by the advances the French were making in exploring the interior of North America.

After Sir Bibye reported to him on the return of the sloops *Churchill* and *Musquash,* Dobbs became convinced that the Hudson's Bay Company was concealing information about the Passage in order to protect its monopoly. He talked with influential merchants and finally persuaded the Government to back an expedition to find the Passage. He also argued for revocation of the Company Charter so that the lands around Hudson Bay might be opened to trade by all British subjects. Although Christopher Middleton agreed that the Admiralty should support the expedition, where exclusive rights to trade were concerned, he sympathized with his employers. But, for reasons now unknown, he overcame his initial reluctance to resign from the Company and in 1741 accepted command of the expedition.

The Company feared that the Admiralty expedition might result in encroachment on its trade, property, and other privileges. It requested the Admiralty to forbid Middleton to do anything that might injure trade or to winter in its harbors unless in distress. In the face of this, it was difficult to accept the Company's protestation that it did not seek to hinder the expedition but simply to protect its own interests. Public opinion, aroused by Dobbs's vigorous campaign, was so strong that the Company was forced to back down and to instruct the post officers to render Middleton whatever assistance they could.

In June 1741, nearly eight years after Arthur Dobbs first brought his memorandum on the Northwest Passage to London, Middleton sailed down the Thames in His Majesty's bomb ketch *Furnace*.* He was accompanied by the smaller *Discovery* under his cousin Captain William Moor, also a former Company employee. Middleton had good ships although supplies were inadequate. He had only three competent officers and a crew made up largely of impressed seamen.

Middleton proceeded directly to Churchill for wintering, as the season was too late for exploration. His old friend James Isham, who arrived shortly thereafter, commanded the post. Harassed by disruption of trade resulting from Indian wars in the interior and from French encroachments, he nevertheless extended his hospitality. The ships were berthed for the winter and the expedition men given quarters in the old fort two miles up river from Fort Prince of Wales.[2]

During the winter, relations between the members of the expedition and the men at the post deteriorated. Expedition supplies, inadequate to begin with, were short and it strained Isham's resources to help the extra men. Middleton did assist

---

* Bomb vessels were more strongly built than other naval ships in order to withstand the firing of bombs — hence their frequent selection for and use in Arctic exploration.

Isham by forbidding his men to trade in any way with the Indians and by confiscating all trade goods on the expedition ships (a move Dobbs criticized later). On the other hand, he issued excessive quantities of spirits—an order popular with the men but one which was detrimental to their health and unfortunate for morale at the fort, where liquor was not rationed as freely and where the men had work to do. Holidays were observed with thirty gallons of brandy and the Christmas celebration was a drunken brawl that lasted a fortnight. By spring, thirteen of the expedition men had died, all but two from scurvy, and many of the rest were too weak to work. Isham helped them prepare to leave and lent Middleton additional men, including three Indians to act as interpreters. On 30 June 1742, no doubt with relief, he watched *Furnace* and *Discovery* sail out of Churchill toward northern discoveries.

It was then that Captain Christopher Middleton showed his great skill as a master mariner and a navigator in the ice. Middleton was diligent in measuring the speed and set of the tides at every opportunity. Later explorers confirmed all of his observations. With his inexperienced and scorbutic crew he sailed up the western shore of Hudson Bay and entered Roes Welcome. Pushing beyond the point Luke Foxe had reached on Monday, 12 July, he named a new headland Cape Dobbs, and just beyond it found an opening into the land. The next two weeks were spent exploring and charting this wide, deep stretch of water. He soon found out that he had not discovered the Passage but a bay, which he named for Sir Charles Wager. After leaving the ice-filled mouth of Wager Bay his way was blocked by ice at Repulse Bay. He then discovered and named Frozen Strait, solid with ice, but which he was able to observe from the top of a high hill. Seeing that further progress was impossible and that most of his men were ill, he decided, after consultation with his officers, to bear away for England, where he arrived at Woolwich on 13 October.

Middleton then wrote Dobbs: 'Undoubtedly there is no Hope of a Passage to encourage any further Trial between Churchill and so far as we have gone; and if there be any further to the Northward, it must be impassable for the Ice.'[3] At first Dobbs seemed satisfied, although disappointed, with Middleton's conclusions. He began inquiring around, however, and after interviewing other officers who had been on the expedition as well as dissatisfied employees of the Hudson's Bay Company, he decided there were inconsistencies in his Captain's report. He accused Middleton of taking a £5000 bribe from Hudson's Bay Company to sail in the wrong direction and to alter his charts, so concealing the fact that a Passage existed. Middleton's statement that the Wager was a bay and not a strait, and that the tides all flowed from Frozen Strait in the east toward the western shore and into Wager Bay, was ridiculed by Dobbs. He pointed to the number of whales in Wager Bay and around Marble Island as proof of a Passage, for they were not commonly seen in Hudson Strait. Middleton refuted the charges with good common sense, and defended himself with dignity when the Admiralty instructed him to answer the charges. Dobbs called Middleton a liar and the ensuing exchange of acrimonious letters developed into a vituperative pamphlet war which seemed as endless as it was libelous.[4] Middleton was publicly discredited although the Navy apparently thought well of him for he kept his commission. He was not given another command until 1745, after the Admiralty Court of Enquiry at which he was cleared and Dobbs defeated.

Dobbs was prominent and, although his stand was absurd, public opinion was with him. The Company was prosperous, secretive, and apparently dilatory in its duties. The attack on Middleton was but another way of getting at the monopolistic Hudson's Bay Company, the principal target. Dobbs fired his biggest gun when he published his book on Hudson Bay. It is a curious work containing a description of the Hudson Bay region based on an account of Joseph La France, a French-Canadian Indian half-breed and includes an abstract of Middleton's journal. It reprints a summary of Bartholomew de Fonte's fictitious voyage through the continent from the Pacific until he met Boston men who had sailed from Hudson Bay, and Dobbs's own abstract of earlier voyages, as well as vocabularies of Indian tribes. The book was useful in its account of resources and trade in the region, which was fuller, if sometimes erroneous, than any then published. 'The whole intended to shew the great Probability of a North-West Passage, so long desired, and which (if discovered) would be of the highest Advantage to these Kingdoms.'[5]

The work is well larded with unprincipled attacks against Middleton and the Hudson's Bay Company. On the second page Dobbs comments that the country is dismal to live in because of the Company monopoly. So wild are some of his words that even today they sound hysterical. Yet when the book was published they were taken seriously. Of Middleton's report he wrote:

I shall here give a short Abstract of the Journal which he has been pleased to give us, wherein, tho' many material Observations have been concealed and omitted, and others have been misrepresented; and the chief Part of the Coast, where the greatest Hopes was of a Passage, was entirely slighted and neglected by him, Part being passed in the Night, and the Remainder sailed along in hazy Weather, at five, six, and eight Leagues Distance, so as to make no Discovery of those broken Lands, of which that whole Coast consists; which seems plainly done with a design in him to compliment the Company at the publick Expense, that he might have it in his power to gratify them by concealing the Discovery; and thought from his Character of being an experienced Sailor, no other after him would pretend to look after it for the future, which would quiet the Company in the possession of their darling Monopoly in the Bay, for

which, no doubt, he had strong Motives to induce him to slight
it, they having offered him before he went the Voyage £5000
not to go, or to slight the Discovery, by going to *Davis's*
Streights, or any other Way but where he was directed, as he
has own'd to several Persons; yet notwithstanding all his Art
in concealing a great deal, and disguising more, in his journal,
enough is discovered in it, to shew he was in the Passage.

And so it goes on and on through a single sentence that runs
a whole quarto page.

Nor is the Company spared the benefit of his polemics:

The Company avoid all they can making Discoveries to Northward of *Churchill,* or extending their Trade that Way for fear
they should discover a Passage to the Western Ocean of America,
and tempt, by that Means, the rest of the *English* Merchants
to lay open their trade, which they know they have no legal Right
to, which, if the Passage was found, would not only animate
the rest of the Merchants to pursue the Trade through that Passage, but also to find out the great Advantages that might be
made of the Trade of the Rivers and Countries adjoining to
the Bay, by which Means they would lose their beloved Monopoly; but the Prospect they have of Gain to be made with trading
with the *Eskimaux Indians,* for Whale-Fin, Whale and Seal
Oil, and Sea-Horse Teeth, induces them to venture a Sloop
annually as far 62°.30′. to *Whale Cove,* where these *Indians* meet
them, and truck their Fin and Oil with them: But tho' they are
fully informed of a fine Copper Mine on a navigable Arm of the
Sea North-westward of *Whale Cove,* and the *Indians* have offered to carry their Sloops to it, yet their Fear of discovering
the Passage puts Bounds to their Avarice, and prevents their
going to the Mine, which by all Accounts is very rich; yet those
who have been at *Whale Cove* own, that from thence North-
wards is all broken Land, and that after passing some Islands,
they from the Hills see the Sea open leading to the Westward;
and the *Indians* who have been often at the Mine say, it is upon
a navigable Arm of the Sea of great Depth leading to the Southwest, where are great Numbers of large black Fish spouting
Water, which confirms the Opinion, that all the Whales seen

betwixt *Whale Cove* and *Wager* River, all come there from the Western Ocean, since none are seen any where else in *Hudson's Bay* or *Strait.*

Besides, they [the Company] have not only neglected to find a Passage to the Western Ocean, but have also refused to look for it, and have discouraged and endeavored to seduce others from finding it, by offering Rewards or Bribes to Captain *Middleton,* who was employed by the Government to make that Discovery. . .

He did not fool the old Hudson Bay hands, however, for Captain Coats remarks about the book:

What Mr. Dobbs has thought fit to call a description of Hudson's Bay, is so erronious, so superficial, and so trifling, in almost every circumstance.

So contrary to the experience and concurrent testimony of every person who have resided in that country, or of those who have used it any considerable time, that when it first appeared it was matter of astonishment to all who may be suppoosed to be competant judges.[6]

By making unsubstantiated accusations and stirring up public opinion against Middleton and the Hudson's Bay Company, Dobbs apparently hoped to get the Government to send out another expedition. He also desired to break the Company monopoly in the fur trade to make way for a company of his own. As he was not successful, we may surmise that the Admiralty had had quite enough of his tirades. He was, however, able to raise funds for another exploring expedition. He was helped in this by an Act of Parliament (1745) offering a reward of £20,000 to any of His Majesty's subjects, except those serving on naval vessels, who discovered a Northwest Passage through Hudson Strait.

Failing to obtain naval vessels for the new expedition but with the incentive offered by the prospect of such a generous reward if the Northwest Passage was discovered, Dobbs raised

£10,000 by public subscription, and a committee of nine of the contributors was appointed to oversee the venture. This 'North West Committee' headed by Dobbs purchased the ships *Dobbs* (180 tons), and *California* (140 tons). Once more the services of two experienced Hudson's Bay Company captains were obtained: Captain William Moor of *Dobbs,* who had been Middleton's second in command but had taken the side of Dobbs during the controversy; Captain Francis Smith of *California,* who annually had sailed Company sloops in the Bay to the north of Churchill for trade and discovery since at least 1737. Very high wages were paid to get seamen for the voyage. As an added incentive premiums were offered in case of success in the discovery, beginning with £500 each for the captains, £200 for the mates, and graduating down to the ordinary seamen. Each ship became a letter of marque and any prizes taken were to be its own.[7]

The captains were instructed to investigate with special thoroughness 'Wager Strait,' which Dobbs believed to be the Passage, and to observe the rise and fall and direction of the tides, which were thought to indicate its location. Precise points of rendezvous were established in case the ships became separated. The instructions gave considerable space to procedures once the ships were through the Passage.

Two accounts of this expedition were published. One by Henry Ellis, a widely traveled young gentleman, who was sent as draftsman and personal agent for the Committee. He sailed with Captain Moor on *Dobbs* to keep a journal and to write the official account of the voyage. The other account was written by a mysterious individual, probably a friend of Dobbs, who called himself simply 'the Clerk of the *California.'*[8] Ellis's is the more straightforward account of the voyage. The clerk's book gives most of its pages to summaries of earlier voyages and great detail to the petty quarrels and disputes between the officers of the expedition, particularly the two captains.

The vessels left London 10 May 1746, sailing in company with four Hudson's Bay Company ships. At the Orkneys they were met, ironically, by Captain Christopher Middleton, now in command of the sloop-of-war *Shark*. By coincidence, perhaps not entirely unpremeditated by someone, the three disparate elements of the famous controversy were brought together— Dobbs's expedition; Middleton; and, in the Company ship *Prince Rupert,* Governor James Isham, officially opposed to both. Middleton performed his duty by convoying the six ships along with two other merchantmen well out into the Atlantic, where he left them on 16 or 17 June. The next day Moor and Smith parted company with the Company ships and did not see them again during the crossing.

The expedition was nearly wrecked on the night of 21 June when the great cabin of *Dobbs* caught fire. The blaze progressed toward the magazine directly below, where there were thirty to forty barrels of powder, candles, spirits, matches, and other combustibles. Ellis says:

> The dangerous Place the Fire was in, gave every one on Board the greatest Reason to expect, that Moment, or the next at most, was their last. You might hear on this Occasion, all the Varieties of Sea-Eloquence; Cries, Prayers, Curses, and scolding, mingled together; yet this did not prevent proper Measures being taken to save the Ship, and our Lives.

The fire was fought by bucket lines but the confusion was intensified when, 'In the midst of all this Hurry, the man at the Helm, reflecting on his Situation, and thinking it more dreadful than any other Persons, having the Fire and Powder immediately under him,' left his post.

> The Ship was now Head to Wind, and the Sails shaking and making a Noise like Thunder; then running right before it, and rolling, every Body upon Deck waiting, and that too in an Agony mixed with a kind of Impatience, for the Blast, that must have put an End to our Fears and Uncertainties.

California was far in the lead at the time and could offer no assistance, but bucket brigades put out the fire.

As they neared Hudson Strait on 5 July, they began to fall in with 'Mountains of Ice' 'of a prodigious size'; three days later they made Resolution Island. They met the usual ice and fog, but by now the captains were experienced in navigating the strait. On the seventeenth, Ellis continues,

> . . . the Ice being very thick about us, we made fast to a very large Piece of it, with several Ice Anchors and Ropes. It is requisite in such Cases to make Choice of the largest Piece that can be found for this Purpose, because having more hold of the Water, it is less affected by Winds and Currents (which generally run on the Surface) so that all the small Ice is drove from about us in Time, and we are left at liberty to proceed. Here we unhung our Rudder, which traversed very stiffly, and made it go easier; and the Crew of the *California,* as well as we in the *Dobbs* Galley, filled our empty Casks with fresh Water out of the Ponds that are commonly found upon the Ice.

They made the western shore 11 August and on the nineteenth reached Marble Island which they explored quite thoroughly. Turning south, they arrived 26 August off Hayes River and anchored *California* in Five Fathoms Hole about seven miles below York Fort. Moor in *Dobbs* ran aground attempting to reach the same anchorage. Seeing the ships coming, Governor Isham pulled up all the buoys, cut down the beacon marking the channel, and loaded his guns. He requested the explorers to come no closer to the Fort without showing proper governmental or Company authority. As Moor and Smith held commissions as privateersmen, which obligated any British subject to assist them, Isham had to let them winter. He lent them necessities and gave the benefit of his advice, but otherwise held himself aloof. After all, he had got himself in the ill favor of the Company by being civil to Middleton and he did not intend to get himself in such circumstances a second time. In any case, he had strict orders about Moor and Smith. They were regarded as competitors, for they had instructions to trade more favorably with the Eskimos than the Company did. Isham, like his superiors, suspected that Dobbs either was obtuse or actually intended his ships only for trade.

The vessels were laid up in Ten Shilling Creek five miles above York Fort. A twelve-foot hole was dug in which to stow their beer to prevent freezing. Then a two-story log cabin was built, twenty by sixteen feet, named Montague House after the Duke of Montague, who headed the list of subscribers.

Unlike Middleton's men, they did not suffer from cold for, while they were inadequately supplied in this respect, Isham gave them proper clothing. Ellis remarks that 'Since, as to any Distresses our People underwent, they occasioned for Want of Proper Food, and an inexcusable Indiscretion in the Use of spirituous Licquors, rather than from the Intenseness of the Cold.' They soon found, nevertheless, at the first cold snap in November, that they must winter in the house, for Captain Smith and his men who were still on their ship found they

> could not be warm, not even in the Cabbin, though a great Fire was continually kept, and Blankets nailed over the Windows. If any Water poured out of one Vessel into another, fell aside, it immediately froze. Brandy was congealed so as to look like Oil. Port Wine froze solid. Licquor, one third Brandy, froze solid. . . . All within Side the Ship, the Ceilings, and the Boltheads, excepting in the Cabbin or the Galley, were thick covered with a white Rind. Upon Waking in the Morning the Blankets would have Icicles upon them near the Mouth, proceeding from the Freezing of the Breath. When we went Abroad, the Eyelashes, the Dropping of the Nose, and the Sweat aside the Wigs, froze.[9]

During the winter, which was passed with some discomfort because of scurvy, the longboat was lengthened and made into a small schooner for inshore exploration. With the coming of

spring the ships were laboriously broken out of the eight feet
of solid ice that had built up around them. On 21 April

> the *California* rose intirely and floated, having come up very
> gently. The Water down the Creek increased very much, bring-
> ing Fleaks of rotten Ice with it, and about Noon several Boards
> of Ice of great Length, being the upper Ice of the Creek; and in
> the Evening much Ground Ice; some of it come down in very
> heavy and large Pieces.

By 28 May, with the river clear, there was a high enough tide to
get the ships out of the creek.

> The *California* floated first, and in a few Minutes after the
> *Dobbs;* both Ships proceeded to get out of the Creek, but the
> *California* could not faster than the *Dobbs,* as the Channel
> was not wide enough to let her pass; the *Dobbs* stopping short
> of the length she might have got that Tide for want of a Long-
> boat, (her Long-boat having been lengthen'd and turned into
> a Scooner; so becoming in a manner useless as a Long-boat.)

Because of having missed this chance it was nearly a month
before another flood tide was high enough for them to drop
down river, where they anchored again at Five Fathoms Hole.
They ate venison supplied by the Governor and in turn were
eaten by mosquitoes.

> They are here so troublesome, that the People cannot sleep be-
> tween Decks, or in their Cabins tho' Smokes were continually
> made to drive the Musketoes out, but are forced to sleep either
> in the Tops, or in the Sails. In the Day Time the People wore
> Crape, or a Piece of Bunting over their Faces, and long Trowsers
> to preserve their Legs; yet with these Precautions they suffer'd
> very much. The Ship lay half a Mile from the Shore, neverthe-
> less the Musketoes would find the Way on Board of themselves.
> But incredible were the Numbers that were brought on the Hats
> and Cloaths of those who came from the Shore in the Boats.

Salutes were exchanged with the Fort 22 June and two days later, with a fair wind, they sailed northward.

On the afternoon of 28 July 'the Sea was feathered with a strong Tide' and the next day the ships entered the mouth of Wager Bay. They were now in the body of water which was the focal point of their expedition and Ellis writes:

> considering the warm Dispute [a precious understatement] there had been about it, between Arthur Dobbs, Esq; and Capt. Middleton; and the great Expectations which the Dispute had raised in the World, as well as the near Relation that it had to the present Expedition; so that the neglecting it might have been looked upon as an inexcusable Omission, and the World have been still left in Suspence, whether it was a Strait as the former of those Gentlemen, from various, very probable Reasons, had concluded it to be; or a fresh Water River, as it was asserted to be by the Captain.

After the ships were safely anchored in Douglas Harbor within Wager Bay, it was agreed in a council held on board *Dobbs* on 30 July to send the two longboats, under the captains, to explore. The ships were to remain in anchorage. If the boats had not returned by 25 August the mates were instructed to sail to England. Moor and Smith performed this part of their assignment thoroughly and well. They were, as Ellis's description attests, impressed by the rushing rivers and the rugged desolation of the landscape.

> But the most tremendous Part of the scene were the shattered Crags which lay at our Feet, and appeared plainly to have burst from the Mountain Tops, thro' the expansive Power of the rigorous Frosts, and so rolled with inexpressible Fury down the Sides, 'till they reached those Places where their Ruins now lay: I call them Ruins; for such they properly were: And if there is something that deeply affects us, when we behold either the Waste of War, or the Devastations of Time, it may be easily

conceived, that something much more terrible must be felt
from the Sight of these amazing Relicks of the Wreck of Nature.

The longboats penetrated to the very western end of Wager
Bay until they could go no further and

> we had the Mortification to see clearly, that our hitherto im-
> agined Strait ended in two small unnavigable Rivers; one of
> which plainly fell from a large Lake, which lay at some Miles
> Distance to the South West. Thus all our Hopes vanished, and
> we had nothing to console us for the Pains we had taken, the
> Time we had spent, and the Dangers we had run, but the Satis-
> faction of having done in this Respect, all that could be looked
> for from us, and having thereby cleared this Point, and left no
> farther room to doubt about the Issue of this Inlet.

The boats returned to the ships 7 August, where a council was
held on board *California.* Captains William Moor and Francis
Smith agreed that there was no opening into Wager Bay other
than the way they had come in. Henry Ellis and the surgeon
Edward Thompson thought, however, that the northern shore
had not been sufficiently explored because of the rough weather
when the boats returned. They were granted permission to explore that shore with one of the boats, and all were finally satisfied that the Wager was a bay.

Ellis having found no opening along the north shore, another
meeting was held on the fourteenth. It was then officially stated
that the Wager could not be a strait. Captain Christopher Middleton's conclusions were completely vindicated and even Ellis,
Dobbs's own man, was forced to admit that 'Mr. Middleton had
quite a contrary Notion [to Dobbs] . . . and he was right.' He
then hedges his remark by saying that Dobbs reasoned rightly
but had been given misinformation. Interest in discovery of the
Passage had been high, even among the common seamen. The
possibility had been discussed endlessly, disappointment was
bitter, and it is amusing to read that aboard *Dobbs*

> there was a very honest Seaman, whose sole Delight was a
> delicious Dram, that one Day heated himself to such a degree,
> in talking over the Business of the Expedition, that in the warm
> Sincerity of his Heart, he could not help saying with a good
> round Oath, *Now had I rather find the* NORTH WEST PASSAGE
> *than* HALF *an* ANCHOR *of* BRANDY.

With the primary purpose of their expedition accomplished
there was some discussion of further exploration either in Repulse Bay or in Chesterfield Inlet, which had been discovered
by *California* on her way north. It was suggested that one ship
go in each direction, but the captains had no authority to separate the vessels. In any case, many of the seamen were ill and
there was a great desire on everyone's part to go home. In fact
the clerk of the *California* indicates that an incipient mutiny
was brewing and had they not sailed for England an ugly situation might have developed. On the eastward passage the two
ships were separated for a fortnight but reunited in the Orkneys.
They proceeded under escort to Yarmouth, arriving 14 October.

In spite of the conclusive proof of the absence of a Passage
through northern Hudson Bay, Ellis concludes his account with
some of the curious double talk peculiar to writers on the subject:

> Thus, I say, ended this Voyage without Success indeed, but not
> without Effect; for though we did not discover a North West
> Passage, yet were we so far from discovering the Impossibility
> or even Improbability of it, that on the contrary, we returned
> with clearer and fuller Proofs, founded on the only Evidence
> that ought to take place in an Enquiry of this Nature, plain
> Facts, and accurate Experiments, that evidently shew such a
> Passage there may be.

Perhaps he wanted to please Dobbs. The clerk flatly states:

> I have . . . entirely excluded there being any Communication
> between Hudson's Bay and the supposed Welcome with the

> Western Ocean, to be judged of from Winds, Tides, or any other
> Phoenomena.

But he too continues:

> But as there is a Possibility of a Communication here though
> these Phoenomena may not appear, it can only be determined,
> if such there is, by finishing the Search of what we left undis-
> covered. All that remains to be searched is between the Latitude
> 62 Deg. and the South Point of Main, and Mr. Bowden's Chester-
> field Inlet: At Repulse Bay should there be an Inlet there, which
> there is no Reason to believe, such a Passage would scarce be
> practicable; and better kept a Secret. . . .

In his summary Ellis, who wanted it both ways, writes, 'it
seems highly probable, that this Passage is not very far to the
Northward,' and gives his reasons; two pages later he is writing,
'If this Passage be not far to the Northward which the Reason
already assigned, seem clearly to prove it is not,' and so forth. In
spite of these remarks, Ellis holds out hope that Chesterfield
Inlet, named for one of the sponsors of the expedition to Repulse Bay, might develop into a Passage.

By the time he got around to writing the preface to his book
he had pretty well convinced himself that he could not believe
his own eyes.

> As to the Dreams of . . . the Danger and Difficulty of the
> Navigation through Hudson's-Straits and Bay, and of the insup-
> portable Rigour of the Cold in those Northern Climates . . .
> we know that this Navigation is far from being so perilous as
> it is represented; and . . . it will be shewn that there are very
> good Grounds to expect, that this Passage is not either narrow
> or encumbered with Ice, but may be both passed and repassed
> in the Compass of the same Summer.

He goes on:

the manner in which the two Ships [*Dobbs* and *California*] Companies wintered in Hudson's-Bay; and the Discoveries they afterwards made; which, though they did not absolutely shew where the Passage lay, yet seem to have firmly established the Certainty, that such a Passage there is.

Finally he writes:

And as upon the Lights derived from the Comparison of these Voyages, and those that were also let in by Capt. Middleton's Informations before his Expedition, and the Facts reported in his Account of his Expedition, the last Voyage was undertaken; so it has clearly verified every Point upon which the Reality of the Passage depended, and has thereby given Certainty to our Hopes, though the issue of it did not altogether correspond with our Expectations.

Dobbs's reaction to these accounts is not known, but he sent out no more expeditions. There is no question about Isham's opinion of the two books. He condemned them with much justification. He remarks first on Ellis:

I observe its a common Rule with some persons that writes a history of Voyages &c. for want of a proper and Just Subject to make a complete Book; they Enlarge upon things which is neither consistant with truth, justice, nor honour . . .[10]

He takes Ellis to task for his lack of knowledge of natural history, Indian customs, the country and its resources. His criticism concludes:

. . . As to mr. Dragg's [clerk of the *California*] Last Book, itt wou'd be only a Repitition of the same thing over again, I therefore do not think it Reasonable to make any Remarks upon itt, more then I can but Observe he is more perticular as to truth then the aforemention'd Author's [11]

After all, both men were working for Dobbs, and Ellis's book contains severe attacks on the Company and its officers. The clerk's poorly written but probably more honest account is marred by savage remarks about Ellis and Captain Moor.

Typically, although Dobbs was disappointed his energy was in no way dissipated. He decided that they had been 'defeated in their Expectations, by the Timidity, ill Conduct, or bad Inclination, of some of the Commanders and Council.'[12] Dobbs thereafter devoted his time to hectoring the Hudson's Bay Company about their monopoly and endeavoring to form a company of his own. His onslaught against Middleton appears to have been a device to raise capital for an expedition. Both expeditions were a means of attacking the Hudson's Bay Company, which he considered, had 'slept on the shores of the Bay' for a generation. A terrific struggle ensued between Dobbs and the Hudson's Bay Company. He accused the Company of various breaches of faith, including failure to search for the Northwest Passage. In spite of his energy and his political influence, Dobbs's petition to the Privy Council was turned down. The Council said he had not proved his case against the Company and he was not granted a new charter.[13] As a sort of consolation prize he was appointed Governor of North Carolina, where his genuine interest in the overseas development of the Empire and his energy and ability found a useful outlet.

Arthur Dobbs was not the only one connected with this expedition to go to America. Henry Ellis later became Governor of Georgia, and the clerk of the *California* too migrated to the New World. And it is to the American colonies we must follow them for the next episode in our story.

18

The American 'Argo'

In 1750 a man who said his name was Charles Swaine called on Governor Samuel Ogle of Maryland. Swaine, only recently come to that Colony, requested permission to raise funds and outfit a vessel to search for the Northwest Passage. He painted a glowing picture of northern fish and fur trade and pointed out the possibility of collecting the English Government's reward for finding the Passage. He clinched his argument by showing evidence that he was the explorer who had been the 'Clerk of the *California*' whose book was then being read in America. He expressed his belief in the existence of the Northwest Passage based on his own experience.

The 'Clerk of the *California*,' as has been indicated, was an elusive individual. Neither in his own book nor that by Ellis is his name mentioned, but less than a score of years after the *Dobbs-California* expedition, John R. Forster wrote that the clerk's name was Theodore Swaine Drage,[1] and that he was also the author of *The Great Probability of a Northwest Passage,*[2] which bears the name Thomas Jefferys on the title page. For many years subsequent authorities, including Sir John Barrow,

211

accepted Forster's identification of this individual.[3] J. E. Nourse published evidence first in 1879 and again in 1884 [4] — although no conclusions were then drawn from it — that the clerk's name was Charles Swaine and that he wrote both the clerk's account and *The Great Probability*. Nourse has been followed by several recent scholars, and it is generally agreed that the same man probably wrote both books, and that Jefferys was the cartographer who did the maps.[5]

New evidence has come to light proving that Forster was correct in giving Drage as the clerk's name. Captain Francis Smith, commander of *California,* in a letter to Governor James Isham writes the name of his clerk as 'mr. Dragg.' [6] Evidently the clerk was the source of much friction between Captain Smith and Captain Moor. At least Moor felt that way about it, and indeed the clerk in his book is constantly making derogatory remarks about Moor. Smith had requested Isham to have Drage as a guest at York Fort in order to remove the irritation and improve relations between himself and his colleague. Again in an exchange of letters between Isham and James Gwynn, surgeon of *California,* the clerk is mentioned in both letters as 'Drage.' [7] Yet again in writing Captain Smith, Isham begins his letter of 26 March 1747, 'I Return you my hearty thanks for the prest. sent by mr. Drag.' [8] We have already seen that Isham referred to 'mr. Dragg's Last Book' in obvious reference to the account by the 'Clerk of the *California.*' [9] It is thus well established that the clerk was a Mr. Drage or Dragg.

Similarly, it is clear that Captain Charles Swaine commanded the only two serious American attempts to discover the Northwest Passage in the eighteenth century. His statement that he was experienced in Hudson Bay apparently influenced Governor Samuel Ogle of Maryland to give him the following commission in November 1750:

> Whereas An Act of Parliament hath been made for the Encouragement of His Majesty's Subjects to attempt a North West

Passage, with a Bounty a purse of Twenty Thousand Pounds
for any Person or Persons who shall discover the same And
Whereas Charles Swaine late Clerk of the Ship *California*
which proceeded on the said Discovery in the Years seventeen
hundred forty-six and seventeen hundred forty-seven, but now
of Chester Town in the Province of Maryland, apprehends that
there is reason to believe that such Design may be by him accomplished, and having made Application to me for my Aid
and Assistance in such his Undertakings Know Ye therefore
that having taken the said Proposal of th[e said] Charles
Swaine into due consideration and being willing and desirous
to give him all the Consideration and Encouragement that in
me lies, I hereby notifie to all whom It may concern such his
Application and all His Majesty's Subjects are hereby requested
to treat him as a person in the legal Prosecution of such a laudable Design, and He the said Charles Swaine is hereby required
to act in due observation of the Rights and Privileges of the
Hudson's Bay Company and the Laws of Great Britain Given
at the City of Annapolis under the Great Seal of the said Province
of Maryland this third Day of November in the Year of Our
Lord One Thousand seven hundred and fiftye.[10]

The commission specifically states that Swaine was the clerk of
the *California*. The same statement is made by Benjamin Franklin in a letter to Cadwalader Colden, dated Philadelphia, 28
February 1753.

. . . I believe I have not before told you, that I have provided a
subscription here of £1,500 to fit out a vessel in search of a
North West passage. She sails in a few days, and is called the
Argo, commanded by Mr. Swaine, who was in the last Expedition in the *California* and author of a Journal of that voyage in
two Volumes. We think the attempt laudable, whatever may be
the success. If she fails, *'magnis tamen excidit ausis.'* [11]

Such testimony is impressive but it does not agree with Captain
Francis Smith or James Isham, who nowhere in their journals
mention a Swaine. It is possible that Swaine was lying to Ogle
and Franklin about his experience on *California*. Yet Swaine's

record from 1753 to 1766 'is fairly well known and he was always regarded as an honest straightforward man.'[12] I have therefore concluded that Theodore Swaine Drage and Charles Swaine are one and the same man, and that Drage was his real name.[13] For an unknown reason he chose to live under the second name for a period of about eighteen years, and for business reasons may have used both names very briefly.

No exact birth date is known. Drage, whose brother William was a London pamphleteer, studied law at Gray's Inn in 1737. In 1746 and 1747 he was clerk of the *California* and in 1748 and 1749 published his account of that voyage. In 1750 Swaine appeared in Maryland and in 1753 and 1754 made his *Argo* voyages. After his return he served as a commissary officer with General Braddock in 1755. He was appointed, in 1757, Clerk of Orphans Court and Register of Deeds in Northampton County, Pennsylvania, where he had settled. The following year he was made Clerk of Courts in Easton, and in that same year the name of Theodore Swaine Drage appears in Philadelphia as a partner in Croghan and Drage, liquor dealers. Also, in 1758 Swaine married Hannah Boyte as his second wife. In 1760 there was a lawsuit against Swaine and his wife. In 1767 Drage was a partner in Spears and Hughes, liquor dealers in Philadelphia, and the same year Swaine sold his house in Easton to John Hughes. Both Swaine and Hughes are referred to at this time as merchants of Philadelphia. Nothing more is ever heard of Swaine, nor does Drage appear in Pennsylvania again. In 1769 Drage is reported in London, presenting to the British Museum a copy of the newly published *The Great Probability of a Northwest Passage* inscribed 'Presented by the author Mr. Drage, June 15, 1769.' While in London he studied for the ministry, which apparently caused some amusement among those who knew him. Samuel Wharton, who reported this unlikely event to George Croghan, Drage's former partner, refers to him as '*Mr. Swaine.*' Drage was ordained and moved to South Carolina, where he died in Camden in 1774. He left his estate to his wife *Hannah Swaine Drage* in Philadelphia. A large lot of manuscripts and papers were shipped to his widow and have disappeared. If they ever turn up they may tell us the full story of the man who commanded *Argo.*

The expedition from the Colonies was obviously promoted in the hope of winning the £20,000 reward posted by Parliament. In his preface to *The Great Probability* the author says the purpose of the voyage was

> not to interfere with the *Hudson's* Bay Trade, or to carry on a clandestine Trade with the Natives of *Greenland,* but to discover a Northwest Passage, and explore the *Labrador* Coast, at that Time supposed to be locked up under a pretended Right, and not frequented by the Subjects of *England,* but a successful Trade carried on by the *French;* to open a Trade there, to improve the Fishery and the Whaling on these Coasts, cultivate a Friendship with the Natives, and make them serviceable in a political Way.

One gets a feeling that Swaine was more interested in the reward, but found in the trading, whaling, and fishing possibilities better reasons for urging merchants to finance the expedition. Swaine was a successful promoter and obtained subscriptions from merchants in Maryland, Pennsylvania, New York, and Boston. As we have seen, Benjamin Franklin had raised £1500 to fit out a vessel. He had long been interested in Arctic exploration for he had read and enjoyed Arthur Dobbs's book and asked to see Captain Middleton's reply.[14] He had also read both the clerk's and Ellis's books.[15]

The merchants purchased the schooner *Argo,* a vessel of about sixty tons built in Newbury, Massachusetts, in 1749,[16] and they found satisfactory Captain Swaine's estimate for stores for the voyage, for repairs on the vessel, and for advance wages for the seamen.[17] The sponsoring group received a scare from the Reverend James Stirling of Charlestown, Maryland. One of the original subscribers, Stirling backed out and, going to England, attempted to obtain an exclusive trading patent to the entire Labrador coast from Hudson Strait to the Strait of Belle Isle. William Allen, who headed the 'North-West Company,' worriedly wrote to Thomas Penn in London explaining the delay in sending out the expedition (largely because of lack of funds) and enclosing a petition that that 'Scoundrell of a parson' Stirling not be granted such a patent.[18] It was not granted.

Two and a half years after Governor Ogle had given Captain Charles Swaine his commission, the expedition finally sailed from Philadelphia on 4 March 1753. They touched at Hyannis on Cape Cod and at Portsmouth, New Hampshire, and then headed for Hudson Strait.

William Allen was able to write his friend Thomas Penn on 7 July 1753:

> We equipped the vessell and dispatched her from this port the beginning of March: As we could not get a proper set of men here to compleat her compliment we ordered the master to go to New England where our Correspondent had procurred for us ten able Whale men, chiefly Harponers, and two cedar whale boats with all necessary tackle The springing of one of the vessells masts detained them till near the middle of Aprill, at which time they set out upon their Voyage in high spirits We have directed them to search Chesterfield inlet and one other that has not been hitherto explored in case they should not find a passage there, then our orders are that they should leave the vessell with eight hands at Marble Iland, and that the Master and six more should take thirty days provisions with them and indeavour to travell by land to make what discovery they can, with relation to any waters that lead in to the South Sea that in case they should not return in six weeks (which time the eight men on board are to employ in whale fishing) they are to make the best of their way home to this port. If all their searches prove fruitless in regard to a passage they are to spend the rest of their time upon the Labradore coast and to indeavour to es-

tablish a trade with the Eskemous Indians, which upon the best information we have had may turn to very good account. We have fitted out the vessell with sixteen months provisions and all necessarys, the cost will be about £900 sterling which is a trifle when compared to the charge of those vessells sent from London I am in great hopes that the long sought for passage will be now discovered we shall however I hope determine the point whether there is any or not.[19]

Argo arrived in Boston on her return on 21 October 1753 and landed in Philadelphia the next month. A résumé of the voyage, probably written by Franklin, was published a few days later in the *Pennsylvania Gazette*.

Sunday last arrived here the Schooner Argo, Captain Charles Swaine, who sail'd from this port last Spring on the Discovery of a North-West Passage. She fell in with the Ice off of Farewell; left the Eastern Ice, and fell in with the Western Ice in Lat. 58 and cruiz'd to the Northward to Lat 63 to clear it, but could not; it then extending to the Eastward. On her Return to the Southward she met with two Danish Ships bound to Ball River and Disco up Davis's Straits, who had been in the Ice fourteen Days off Farewell, and had then stood to Westward, and assured the Commander that the Ice was fast to the Shore all above Hudson's Straits to the Distance of 40 Leagues out, and that there had not been such a severe Winter as the last these 24 Years that they had used that Trade; they had been 9 Weeks from Copenhagen. The Argo finding she could not get round the Ice, pres'd thro' it, and got into the Straits Mouth the 26th of June, and made the Island Resolution but was forc'd out by vast Quantities of driving Ice, and got into a clear Sea the first of July. On the 14th, cruising the Ice for an Opening to get in again she met 4 Sail of Hudson's Bay Ships, endeavouring to get in, and continued with them till the 19th when they parted in thick weather in lat 62 and a Half; which thick Weather continued to the 7th of August; the Hudson's Bay-men supposed themselves 40 Leagues from the Western Land. The Argo ran down the Ice from 63 to 57,30 and, after repeated attempts to enter the Straits in vain, as the Season for Descovery on the

Western Side of the Bay was over, she went on the Labradore
Coast, and discover'd it perfectly from 56 to 55, finding no less
than 6 Inlets, to the Heads of all which they went, and of which
we hear they have made a very good chart, and have a better
Account of the Country its Soil, Produce, &c than has hitherto
been published. The Captain says 'tis much like Norway's and
that there is no Communication with Hudson's Bay thro' Labrador where one has been hitherto imagined, a high Ridge of
mountains running North and South about 50 Leagues within
the Coast. In one of the Harbours they found a deserted Wooden
House with a Brick Chimney which had been built by some
English as appear'd by Sundry Things they left behind; and
afterwards in another Harbour they met with Capt Goff in a
Snow from London, who inform'd, that the same Snow had
been there last year and landed some of the Moravian Brethren,
who had built that House; But the Natives having decoy'd the
then Captain of the Snow, and 5 or 6 of his Hands in their Boat
round a Point of Land at a Distance from the Snow, under
Pretense of Trade and carry'd them all off (they having gone
imprudently without Arms) the Snow, after waiting 16 Days
without hearing of them went home, and was oblig'd to take
away the Moravians to help work the Vessel. Part of her Business this year was to enquire after those men. Captain Swaine
discover'd a fine Fishing Bank, which lies but 6 Leagues off the
Coast, and extends from Lat 57 to 54, supposed to be the same
hinted at in Capt Davis's second Voyage. No bad accident
happen'd to the Vessel, and the Men kept in perfect Health
during the whole Voyage, and return'd all well.[20]

Part of the journal of this voyage was printed as an appendix
in *The Great Probability*. It describes in detail the explorations
on the Labrador coast and trade with the Eskimos. After several
trips inland Swaine decided that, because of the mountain range
running parallel to the coast, there could be no strait between
the Labrador coast and Hudson Bay south of Hudson Strait, a
theory that had been widely speculated on. On 29 August *Argo*
was nearly lost in a gale but managed to reach the shelter of a
harbor. The men visited a good deal with Captain Elijah Goff
of the English brig *Hope,* who told them that on 9 July he had

joined Capt. Taylor in a Sloop of about 35 Tons, fitted out from
Rhode Island to go in Pursuit of a *North-west Passage;* and if
not successful to come down the Coast of *Labrador*. Capt. Goff
said he had learned by Capt. *Taylor* that the *Philadelphia*
Schooner would be out, and he should have suspected this to
be her, but she entered the Inlet so readily, and came up with
that Boldness as could not but think that the Schooner was a
French Vessel acquainted with the Coast; and he had received
Orders to avoid any Harbour in which a French Ship should appear.[21]

Goff and Taylor had agreed to associate in their explorations,
which they did until 11 August when Captain Taylor left Goff
a few days before Swaine showed up. This is all that is known of
another obscure American voyage. But Taylor, whoever he was,
apparently knew of the *Argo* venture. Goff arrived in New
York in late October and reported his meeting with Swaine, not
knowing that *Argo* had arrived in Boston a few days before.

The local subscribers lost no time getting a first-hand account
of the voyage. On 23 November they met at the Bull's Head in
Philadelphia 'and expressed a general Satisfaction with Captain
Swaine's Proceedings during his Voyage, tho' he could not accomplish his Purpose and unanimously voted him a very handsome Present.' [22] Obviously they were satisfied that Swaine had
done his best. He was unfortunate in attempting to pass through
Hudson Strait in one of the worst seasons for ice in years, so that
he could reach only as far as Resolution Island. With the Eskimos he had found a source of furs, whalebone, and oil, and had
discovered a new fishing bank, not an altogether profitless
voyage.

The following year Captain Charles Swaine sailed once more
in *Argo* for another attempt at the Passage. Very little is known
of this second expedition. He sailed from Philadelphia 2 May and
returned in October.[23] Three men, including John Patten who
was on both *Argo* voyages and made charts of the sections of
the Labrador coast they had explored, were killed by Eskimos

and their boat lost. Disobeying orders, they may have ventured too far inland in search of a mine from which ore samples had been taken the year before. Someone in Philadelphia had requested this search, quite unknown to the Captain.[24] Another report states they were fishing on an island some distance from the schooner.[25]

The sponsors salvaged some of their funds by selling all surplus stores from *Argo* at auction soon after her return, and on 23 November the schooner with her boats and gear was put up for sale.[26] Captain Swaine presented a collection of Eskimo ethnological specimens to the Library Company of Philadelphia, on behalf of the North-West Company.[27] So ended the only serious American attempts to discover the Northwest Passage— and to win £20,000.

Unfortunately, Swaine's original journals and papers have disappeared. Franklin wrote to Peter Collinson on 26 June 1755:

> I will some Day muster up all the Papers and Letters I have relating to Swain's fruitless Expeditions and send them to you.[28]

In 1762 Franklin was in London and on 27 May he wrote to Dr. John Pringle (later Sir John and President of the Royal Society) about some other papers and said,

> [they] are bundled together with the manuscript journals of the two voyages I prompted from Philadelphia, which proved, indeed, unsuccessful, but the journals contain some valuable information.[29]

Franklin adds that he wished them in the possession of Dr. Pringle and if any accident should happen to him on his return to America he desired his executors to send them to Pringle. Possibly copies of them were in the chest of Drage papers sent to Hannah. Repeated search by various scholars has failed to locate the missing journals.

19

Old Hopes Revived

*A*t the close of the eighteenth century two old theories were revived: that the Northwest Passage might be reached by way of the open sea toward the North Pole, and that it might be reached by penetrating the northwest coast of America. The English were not alone in these speculations, for the question of the existence of a strait between Asia and America also interested Czar Peter the Great. Although Semyon Ivanovich Deshnev had already, in 1655, sailed around the East Cape — then called Cape Chukchi — (or Chukchee) the point in Asia nearest to America, his report on it lay buried in government archives for over eighty years. Similarly inaccessible to the Czar was the report of a Swedish explorer, Henrich Bush. Sent by the Russian Governor of Siberia, Bush apparently sailed, in a boat of his own building, across to Alaska and back. There were other reports and maps which, however, might have indicated to Peter the separation of the continents.

Before his death, 28 January 1725, Peter I drew up instructions — subsequently signed by his widow Catherine I — for Fleet Captain Vitus Bering. On 5 February 1725, the fifty-four-year-old Dane left St. Petersburg to begin the 6000-mile trek across the continent. He arrived in Kamchatka early in 1728, where construction on the ship *St. Gabriel* was speedily completed. On 14 July 1728, Bering set sail, passing the easternmost extension of Asia on 13 August.

As the season was getting late, they continued to a latitude of 67° 18' and then returned to their home port. Bering had accomplished his mission, which had been to discover whether or not the two continents were connected. He was certain they were separate, but failed to convince anyone. He was sent in command of a second undertaking during which he died, December 1741, on the island in the sea that both now bear his name.[1] On his second voyage the ships *St. Peter* and *St. Paul* reached the Alaskan coast. Russian traders and trappers soon followed, but they made no attempt to sail around the northern part of America or to establish permanent settlements — at least not for another forty years. However, the second Bering expedition turned into a geographical and scientific survey of eastern Asia which continued officially for twenty-five years.

The English too wanted to determine whether or not a Strait of Anian opened up a passage from the Pacific. For many years the Indians bringing their furs to trade at Churchill had been telling the English of a large river to the westward, with copper deposits along its banks, emptying into a northern ocean. In the spring of 1768, a group of northern Indians arrived at Churchill with additional accounts of the river and, what was more exciting, with samples of the copper ore. Moses Norton, the Governor, thought that someone should be sent to discover and investigate the copper mines. When he suggested the plan to the Company's Committee in England that same summer, it was enthusiastically endorsed. Samuel Hearne, one of the Company's veteran employees, was selected to undertake the overland journey. His instructions emphasized that he should ascertain the latitude and longitude of the mouth of the river and make a chart and keep a journal of his journey.[2] He was also to create and maintain good relations with the Indians, and investigate the fur-bearing animal population and copper ore reports. The instructions go on:

> Another material point which is recommended to you, is to find out, if you can, either by your own travels, or by information from the Indians, whether there is a passage through this continent. It will be useful to clear up this point, if possible, in order to prevent farther doubts from arising hereafter respecting a passage out of Hudson's Bay into the Western Ocean.

Hearne adds two footnotes to this section of his orders, saying that the continent is much wider than many people imagine and that when he was 500 miles west of Hudson Bay he failed to meet any Indians who knew of any end to the land in that direction, but that he saw several Indians who had been westward to a great chain of mountains from which all the rivers flowed westward.

Hearne made a late start from Fort Prince of Wales on Churchill Bay in November 1769 and after going about 200 miles returned when his Indians left him. Another start the following year was also abortive. He set out for the third time 7 December 1770 with his Indians, proceeding slowly all winter and arriving at the Coppermine River 13 July 1771. He descended it for five days until he came to its mouth on the Arctic Ocean. Hearne, displaying the practical knowledge of the men employed in Hudson Bay, gives his own opinion.

> As to a passage through the continent of America by the way of Hudson's Bay, it has for long been exploded, notwithstanding what Mr. Ellis has urged in its favour . . . that any comment on it would be quite unnecessary. My latitude only will be a sufficient proof that no such passage is in existence.

His latitude and longitude (71° 34′ N., 120° 30′ W.) were erroneous for the mouth of the Coppermine, for he computed them by dead reckoning rather than by astronomical observations. It is actually 67° 48′ N., 115° 47′ W., but Hearne was sufficiently close to prove his point as far as a Northwest Passage was concerned.

In concluding the excellent account of his journey, Hearne wrote:

> Though my discoveries are not likely to prove of any material advantage to the Nation at large, or indeed to the Hudson's Bay Company, yet I have the pleasure to think that I have fully complied with the orders of my Masters, and that it has put a final end to all disputes concerning a North West Passage through Hudson's Bay. It will also wipe off, in some measure, the ill-grounded and unjust aspersions of Dobbs, Ellis, Robson, and the American Traveller; who have all taken much pains to condemn the conduct of the Hudson's Bay Company, as being averse from discoveries, and from enlarging their trade.

Since he had walked the land from Churchill to the Arctic Ocean, the Strait of Anian disappeared from maps of North America.

Twenty years later Alexander Mackenzie, fur trader employed by the Hudson's Bay Company's great rival, the North-West Company, made two historic journeys.[3] The first from Fort Chepewyan, down the river that bears his name, established another point of contact with the Arctic Ocean. He reached Whale Island in the river's delta 12 July 1789. In 1793 Mackenzie made the first trip across the continent north of Mexico and reached the Pacific at the mouth of the Bella Coola River. These two canoe voyages established the vast unbroken extent of the northwestern part of North America. If a sea passage existed it now had to be north of the contact points established by Hearne and Mackenzie at the mouths of the Coppermine and Mackenzie rivers, as well as north of Hudson Bay.

In 1773 the British Admiralty determined to attempt the passage by way of the North Pole. The man responsible for reviving Robert Thorne's plan was Daines Barrington, an eminent lawyer and member of the Council of the Royal Society. One of his many interests was collecting information relating to the practicability of navigating the Polar Sea beyond 80°. He concluded that in certain seasons the sea was open far beyond Spitsbergen and that there was a good possibility of sailing to the Pole and beyond. Early in 1773 he presented his plan to the Council members of the Royal Society, who were sufficiently impressed to urge the Earl of Sandwich, First Lord of the Admiralty, to consider the matter. Sandwich, who did so much to promote British voyages of exploration, proposed a plan 'for an expedition to try how far navigation was practicable towards the North Pole.'[4]

Careful preparations were made for the expedition. Two strong naval bomb ships, *Racehorse* and *Carcass,* were selected, strengthened for use in the ice, and substantially equipped. Constantine John Phipps, later Lord Mulgrave, was appointed commander of the expedition on *Racehorse* with Captain Skiffington Lutwidge in command of *Carcass.* Proper observations were ensured by engaging the astronomer Israel Lyons and providing him with impressive and elaborate instruments. It was apparently felt that improvements in ships and navigation since the last attempt to sail across the North Pole in the early seventeenth century promised a chance of success. Probably any of the Spitsbergen whalers could have told them otherwise. Several of these men were employed as pilots, but their opinions were not asked.

Phipps reached the edge of the ice west of Spitsbergen 6 July and for the next month worked back and forth trying to get east beyond the ice. It proved impenetrable and the weather foggy. He landed several times on various islands of the group to make observations and to establish the positions of points and the height of mountains. Except for foggy days, Phipps's description of 30 July is typical of his entire stay north of Spitsbergen:

> The weather exceedingly fine and mild, and unusually clear. The scene was beautiful and picturesque; the two ships becalmed in a large bay, with three apparent openings between the islands which formed it, but every-where surrounded with ice as far as we could see, with some streams of water; not a breath of air; the water perfectly smooth; the ice covered with snow, low, and even, except a few broken pieces near the edges: the pools of water in the middle of the pieces were frozen over with young ice.

By 6 August he began to make preparations to abandon his ships which were both held fast in the ice. Luckily on the tenth the pack drifted west, and the ships were forced through the ice and managed to escape. Twelve days later he began the voyage home.

Aside from resulting in one of the handsomest books on eighteenth-century exploration, this voyage is perhaps most notable for the training it gave to two future naval heroes, one English and one American. Horatio Nelson and Nicholas Biddle, later a Revolutionary War captain who lost his life when his command, the Continental frigate *Randolph* blew up during her engagement with H.M.S. *Yarmouth,* were shipmates under Captain Lutwidge in *Carcass.* Nelson was a midshipman and Biddle, who had been serving as a midshipman, took a voluntary demotion to a seaman in order to go on the expedition for which the complement of midshipmen was already filled. Nelson, then a boy of fifteen, serving as Captain Lutwidge's coxswain, nearly lost his life when he and a shipmate took off over the ice after a large polar bear. Nelson's musket flashed in the pan and a chasm in the ice between him and the bear probably saved his life. Nelson was reprimanded by his captain, who asked why he had gone bear hunting. 'Sir,' he said, 'I wished to kill the bear that I might carry the skin to my father.'

The Honorable Daines Barrington was still not convinced by Phipps's failure to get much north of 80°. Good lawyer that he was, he began accumulating evidence to support his theory that a ship could sail to the North Pole. He combed the literature and interviewed whaling captains who claimed to have sailed beyond 80°. Some men said they had sailed beyond 83°, and one Dutch account mentions going within half a degree of the Pole. Barrington believed them, although their evidence was all circumstantial — either verbal, based on the memory of voyages taken many years before, or second- and third-hand. He could not produce one instance of a documented voyage beyond Phipps's.[5] Nevertheless he thought another expedition should be sent out. Marshaling all his evidence he delivered two papers, in May and December 1774, before the Council of the Royal Society.

Meanwhile the Council submitted another plan to the Admiralty. It was proposed to reverse these time-tested but unproductive courses to the Northwest and to the Pole and to enter the high latitudes from the Pacific. The obvious choice for such an expedition was Captain James Cook, who had just completed his second circumnavigation and who knew the Pacific so well. On his voyages Captain Cook had discovered more islands, surveyed more coasts, charted more waters, and cleared up more geographical nonsense than any single man before or since. The Admiralty was, however, reluctant to ask Cook directly since he had already served so long. Sandwich therefore invited the explorer to dinner, during the course of which he explained the plan and, as expected, Cook volunteered. The Government gave a further incentive. It amended the Parliamentary Act offering a £20,000 prize to British merchant ships passing from the Atlantic to the Pacific by way of Hudson Bay: this Hudson Bay restriction was removed and north of 50° in any direction substituted. In addition, a reward of £5000 was offered to any vessel passing within one degree of the North Pole; now vessels of the Royal Navy were also included.

In 1776 when Captain Cook was sent to the Pacific, His Majesty's armed brig *Lion* under Lieutenant Richard Pickersgill also sailed with orders to protect the British whaling fleet from American privateers and to continue up Davis Strait and into Baffin Bay. Pickersgill was to chart the bay shores and to look for harbors, a Passage entrance, and similar features. This information would help the vessel which would be sent there the following year to meet Captain Cook if he emerged into Baffin Bay. Pickersgill, who had sailed with Cook on his previous voyage, left Deptford 25 May. He struck soundings southwesterly of Iceland which he speculated might be the remains of Buss Island. Passing Cape Farewell, 7 July, and keeping close to shore, he made his way slowly up the Greenland coast. The grandeur of the scenery astonished him. Occasionally he fished, catching in one day thirty-six 'hollybutts' weighing from 100 to 300 pounds each. Leaving the shore when the ice cleared he made better progress, but after a run of seventy-seven miles he returned to the coast. His farthest north was 68° 10'. Then

> At twelve, having passed a number of the highest ice-islands I ever saw, and meeting with many more, bigger and bigger, and every hour visibly increasing their number, with a very heavy sea from the southward and a hard gale, the nights growing dark very fast, and the season far spent, a number of our men sick, a putrid fever raging in the vessel, and numbers complaining for want of clothing and with pains in their limbs, which seems to be in this country a general complaint, — the vessel very wet and single-bottomed, without being provided for wintering if we had been caught in the ice; in this situation, I thought it necessary to return.[6]

By 4 September he was in Porcupine Harbor on the Labrador coast, where he was taken ill, and on the 27th sailed for home.

The following year *Lion* sailed under Lieutenant Walter Young from the Nore on 23 March to meet Cook in Baffin Bay and to attempt the Northwest Passage if he found a propitious opening. Sailing up the middle of the Bay he reached a latitude of 72° 42′ but hurried home without pressing his advantage, and arrived at the early date of 26 August. Pickersgill had been strongly criticized for his lack of accomplishment, although he had been specifically instructed not to sail through a Passage if he found one, which he had not.[7] Dr. John Douglas, Bishop of Salisbury, remarked that Pickersgill deserved the censure he received for improper behavior in Davis Strait and that Young's talents were more suited to naval battle than geographical exploration.[8]

Cook's instructions were also specific but, as befitting orders to a man of his experience and competence, gave him ample latitude to use his judgment. He was expected to arrive on the northwest coast in June 1777, and to sail north without searching rivers or inlets until he reached 65°. At that point he was to explore every opening pointing toward Hudson Bay or Baffin Bay, obtain information from the natives if possible, and to attempt passages too shallow for his ships in small boats. If no strait was found, he should go to the port of St. Peter and St. Paul on the Kamchatka coast for the winter. The following spring, 1778, he was to sail through Bering Strait and proceed as far as possible. If he then failed to sail through the Polar Sea he was to return to England as best he could. Cook's instructions, in which it is suspected that he himself had a hand, were drawn up with uncommon good sense. Cook was not sent through Hudson Bay, as some wished, because Dobbs's expeditions and Captain Christopher's survey of Chesterfield Inlet in 1761 had sufficiently proved that there was no Northwest Passage in that region. Also the Spanish, at last aroused from their lethargy by English voyages, had explored the coast to the north of California. Samuel Hearne's discovery of the mouth of the Coppermine River also showed the futility of commencing to search for a Passage lower than 65°. By starting beyond 65° Cook could gain more accurate information about the relationship between the two continents than was available from Bering's reports. In short, 'Captain Cook's instructions were founded on an accurate knowledge of what had been already done, and of what still remained to do.'

Cook sailed in June 1776 with two ships, *Resolution* and *Discovery*. After a leisurely voyage through the Pacific and the discovery of the Hawaiian Islands, Cook arrived on the northwest coast in March 1778, a year later than the Admiralty had planned. On reaching 48° 15′ he commented:

> It is in this very latitude where we now were, that geographers have placed the pretended strait of Juan de Fuca. But we saw nothing like it; nor is there the least probability that ever any such thing existed.[9]

The trend of the coast forced Cook to begin his detailed search long before reaching 65°. He carefully explored Prince William Sound and ran up into Cook Inlet. Even before he reached its head, where he remarked 'All hope [sic] of finding a passage were now given up,' he wrote:

> We were now upward of five hundred and twenty leagues to the Westward of any part of Baffin's, or of Hudson's Bay. And whatever passage there may be, it must be, or, at least, part of it, must lie to the North of latitude 72°. Who could expect to find a passage or strait of such extent.

Cook did not consider his patient exploration of Cook Inlet wasted, for he hard-headedly wrote:

> . . . we were now convinced, that the continent of North America extended farther to the West, than, from the modern most reputable charts, we had reason to expect. This made the existence of a passage into Baffin's or Hudson's Bays less probable; or, at least, shewed it to be of greater extent. It was a satis-

faction to me, however, to reflect, that, if I had not examined this very considerable inlet, it would have been assumed, by speculative fabricators of geography, as a fact, that it communicated with Baffin's or Hudson's Bay to the East; and been marked, perhaps, on future maps of the world, with greater precision, and more certain signs of reality, than the invisible, because imaginary, Straits of de Fuca, and de Fonte.

Working his way through the great barrier of the Aleutian Islands, Cook rounded the Alaska Peninsula on 28 June. By 17 July he had completed a circuit of Bristol Bay, when he passed Cape Newenham. Passing and naming Cape Prince of Wales, the westernmost extremity of North America, 9 August, he crossed over to the Siberian shore, sighting the Diomede Islands on the way. Two days later he sailed through Bering Strait with both coasts simultaneously in sight. Keeping along the American side he passed latitude 70° 33' on 17 August, and before noon that day saw the reflection from the ice called 'ice blink.' About 2:30 that same afternoon he reached the ice and also his farthest north at 70° 41' near a point which he named Icy Cape. Finding himself in shoal water, on a lee shore with ice driving down on him, Cook took the only course open, to the southwest. He named Cape Lisburne on his way south and then worked his way along the ice's edge westward to Cape North on the Siberian Arctic coast. With the ice barrier solid and the season far advanced, he decided to find a good wintering place and return north the following summer for an attempt at passage to the Atlantic. Anchoring in a bay, 10 August, St. Lawrence Day, he named it for that saint. Exactly fifty years earlier, 1728, Bering had named the nearby island for the same saint. Cook paid tribute to the work of his courageous predecessor:

> . . . he has delineated the coast very well, and fixed the latitude and longitude of the points better than could be expected from the methods he had to go by.

He departed Unalaska the last of October and by late November was back in the Hawaiian Islands, a perfect place for his wintering. Here Cook was killed by natives.

Although his successor Captain Charles Clerke was in the last stages of consumption, he took the two ships north as planned the following spring. He found impenetrable ice about three degrees farther south than the previous summer, slightly beyond 69°. This competent officer, who had circumnavigated the world three times, with Commodore Byron on *Dolphin* and on both of Cook's previous voyages, died 22 August. Captain James King, who succceeded Clerke and wrote the third volume of Cook's voyage, said of him:

> It would be doing his memory extreme injustice not to say, that during the short time the expedition was under his direction, he was most zealous and anxious for its success. His health, about the time the principal command devolved upon him, began to decline very rapidly, and was every way unequal to encounter the rigours of a high Northern climate. But the vigour and activity of his mind had, in no shape, suffered by the decay of his body: and though he knew, that by delaying his return to a warmer climate, he was giving up the only chance that remained for his recovery, yet, careful and zealous to the last degree, that a regard to his own situation should never bias his judgment to the prejudice of the service, he persevered in the search of a passage, till it was the opinion of every officer in both ships, that it was impracticable, and that any farther attempts would not only be fruitless, but dangerous.[10]

The caliber and common sense of Cook and his officers is no better shown than in Captain King's conclusions on the problem. He wrote:

> The evidence that has been so fully and judiciously stated in the introduction, amounts to the highest degree of probability, that a North West passage, from the Atlantic into the Pacific Ocean, cannot exist to the Southward of 65° of latitude. If then

there exists a passage, it must be either through Baffin's Bay, or round by the North of Greenland, in the Western hemisphere; or else through the Frozen Ocean, to the Northward of Siberia, in the Eastern; and on whichever side it lies, the navigator must necessarily pass through Beering's Straits. The impracticability of penetrating into the Atlantic on either side, through this strait, is therefore all that remains to be submitted to the consideration of the Public.

The expedition returned to England under the command of Captain James Gore.

While the geographical outlines of the northwest coast and Alaska were by no means filled in, search for a strait entering the Pacific from North America ended with Cook's death. Bering's discovery was confirmed and, coupled with the journey by Hearne, demonstrated that passage by water would be unsuited to commercial traffic.

Cook's third voyage was more successful in other respects. He surveyed a large portion of the northwest coast and proved that North America extended, by the Alaskan Peninsula, much nearer Asia than had been supposed. As Bishop John Douglas, who edited Cook's third voyage, remarks, Cook balanced his discoveries by annihilating imaginary southern lands on his second voyage and by doing the same to imaginary northern seas on his third. There were also unexpected commercial developments. In Canton some of Cook's sailors sold a few sea otter skins, skins which had hitherto come in overland from Kamchatka. The prices received for the new skins set off the great northwest coast-China trade that was to flourish for nearly half a century. English and American ships swarmed to the coast. The Spanish attempted briefly and unsuccessfully to stop them.[11] Among voyages published by the adventurous captains participating in the business, that by Captain John Meares in 1790, ten years after Cook, includes a section on the probable existence of a Northwest Passage,[12] in which he apparently believed. The section is mostly wind and adds nothing new. More substantial is the work of Captain George Vancouver. An officer with Cook, he was sent with the ships *Discovery* and *Chatham* in 1790 to the northwest coast to deal with the Spaniards and to chart the coast south of where Cook began his survey. He was particularly instructed to search for navigable rivers which might serve as routes of communication between the sea and inland lakes, and to explore the region of the Strait of Juan de Fuca. The competent results of this voyage isolated Vancouver Island from the mainland but otherwise showed a solid, mountainous, if deeply indented, coastline.[13]

Spanish exploration of the west coast of North America was not, as many writers have assumed, for a Northwest Passage. Rather, the Spaniards seem to have been exploring the coast in search of prosperous and fabulous cities and investigating the possibilities of pearl fishing. Although they were interested in the English attempts, they obviously hoped that no passage would be discovered, for the continent protected their Pacific commerce from English raiders.

20

The Twin Attack

During the eighteenth century the magic words 'Northwest Passage' summoned up an image quite different from the romantic one of the early explorers. It no longer evoked that of a clear open-water channel to warm seas and Eastern riches, but of an ice-choked route among barren Arctic lands. Although a Passage was no longer commercially important, it did present a geographical challenge.

In the past all great Arctic voyages had behind them a 'true believer' in the Northwest Passage, an intellectual, often wealthy, always with close friends in high places. Voyages were stimulated and their momentum perpetuated by men like Michael Lok, Sir William Sanderson, Dudley Digges, Sir John Wolstenholm, Arthur Dobbs, and Daines Barrington. The remarkable British voyages in the nineteenth century had similar backing. Now the part was to be played by Sir John Barrow, for forty years Second Secretary of the Admiralty. Barrow, a Lancashire man born in 1764, was a serious student of astronomy and navigation. As a young man he shipped on a whaler for Spitsbergen, and thus acquired practical experience in these sub-

jects and in Arctic conditions. His consequent interest in the
North continued until his death in 1848.

In the late 1790's he acquired an excellent reputation for his
survey of the Cape Colony while in the household of Lord
Macarteney, who was attempting to make peace between the
Boers and Kaffirs. There in 1800 he married, but his plans for
a pastoral life on Table Mountain were frustrated two years
later by the Treaty of Amiens, which required all Englishmen
to leave Cape Town. Returning to England, he was appointed
to the Admiralty post in 1804. From this influential position
Barrow promoted a series of Arctic explorations both by land
and by sea. On the basis of his single whaling voyage he set
himself up as the ultimate authority on Arctic exploration and
geography. In him all those who wished to search for a Northwest Passage and those who believed there was an open Polar
Sea found a reliable friend. Those who opposed his theories
had an irascible enemy.

At this time the authenticity of Baffin's discovery was in grave
doubt. In the new edition of Daines Barrington's book, reissued in 1818 because of its timely interest, there is a map of
the Arctic regions showing a hazy rendition of Baffin Bay with
the note, 'According to the relations of W. Baffin in 1616 but
not now believed.'[1] Even Barrow, always eager for any clue
of an opening through the northern islands, was doubtful, and
in his history, published the same year, he makes uncomplimen-
tary remarks about the authenticity of Baffin's discoveries.[2]

Barrow was well established in the Admiralty when a report
came in 1817 that an unprecedented breakup of ice over the
past two years had left the sea between Greenland and Spitsbergen, from 74° to 80° latitude, perfectly clear. Great icebergs
in unusual abundance were floating about the North Atlantic.
The captain of the brig *Bremen* reported that he had sailed up
the east coast of Greenland and, rounding the land to the northeast, sailed west for three days out of sight of land. On the basis

of this report Barrow concluded that Greenland was an island. He further concluded from the quantities of driftwood deposited along the shores of Greenland and Iceland that a current must flow down through Baffin Bay, which therefore could not be enclosed. It must, he maintained, connect with the Polar Sea. Barrow also believed that once the ice barrier was passed the Polar Sea would be open.

He found further confirmation of his argument in a similar report by William Scoresby, Jr. (just returned from his annual whaling voyage) to Sir Joseph Banks, President of the Royal Society. Scoresby expressed opinions very like those of Barrow, although he did not believe the Polar Sea was open. He gave five reasons in support of the Northwest Passage theory: (1) a strong current flowed from northeast to southwest past Spitsbergen, and also north through Bering Strait; (2) the large quantity of ice brought south and dissolved each year could only come from a Polar Sea; (3) large tropical logs and quantities of driftwood were found on the west coast of Greenland where current always flows southwest; (4) the known northern coasts of Eurasia and North America indicated the absence of a land connection between them; (5) whales harpooned off Greenland were found in the Pacific, while whales with stone lance heads in them were found off Spitsbergen. While all the indications were that a water connection existed, Scoresby said, it would not, if found, be open more than eight to ten weeks and then only at intervals of several years. 'Hence, as affording a navigation to the Pacific Ocean, the discovery of a north-west passage could be of no service.' Nevertheless, he thought it worth exploring for the increase in geographical knowledge. He ventured to add that had he been exploring instead of 'fishing' he might have solved the Northwest Passage problem. He also expressed his desire to command an expedition to survey eastern Spitsbergen and the east coast of Greenland, to search for the lost Iceland colonies in Greenland, and to explore for the Northeast and Northwest Passages.

Scoresby paid tribute to the old navigators who did so much in tiny vessels. Their experiences, he pointed out, proved that small vessels, preferably between 100 and 200 tons, were much better than large ships for Arctic use. Such ships are stronger, more easily managed, and in less danger of being stove by ice, as well as being less expensive. Ships become weaker as they increase in magnitude. A small sloop can lie aground, fully laden, on rough bottom and sustain no injury, whereas a large ship would be lost.[3]

Although some whalers might have reached 82° — and Scoresby had himself achieved about 81° 30' on a voyage in 1806 as mate of his father's whaler *Resolution* — he thought that to expect an open sea around the Pole or even in 83° to 84° was wishful thinking. In pointing out the futility of the £5000 reward for reaching 89° he observes:

> No one employed in the whalefishery, who had the opportunity, would hazard his life, his property, and the success of his voyage, in seeking after a reward which he had every reason to believe was quite beyond his reach; especially as he well knew, that although he should sail to within a few miles of the extent, which would entitle him to the premium, and there be interrupted by some insurmountable obstacle, yet he could have no claim on the reward.

He suggested a new schedule of rewards. Finally, and despite Barrow's disagreement, he stated that if no land was found beyond 82° they should conclude the sea frozen and the Pole not to be reached except by crossing the ice.[4]

Sir Joseph Banks, inspired by Scoresby's news and by his *Treatise on the Northern Ice* which accompanied it, wrote to the First Lord of the Admiralty, expressing the hope that the Government would take advantage of the propitious circumstances to correct northern geography and determine whether or not Baffin Bay provided an open passage to the Arctic Ocean.

Banks offered the co-operation of the Royal Society with any Government-sponsored expedition. The Admiralty was enormously impressed.

By December 1817 plans were already well along for two expeditions — one to sail to and across the Pole and the other to sail through the Northwest Passage. After submitting a plan for an exploring expedition to collect scientific data to Sir Joseph Banks and being invited to London to present it to the Royal Society, Scoresby was bitterly disappointed to find that the expedition was to be under the auspices of the Navy with naval officers in command of the ships. He had supposed that, as an authority on the Arctic with more experience than any other captain in northern navigation, he would of course be chosen. Probably Barrow had a hand in making certain he was not.

Along with the plans for the expedition laid out by Barrow and submitted for suggestions to Banks and the Royal Society went alterations in the scale of prizes offered. A more attractive sliding scale replaced the flat £5000 reward for reaching 89°. Ships reaching 83° would receive £1000; 85°, £2000; to 88°, £4000; and 89°, the £5000 as before. There were also rewards for pushing westward. The mouth of the Coppermine River was worth £5000; the Mackenzie, £10,000; to 150° W., £15,000; and the Pacific, £20,000. The oath taken by owners and masters of whalers restricting their activities to whaling was altered to allow them to try for the rewards when conditions seemed suitable.

The plans approved, the Admiralty issued the necessary orders, and four vessels were selected and commissioned 15 January 1818. Two, *Isabella* and *Dorothea,* were over 380 tons each, while *Alexander* and *Trent* were about 250 tons. The vessels were heavily strengthened both inside and out to withstand the pressure and buffeting of the ice.

An unusually able group of officers was chosen, including

several who would be active in, and whose names would be virtually synonymous with, Arctic exploration for the next twenty-five years. The senior commander, Sir John Ross, was to lead the northwestern contingent as Captain of *Isabella*, accompanied by Lieutenant W. E. Parry in *Alexander* with Lieutenant H. P. Hoppner as his second in command. James C. Ross was a midshipman with his uncle. The Polar half of the expedition was commanded by Captain David Buchan in *Dorothea*, with Lieutenant John Franklin as Captain of *Trent*. Buchan's officers also included Lieutenants Frederick W. Beechey and George Back. Both Hoppner and Beechey were sons of distinguished artists and, possessing unusual talent in drawing themselves, served also as official draftsmen. Midshipman A. M. Skene on Ross's ship was another competent draftsman, and Sir John himself was an artist of no small accomplishment. The two scientists recommended by the Royal Society were Captain Edward Sabine of the Royal Artillery who sailed with Ross, and George Fisher, who accompanied Buchan. Aboard each ship were a whaling master and mate familiar with Greenland waters. An Eskimo, John Sacheuse, who had come to England on a Leith whaler and had learned English, was taken on *Isabella* as an interpreter.

Similar instructions were issued to the commanders of the two expeditions. If Ross in rounding the northeast point of the American continent, which, it was thought, might be in about 72°, found an open sea, he was to keep well offshore and steer for Bering Strait. After passing through the Strait he was to go to Kamchatka and deliver duplicates of all his journals to the Russian Governor for forwarding overland to London. After resting and refitting at the Hawaiian Islands or on the California coast he should, if possible, sail back through Bering Strait, following the American coastline. If this did not seem prudent, he was to return round Cape Horn. While in the Pacific, duplicate journals were to be sent back by another ship if there was an opportunity.

If Buchan succeeded in sailing across the Pole and through Bering Strait, the two expeditions were to rendezvous in the Pacific, and Ross would assume command of the four ships. He was then to send one vessel with a set of dispatches home by the Horn and attempt to bring the rest of the fleet back through the Arctic. If the four came by the Horn, Ross and Buchan were to deposit copies of their journals and observations with each other as an added precaution to ensure their safety.

Ross was given permission to winter if he got part way through the Passage. On no account, however, was he to winter on the eastern coast of America or western coast of Greenland. If he was unable to double the northeast extremity of the continent and penetrate partway to the Pacific, he should explore the coasts and islands as extensively as possible, departing for England no later than 1 October.

> Although the first, and most important, object of this voyage, is the discovery of a passage from Davis' Strait, along the northern coast of America, and through Behring's Strait into the Pacific; it is hoped, at the same time, that it may likewise be the means of improving the geography and hydrography of the Arctic Regions, of which so little is hitherto known, and contribute to the advancement of science and natural knowledge.[5]

In Buchan's instructions, 'as near the Pole as may be' is substituted for Davis Strait, and so on.

The variation and inclination of the magnetic needle was to receive particular attention. Temperature records of the air and sea, both at the surface and at different depths, were to be kept; refraction of objects was to be studied, and as always the height, direction, and strength of tides and the set and velocity of currents noted. Soundings and samples of the ocean bottom were to be taken. (Each day north of 65° a carefully prepared bottle was to be thrown overboard.) It was to contain a paper giving the date and position of the ships and a request in six languages that it be sent to the Admiralty with a note giving the time and place where it was found. Natural history and geological specimens were to be collected. The governments of Russia, Denmark, and Sweden were requested to give the explorers any assistance they could.

The ships were ready two months before sailing time. Captain David Buchan and his fifty-five officers and men awaited their North Pole attempt in the wall-sided *Dorothea* and the brig *Trent,* a rig they later found unsuitable for ice navigation. Dropping down river 25 April Buchan arrived at Lerwick, Shetland Islands, on May Day. Ten days were spent looking for a troublesome leak that developed in *Trent.* She was careened and carefully examined but no trace of the leak could be found, although it was sufficiently serious to keep the pumps going for half of each watch. It was decided to proceed and keep pumping. The cautious seamen of Lerwick, where Buchan, as was common practice for the whalers, expected to fill out the *Trent* crew, refused to sail into the Arctic ice in a leaky vessel. They were obliged to proceed short-handed.

Crossing the Arctic circle 14 May they shaped their course for Spitsbergen. Contrary wind forced them far enough eastward to sight snow-covered, uninhabited Bear Island. A solid curve of ice connected the Island with Spitsbergen and blocked all access northeasterly.

Threading their way through labyrinths of ice, the two ships approached Spitsbergen, which was sighted 26 May. Working up the western coast, the vessels, heavily iced, became separated during thick snows and rough weather, but met at Magdalena Bay, where they anchored 3 June. Here they remained four days to survey the port and enjoy some good weather. Beechey, describing the climate, writes:

In cloudy or misty weather, when the hills are clothed with newly-fallen snow, nothing can be more dreary than the appearance of the shores of Spitzbergen; whereas, on the contrary, it is scarcely possible to conceive a more brilliant and lively effect than that which occurs on a fine day, when the sun shines forth and blends its rays with that peculiarly soft, bright atmosphere which overhangs a country deeply-bedded in snow; and with a pure sky, whose azure hue is so intense as to find no parallel in nature. On such an occasion the winds, near the land at least, are very light, or entirely hushed, and the shores teem with living objects. All nature seems to acknowledge the glorious sunshine, and the animated part of creation to set no bounds to its delight.[6]

On the seventh they quit the anchorage, where they had made the acquaintance of belligerent walruses and peaceful Russian hunters. Ice conditions were unchanged, and they ran into a heavy swell which drove the ships into the ice pack. Getting off with a light breeze, they were again becalmed and driven into the ice where they banged around, and the crew of *Trent* pumped steadily all night. Free again by morning, and steering westward, they fell in with several whalers who informed them that ice was solid to the west, and that fifteen whale ships were fast in it. Still inching north, taking advantage of every opening, Captain Buchan found himself stopped at Red Bay in northwestern Spitsbergen 12 June. While *Trent* was made fast to a floe in the frozen stillness, one of her officers heard a rushing of water and traced it to the spirit room. The ceiling was removed and a stream of water four feet high shot into the ship. The annoying leak that had kept the crew at the pumps was at last discovered; it proved to be an open bolt hole in the vessel's bottom, apparently originally pitched over on the outside. Once plugged, *Trent* was sound and dry. A party of men from *Dorothea* went ashore over the ice on the thirteenth and were nearly lost when an impenetrable fog shut down on them before they could return. After eighteen nerve-racking hours they were recovered close by the ship, which they had been unable to see.

It was well the vessels had been strengthened, for the ice pressure lifted *Trent* four feet, and ice rose up thirty-five feet high beside *Dorothea,* bearing the imprint of the planks and bolts of her bottom. On 23 June the pack, which was drifting south, opened up and the expedition was again at sea. Five days later they were once more anchored back at Fair Haven.

Climbing the hills of Fair Haven each day to watch the ice, they were rewarded on 6 July by seeing that it had been driven northward, and putting to sea they sailed as far as 80° 15′ N. But July turned out to be even worse than June. By pressing on all sail and forcing his ship through the narrow channels, Buchan managed to reach about 80° 34′, his farthest. During a week of thick weather, sounds of springing beams, splitting planks, and cracking timbers indicated severe damage from the increasing pressure. On 19 July it cleared and after nine days of hard labor the ships were extricated from the ice, which for three weeks had extended in every direction to the horizon.

They were clear only for a short time when both ships were nearly wrecked by a gale on 30 July, which forced them again into the ice. Fenders of walrus hides absorbed some of the constant beating against the sides of the vessels. Nevertheless, *Dorothea* was so damaged when they reached South Gat anchorage in Spitsbergen that it was obvious there would be no more exploring that season. Captain Buchan might have attempted further exploring in *Trent* and he was embarrassed by Franklin's request to continue alone. Granting the request would have meant leaving the unseaworthy *Dorothea* to reach England unaccompanied. Her crew would have been greatly endangered and the season was in any case nearly over. Captain Buchan wisely decided to take the expedition home. Putting to sea 20 August, they followed the ice westward to within a dozen leagues of Greenland and then turned south for the homeward voyage. They arrived at Deptford 22 October.

The ice had stopped Buchan's ships in about the same northern latitude where it had forced others to turn back. A vast ice barrier, as was coming to be apparent, stretched from Novaya Zemlya to Greenland. It could only be penetrated successfully for a limited distance up the westward coast of each land area — that is, Greenland, Spitsbergen, and Novaya Zemlya. The eastern shores of these islands were almost perpetually icebound by the currents carrying the ice against the land.

A few days after Buchan's departure, the two ships under Captain John Ross had dropped down to Galleons Reach, 18 April, and left their pilot on the twenty-fourth off Cromer. Even so, they made better time to the Shetlands, reaching Lerwick on the thirtieth, where Buchan's ships joined them the next day.

Accepting the hospitality of his old friend William Mouart of Brassa Island, Ross and his astronomers set up their instruments in his commodious house. While Sabine and the officers made observations the energetic young midshipmen, Skene, Ross, and Bushnan, searched Brassa for curiosities and specimens of natural history. Their enthusiasm was somewhat checked when a large hunk of bone, laboriously brought some distance to the ship with the notion that it was part of a mammoth skeleton, turned out to be the vertebrae of a whale. Ross was cheered to obtain an excellent violin player who volunteered to transfer from the revenue cruiser *Prince of Wales*. The warm Mouart household was left 3 May, with a gift from their host of a large bullock named Matchless. Matchless did not last long, for two evenings after the ships put to sea the crew of *Alexander* was invited to share him.

Soundings were taken passing over the sunken island of Buss, but there was no bottom at 180 fathoms where the chart showed a shoal. The first of the bottles supplied by the Admiralty was tossed overboard 24 May. During the run up the Greenland coast Ross was indefatigable in collecting specimens of everything from stones to sea-water samples. Excellent observations were taken from a grounded iceberg where the ships moored 9 June. Interested Eskimos, who stood around to see the fun, informed them that ice was solid to Disko Bay.

The next day a whaler from Dundee and several from Hull confirmed the Eskimos' report, but told Ross that he could find a good anchorage nearby. On 13 June, Disko Island was visible, and the following day they saluted the Danish flag on Whale Islands.

On 17 June they came upon forty-five whale ships, all delayed by the ice near Vaygach Strait north of Disko. Captain Muirhead of the whaler *Larkins,* who had been beyond 75° N. his last voyage, told Ross he thought his only chance of working north was to keep close to the land. There was consternation on 24 June when moving ice pushed the ships into shallow water and *Alexander* grounded. Boats from the whaling fleet quickly came to the rescue and pulled her off. Ross especially commended the captains of several whalers for their conduct. Two mornings later *Isabella* led forty-one sails north a short distance to compact ice.

By 3 July the ships were abreast of Hope Sanderson and in sight of Women's Islands, and on the seventh they recognized the 'Three Islands' described by Baffin. The fifteenth they learned from the whale ship *Zephyr* that *Three Brothers* of Hull had been crushed by the ice but the crew had escaped. Forty whalers were still in company and several large whales had been killed. To bring up samples from the sea bottom, Ross invented a useful contrivance called a deep-sea clam.*

On 22 June, Ross passed 75° 12', the highest latitude actually known to have been reached by whalers up to that time. The next day the crews were turned out to haul the ships through

---

* This device for dredging samples had forceps-like jaws which closed automatically when they touched bottom. Ross used it in over a thousand fathoms of water. He gives a detailed description of his invention in *A Voyage of Discovery . . . of a North-West Passage* (London, 1819).

the ice by cables. Led by the fiddler, the men cheered lustily when his music was interrupted as he dropped through a snow-covered hole for an icy ducking. Ross believed he would outrun the whale ships as all, with the exception of *Dexterity* of Leith were trailing him; so he sent dispatches home aboard her. Discovering and naming Melville Bay, he also named a remarkable peaked spiral rock in its midst, Melville's Monument.

James Clark Ross successfully harpooned a peculiarly marked, forty-six-foot, black and white whale, 30 July, which yielded nine tons of blubber retained to use for light and fuel should the expedition be obliged to winter. Whalers still kept company and *Bon Accord* of Aberdeen killed nine whales on 31 July and parted company with three cheers.

As they worked up the Greenland coast, myriads of little auks swam among vast numbers of whales and sea unicorns in the channels opening in the slowly disintegrating ice. Hundreds of the birds were shot and served to the ships' companies. New bay ice, forming on the open channels, was shattered by a wave ahead of the ship made by rolling a boat suspended from the jib boom. Three small islands off Cape Melville were named for Midshipman Skene who discovered them. At one point ice six feet thick lifted *Isabella* several feet, broke against her sides, and curled back on itself. The two ships collided and were then torn apart with their anchors fouled in each other, and so they strained at the taut cables between them until one of the cables parted. The moving force of the ice was almost incredible and, without admirable strengthening, the ships would have been lost at this time. Even as docks were being cut in an ice field it began to move rapidly and violently and, coming in contact with a berg, rose against its side over fifty feet and fell back on the very spot where Ross had meant to berth the ships.

At northern Melville Bay a group of shy Eskimos appeared who inquired if the ships came from the sun or the moon. These were the Etah Eskimos, later made famous by Admiral Peary, but Ross called them the Arctic Highlanders. They had never before seen white men and would not come to the ships until Ross and Parry, accompanied by Sacheuse, went on the ice and, slowly pulling their noses and shouting in the local manner, demonstrated their friendship. Sacheuse presented to Ross a picture of this scene. The Eskimos thought little of a terrier dog, a puny creature compared with theirs, but they were terrified by the grunt and fierce appearance of a Shetland pig. As they left the ship they attempted to carry off an anvil, but managed to take only the hammer which was recovered from a snow bank later.

This coast from Cape Melville to Wolstenholm Sound, including Prince Regent Inlet cut off from the south by glaciers meeting the sea, Ross called the Arctic Highlands. To supplement the crew's diet, 3000 little auks were killed 17 August and three birds were issued daily to each man. The following day between Cape York and Cape Dudley Digges the explorers saw 600-foot cliffs spectacularly covered with crimson snow with high white mountains rising beyond.*

After passing Wolstenholm Sound and Cape Dudley Digges, 18 August, Ross was beginning the first circuit of Baffin Bay since its discovery. His bearings agreed with Baffin's. Carey's Islands and Hakluyt Island were recognized as was Smith Sound, which Ross from a distance of about eighteen leagues considered landlocked — this was his first error. He named the capes on either side of it for his ships and concluded that there was no opening in the northern end of Baffin Bay from Hakluyt Island to lofty Cape Clarence. Parry, never directly critical of his commander, had this to say about Smith Sound:

> During the remainder of the day, I passed the greater part of my time on deck, anxious to see whether the mainland to the eastward, that is, the Coast of Greenland, and that to the west-

* The 'red snow' of the Arctic is caused by *Protococcus nivalis,* a rapidly multiplying unicellular plant.

ward, joined; but this I had not, at any time, the good fortune to see, although from ten o'clock until midnight the weather was remarkably fine and clear. It is probable that the chasm, or open space, to the northward, where not any land could be traced *by me,* might be that which Baffin calls Sir Thomas Smith's Sound; and if, agreeably to his relation, this is the 'deepest and largest sound in all this bay,' it is not likely that we should have seen the bottom of it at such a distance, as we estimate that we are twenty leagues from the northern extreme of the west land visible.[7]

And he continues:

Between eleven and twelve o'clock, P.M. we made sail to the southward, and abandoned the search for a passage in this quarter, from a thorough conviction, I should hope, that not any such passage exists here. I am perfectly satisfied myself that this is not the place to look for it, although I must confess that I did not see the continuity of land all around the top of this bay, if it may be so termed.

On 23 August, Ross claimed he saw mountains across the bottom of Jones Sound and called it a bay. This was his second error. A week later they were off Lancaster Sound, which Ross says in the general opinion of all was an inlet. He cites Captain Sabine especially as of the opinion that there was no strait here. The thirty-first they sailed into the sound leaving *Alexander,* a duller sailer, astern. Next day at 3:00 p.m. as the weather was clearing, Ross distinctly saw a range of mountains across Lancaster Sound. He named the range Croker's Mountains after the Secretary of the Admiralty, but no one has seen them since. This mirage resulted in Ross's greatest mistake: he turned his back on the only feasible Passage and sailed out of the Sound. Ross gives many reasons for leaving this 'bay' at once — the short time left to explore the remainder of the western shore of Baffin Bay being the principal one — and he wrote in self-justification of his decision to leave Lancaster Sound:

Yet my anxiety, on the other hand, to leave no part of the coast unexplored, even after all hopes of a passage were given up, determined me to persevere as I did, notwithstanding there was no current, a material decrease in the temperature of the sea, and no driftwood, or other indication of a passage, until I actually saw the barrier of high mountains, and the continuity of ice, which put the question at rest.[8]

Unfortunately it did not, as Ross soon discovered after his return.

Again, Parry was more cautious in his account [9] and wrote:

. . . it certainly has more the appearance of being the entrance of the wished-for straits, than any place we have yet seen. . . . we stood into the inlet [30 August] . . . and the more we advanced, the more sanguine our hopes were that we had at last found what has been for ages sought in vain. Every thing, indeed, tended to confirm this our belief; at noon we tried for soundings with two hundred and thirty-five fathoms of line, without finding bottom; and in the evening, when the sun was getting low, the weather being remarkably clear, we could see the land on both sides of the inlet for a very great distance, but not any at the bottom of it.

He continued the following day:

. . . but, alas! the sanguine hopes and high expectations excited by this promising appearance of things were but of a short duration, for, about three o'clock in the afternoon, the Isabella tacked, very much to our surprise indeed, as we could not see any thing like land at the bottom of the inlet, nor was the weather well calculated at the time for seeing any object at a great distance, it being somewhat hazy. When she tacked, the Isabella was about three or four miles ahead of us, so that, considering the state of the weather, and a part of this additional distance, for we did not tack immediately on her tacking, but stood on towards her, some allowance is to be made for our not seeing the land all around.

Coasting down Baffin Island, Ross collected a 1131-pound bear for the British Museum. By crossing to Greenland and back again to Baffin Island, he could eliminate James Island from the charts. Off Cape Farewell, *Isabella* weathered a heavy storm and anchored in Brassa Sound, Shetland Islands, 30 October, where *Alexander* had arrived a few hours before. Ross could report with pride to the Secretary of the Admiralty:

> Not an instance of punishment has taken place in this ship, nor has there been an officer, or man, in the sick list; and it is with a feeling not to be expressed, that I have to conclude this letter, by reporting that the service has been performed, and the expedition, I had the honour to command, has returned, without the loss of a man.

After a week at Brassa they sailed, 7 November, and a week later anchored in Grimsby Roads. Two days afterward Ross was reporting to the Lords of the Admiralty in London.

Ross's report infuriated Sir John Barrow, who almost immediately began attacking the explorer for mismanaging the expedition and ignoring his instructions. He had, said Barrow, wasted too much time pulling noses with Eskimos when he should have been getting on with his explorations on the western side of Baffin Bay. Just about everything Ross did, according to Barrow, was wrong. The investigation of Smith Sound was inadequate. His most serious charge, that Ross had failed to explore Lancaster Sound sufficiently, was of course true, although no one knew it at that time. Ross defended himself in a restrained and dignified manner, much the way Middleton had received the attacks of Arthur Dobbs. But the two men were never friends again. Barrow could not believe the Ross statement 'that the land is here continuous, and there is no opening at the northernmost part of Baffin Bay.' Nor could he accept Croker's Mountains stretching across Lancaster Sound.

At the most critical points of his exploration Ross seems to have had the good sailor's shyness of land. Cook's ability to navigate his ships carefully close to shore is one that gives most deep-water men gray hairs. This was Ross's first experience at probing along coasts. One of the most baffling aspects — certainly one of the most damaging to Ross in the discussions — was the way most of his officers changed their minds about what they had or had not seen in Lancaster Sound. While Ross says only one other man actually saw Croker's Mountains, no one had questioned his announcement, and the officers of *Isabella,* who were at dinner at the time, neglected his invitation to go on deck to view them. *Alexander* was, according to Ross, eight miles astern of *Isabella,* so no officer there could see the alleged mountains in any case. Parry placed the distance between the ships only half as far. On the voyage home there was apparently plenty of discussion in the wardrooms about the possibility of a Passage through Lancaster Sound and whether or not the mountains really closed it in. Some of the officers began to have their doubts. Captain Sabine published a pamphlet expressing hope that Lancaster Sound would be the Passage and citing deep, open water as an encouraging indication. He also accused Ross of unauthorized use of his tables and other similar irregularities.[10] Ross publicly refuted Sabine's accusations. Previously in his journal he had specifically written that Sabine had been satisfied at the time that no Passage existed in that region, but had recommended that they move south to Cumberland Sound. With hindsight one suspects Ross agreed with the reviewer of his book, who wrote:

> There occur unfortunate moments in the history of a man's life when he is himself unable to account for his actions; and the moment of putting about the *Isabella* would appear to be one of them: for had Captain Ross then felt what he professes to feel in the Introduction to his book, that 'his nautical education had taught him to act and not to question; to obey orders, as

far as possible, not to discuss probabilities' we are quite certain
that he would not have stopped short where he did.[11]

While his work as an explorer was discredited, the Navy
recognized his worth by promoting him to Captain. It is only
in quite recent years that Ross has been given credit for his
substantial accomplishments. Besides eliminating James Island
from the charts, he charted the west coast of Davis Strait;
learned about the hitherto unknown Etah Eskimos; extended
the whaling grounds; invented the deep-sea clam; made valuable magnetic, meteorological, and hydrographic observations;
and confirmed the discoveries of Baffin. Morevoer, the joint
expedition had given invaluable training to a group of officers
who were to carry on Arctic explorations for many years. Nearly
all of them went on succeeding expeditions and nearly all gave
credit to the experience they had gained with John Ross. He
was not however, selected to command the expedition that
Barrow planned to send out the following year. That honor
went to his lieutenant, William Edward Parry, destined to become one of the greatest Arctic voyagers.

21

Opening the Door

*N*ot since the days of Captain Cook's reports on his Pacific discoveries had there been as much excitement generated by exploration as that created by the expeditions seeking the Northwest Passage during the next decade. The discovery of Hudson Bay in 1610 had been a tremendous push by sea westward, but the fact that it was a bay halted any further advance. For over two hundred years each explorer had added to the knowledge of the northern North American shores, but there had been no big advance to capture people's imagination. The next voyage stimulated enthusiasm that lasted until the Arctic was a mystery no more.

John Barrow pushed through his plans for another expedition rapidly. By 16 January 1819 Lieutenant William Edward Parry had his commission for *Hecla.* Five days later he was aboard. The four-year-old *Hecla,* a strong, roomy bomb vessel of 375 tons, was well suited for Arctic service. The 180-ton gun-brig *Griper,* a less happy choice, was selected as her consort, under Lieutenant Matthew Liddon. Both vessels were strengthened as the four ships the previous year had been, and their rigs changed to barks — a handier rig requiring a smaller crew. The Admiralty offered double Navy pay; nearly all of the men who had been with Ross and Buchan volunteered for the new expedition. Captain Edward Sabine was again appointed astronomer and scientist, and the two artists, Lieutenants Frederick William Beechey and Henry Parkyns Hoppner, seconds in command of the two vessels. No less than nineteen of the officers were veterans of the previous year, including Alexander Fisher, assistant surgeon, and James Clark Ross, John Bushnan, and A. M. Skene among the midshipmen. Altogether the complement was ninety-four men; fifty-eight on *Hecla* and thirty-six on *Griper*.[1] The ships, provisioned and supplied for two years, were ballasted with coal which, with a large quantity of firewood, would carry them through an Arctic winter. As additional winter comfort, housing cloths to tent in the decks were prepared for both vessels. Warm clothing and antiscorbutics were plentiful, and a wolf skin would cheer each man's bed.

Parry's instructions specifically ordered him to search Lancaster Sound thoroughly; if he found it blocked, he was to go to Jones Sound, and if turned back there, to continue on to Smith Sound. If he found an opening, he was to proceed as rapidly as possible westward to Bering Strait, not stopping to explore the northern American coast. Otherwise his instructions and procedure, once through the Passage, were nearly identical with those of the previous year. The Northwest Passage was still the primary goal, but 'the improvement of geography and navigation, as well as the general interests of science, were considered as of scarcely less importance.' To facilitate this work Captain Sabine was provided with a large variety of scientific instruments. Captain Ross's deep-sea clam was again to be used to obtain bottom samples, and bottles with messages to be thrown overboard each day.

A steamboat was hired to tow the ships from Deptford to Northfleet, where guns and gunners' stores were taken on and

the compasses corrected. Sailing on 11 May 1819, Parry early
found that *Griper* was impossibly slow. She was so slow that
Hecla towed her through Yarmouth Roads and continued towing her about half the way across the Atlantic. He made a pass
at the elusive Sunken Island of Buss, with the usual result.

On the nineteenth of June he entered Davis Strait and saw
his first ice the following day. After sailing west northwest for
four days, he ran into icebergs and altered his course northerly.
Soon thereafter Parry attempted, without success, to force his
way through to the western shore of Davis Strait, but the ice
was impenetrable. On the advice of his whaling master, he
cleared his ships and, skirting the ice, sailed up the middle of
the Strait, gradually forced by ice conditions over toward the
Greenland shore. From a passing whaler, 16 July, news was
received of a large fleet of whale ships unable to get north of
about 74°. Since this was the latitude where the ships were held
up in 1818, Parry concluded that this was the prevailing condition for that latitude.

After a period of fog the weather cleared on 21 July, revealing
from the crow's nest eighty-eight high icebergs. Parry found
himself off Hope Sanderson and Women's Islands, and having
now reached 73°, he decided to force his way westward through
the middle pack to the entrance of Lancaster Sound. The ships
battled through eighty miles of ice; on the twenty-eighth they
emerged into clear water. Never before had Baffin Bay been
crossed in that latitude at that season. Modestly, Parry wrote:

> By taking advantage of every little opening that is afforded, I
> believe that a strong-built vessel of proper size and weight may,
> in most seasons, be pushed through this barrier which occupies
> the centre part of Baffin's Bay, about this parallel of latitude.
> It must, at the same time, be confessed, that, had we not been
> favoured with strong south-easterly winds, it would probably
> have required several days longer to effect this passage.

Lancaster Sound, alive with whales, opened before him, and stodgy *Griper* was again put on the end of a towline. Although Parry had left England a fortnight later than Ross, he arrived off Lancaster Sound exactly a month earlier than his old commander had. He generously admits that:

> This difference is to be attributed entirely to the confidence which I felt, from the experience gained on the former voyage, that an open sea would be found to the westward of the barrier of ice which occupies the middle of Baffin's Bay. Without that confidence, it would have been little better than madness to have attempted a passage through so compact a body of ice, when no indication of a clear sea appeared beyond it.

At Possession Bay, with lofty Cape Byam Martin towering beside, they found the flagstaff erected the previous year. The sea was clear to the west.

This was the crucial point of the voyage. Would Croker's Mountains stop them? Parry decided to sail on as quickly as possible and leave *Griper* behind, placing a rendezvous at 85°W. near the middle of the Sound. Working slowly against a westerly wind that prevailed for several days, *Hecla* gained only eight or nine miles on her consort. Looking astern, they saw in astonishment *Griper* bowling along under a fresh east wind with all studding sails set, while *Hecla* hung in the westerly. Soon the fair breeze reached them and as they crowded all sail for the westward, the mastheads swarmed with officers and men eagerly searching the horizon ahead.

Nothing barred the way, and christening Croker Bay for the Secretary of the Admiralty, in recompense for his now vanished mountains, Parry hurried westward. The wind increased, sails were reefed, and westward they went. *Griper,* which had been outrun, again caught up. Beyond 86° W. no land had been sighted; the sea was as free of ice as any part of the Atlantic.

Thinking they might now be in the open Polar Sea postulated by Barrow, some of the officers began calculating the course to Cook's Icy Cape in Alaska. But by 10:00 p.m. 4 August they came to compact, impenetrable floes across the Strait. For sport, while delayed, they endeavored to kill the eighteen- to twenty-foot white whales which surrounded them in great numbers. Mr. Fisher heard these beluga emit a shrill, ringing sound, like 'musical glasses when badly played.' The whale song, as the sailors called it, was especially distinct when the whales swam directly beneath the boat several feet under water and ceased when they surfaced. Shoals of narwhals swam by. They discovered a small island which they named for Prince Leopold.

The evening of the sixth, with a favorable breeze, Parry stood southward and, after picking up the land, discovered he was entering a broad inlet. An ice-bound western coastline was visible as the ships sailed down an open channel along the opposite shore. After two days Parry concluded that to go further would be hazardous and waste time. He named the inlet for the Prince Regent and guessed that it communicated with Hudson Bay through Roes Welcome or Repulse Bay. Actually it does so through Fury and Hecla Strait. He also thought the land to the west was an island, his new inlet connecting with the sea around its southern end. He was again partially correct, but the connection, Bellot Strait, is narrow and unsuitable for navigation.

Having sailed about 120 miles down Prince Regent Inlet, he retraced his way. By the fourteenth Parry was back in Lancaster Sound probing for a westward opening in the ice. Because of the closeness to the magnetic pole, compasses were useless. Headway westward came slowly, but by 20 August Maxwell Bay was passed. The ice cleared the next day, but they lay becalmed. On 22 August a small island was named Beechey in honor of Sir William, father of the expedition's talented lieutenant. Beyond Beechey Island it was soon dis-

covered that a broad channel opened to the north, with land
visible in the distance westerly. Parry was delighted for he
had feared he might be embayed if the shore of Devon Island,
which he had been following, continued southward to join
the mainland. He named the new opening Wellington Channel and the continuation of Lancaster Sound, Barrow Strait
after Sir John, 'as a public acknowledgment due to him for
his zeal and exertions in the promotion of Northern Discovery.'
The land beyond Wellington Channel was called Cornwallis
Island after Admiral Sir William, Parry's first naval friend
and patron. Everything looked propitious and Parry, calculating there were still six weeks of good sailing, wrote:

> our prospects, indeed, were truly exhilarating; the ships had suf-
> fered no injury; we had plenty of provisions; crews in high health
> and spirits; a sea, if not open, at least navigable; and a zealous
> and unanimous determination in both officers and men to ac-
> complish, by all possible means, the grand object on which we
> had the happiness to be employed.

Choosing the west channel south of Cornwallis Island, rather
than Wellington, which headed due north, Parry bored
through a neck of ice and there again was open water. From
the broken character of the land Parry concluded that the
whole region was made up of islands and channels. He named
Bathurst Island and several small islands, 24 August, and
weathering Cape Cockburn, approached and named Byam
Martin Island for Sir Thomas, Comptroller of the Navy. Captain Sabine, James Clark Ross, and Messrs. Edwards and Fiske
landed on Byam Martin, where they found remains of Eskimo
dwellings and many caribou and musk ox horns. Continuing
west to Melville Island, along which he sailed the first few
days of September, Parry crossed 110° W. of Greenwich, in
latitude 74° 44′ 20″, 4 September, at 9:15 p.m. His ships were
now entitled to the reward of £5000 for penetrating that far

westward within the Arctic Circle. To mark this important achievement Parry made an official announcement to the crew and complimented them on their past conduct and expressed his belief that by their efforts the expedition would ultimately reach its goal and they would be entitled to the whole reward.

> The enthusiasm excited by this short, but pathetic speech, was truly astonishing, for the ardour that it inspired might be seen in every countenance; and I have no doubt whenever an opportunity occurs of showing the impression it made, its good effects will be very evident; but, to do every officer and man on the expedition justice, I firmly believe they require no stimulus to urge them to their duty.[2]

The event was further commemorated by naming a bluff headland Bounty Cape and by serving extra meat and beer at Sunday dinner. At Melville Island the two ships anchored for the first time since leaving the Norfolk coast. The first stage of the voyage was completed.

Further penetration to the westward was unsuccessful. The nights were getting longer, the weather colder, and the Pacific was still far away. Hunting yielded a few hares, grouse, and a musk ox. A party of seven men from *Griper* got lost and was out over three nights before being found. In gratitude for their rescue the headland to the westward was called Cape Providence. At noontime 16 September the ships were almost abreast this cape. By the eighteenth the rapidly forming, tough, 'young ice' was giving trouble and forced Parry to look for winter quarters. Returning eastward to Hecla and Griper Bay, as he called his first anchorage, he found a good location and for two and a half days all hands were employed cutting a canal over two miles long through seven inches of ice to the chosen spot. They rigged sails on blocks of ice and were aided by a helpful fair wind in clearing the channel. Other blocks of ice were sunk under the edge of the floe. By working long hours and 'splicing the main brace' at the day's end the job was finished on 26 September. That very night the temperature dropped a degree below zero and the following morning no open water was in sight, nor was any seen again that season. The ships were prepared for winter by sending down spars (except lower masts and *Hecla*'s topmast), housing them in with cloth, and sending spare gear ashore to give clear decks. A line was stretched between the two ships as a guide, and poles were set up on the hills as bearings for shore parties. All was snug at Winter Harbour.

The sun was seen for the last time without refraction 4 November and would not again appear for ninety-six days. The theatrical season began the next day with the presentation of *Miss in her Teens,* directed by Lieutenant Beechey. The venture into theatricals induced Alexander Fisher to remark rather sourly that as 'intended sources of amusement, I have no doubt but it will answer its end, that is, of diverting the men.' These performances were continued every fortnight and furnished enjoyment and activity for everyone. As further recreation *The North Georgia Gazette and Winter Chronicle,* with all contributions by the officers, was issued under the editorship of Captain Sabine.[3] On clear days an arc of red light glowed in the south and for about two hours it was possible to read rather fine print.

> To the southward was the sea, covered with one unbroken surface of ice, uniform in its dazzling whiteness, except that, in some parts a few hummocks were seen thrown up somewhat above the general level. Nor did the land offer much greater variety, being almost entirely covered with snow, except here and there a brown patch of bare ground in some exposed situations, where the wind had not allowed the snow to remain.[4]

Hopefully the men cheered themselves by imagining that the next winter would be spent in the South Seas islands.

The first signs of scurvy which appeared 2 January 1820 were cured by prompt use of antiscorbutics. Parry grew a little mustard and cress in boxes on his heating pipes and even this small amount of fresh leaves was helpful. The sun returned in early February and on the fourteenth Parry gave two marines thirty-six lashes for drunkenness — the only punishment inflicted on the voyage. Near disaster was averted a week later when the storehouse on shore caught fire. The flames were brought under control in less than an hour, but sixteen men were on the sick list with frostbite as a consequence.

In early March the weather began to moderate, but it was 6 May before they could start cutting the ships out of the six-foot ice. No open water was yet in sight. By the middle of the month, musk ox and caribou tracks recorded the return of these animals to Melville Island, and on the seventeenth the ships were afloat again, rising some ten to eighteen inches after being freed.

While waiting for suitable sailing conditions Parry decided to explore Melville Island. On 1 June, leaving the ship with a party, he crossed to the north side of the island in five days. To the west was high land which he called the Blue Hills. Turning back through the hilly country he came upon Liddon Gulf, and, crossing it, he returned to his ships 15 June. He then surveyed Winter Harbour since the ice had not yet thawed sufficiently for passage through it.

As July wore on, there was little change. By the twenty-fourth, however, conditions were so improved that sails were bent and the ships made ready to leave. Winter Harbour was free of ice and anchors were weighed 1 August. Distant land seen through the haze on the eighth was named Banks Land (now called Banks Island). By the sixteenth there seemed little hope of getting farther westward because of ice. The ships had reached 113° 46′ 43″, farther west than anyone had navigated north of continental North America.

Thinking he might find a channel running south, Parry consulted with his officers and decided, 26 August, to turn east and look for such an opening. They found none. Upon reaching 90° W., Parry issued full rations and announced they would turn back. During the six days (as opposed to the five weeks on the voyage out) it took to sail from Winter Harbour to Baffin Bay they discovered Admiralty Inlet and Navy Board Inlet. On the fifth they met the whaler *Lee* of Hull, from whom they learned of the death of King George III.

Parry concluded, 26 September, the season was too far gone for further examination of the coast of Baffin Island. The boats were hoisted in, the ships made snug, and they bore away for England. In a gale, which separated the two vessels, *Hecla* lost her bowsprit, foremast, and main topmast but in two days she was on her way under jury rig. On 30 October Parry collected all journals and landed at Peterhead, and by 3 November he was in London. Both ships were paid off at Deptford, 20 December.

After this remarkable voyage Parry concluded a Passage between the two oceans probably existed, but could better be attempted through northern Hudson Bay, keeping as close to the continental coast as possible. He theorized that north of the region where Hearne and Mackenzie had found the ocean was a maze of islands and channels. On the basis of his experience in Baffin Bay, Parry urged whalers to begin their operations later in the season and, by pushing through the middle pack, to get a quick cargo among the multitude of whales in western Baffin Bay and Lancaster Sound.

Parry's amazing success in pushing halfway through the Northwest Passage created enormous enthusiasm and stimulated the immediate fitting out of another expedition to leave early in 1821.[5] The Admiralty adopted the explorer's recommendation to try the route through northern Hudson Bay. Certain alterations were made in equipment, based on Parry's experience. *Fury,* a bomb vessel the size of *Hecla,* was selected as the flagship, replacing the unfortunate *Griper.* Command of *Hecla* was given to Lieutenant George Francis Lyon. The two barks were sister ships of the same size, identically fitted out. The fore- and main-masts in both ships were interchangeable, a style being adopted at that time in the Royal Navy on the recommendation of Sir Thomas Byam Martin, Comptroller. Besides masts, all gear that would fit one ship would fit the other — a decided advantage, for either vessel could furnish her consort with any necessities without alteration. Parry claimed that the old notion of having one ship larger than the other in order that the smaller one could work in more shallow water was not supported by experience. There was not enough difference in draft between a large ship and a smaller one; boats were better for inshore work. The ships were strengthened with oak and iron as before, and other alterations included a thick lining of cork applied all around the ships' sides and under the upper decks; shutters of the same material fitted to every window and skylight so that all the living parts of the ships were insulated; and a more efficient heater rigged up to combat the dampness caused by condensation. The men were given hammocks, and the officers were given cots to replace the damp bunks. The stores were more compact. Higher proof spirits that could be diluted, flour instead of biscuits, and more canned meat in place of 'salt Horse' saved enough space so that the ships could be victualed for three years. To prevent overloading the vessels for the Atlantic crossing, the transport *Nautilus* took part of the cargo as far as Hudson Strait.

Again many of the old experienced hands signed on. Hoppner now was Lyon's second in command on *Hecla*. James Clark Ross and John Bushnan, who had been on the two previous voyages, were joined, among other midshipmen, by Francis R. M. Crozier. George Fisher, who had been with Buchan, was appointed astronomer and chaplain. John Edwards and Alexander Fisher were again ships' surgeons. Other familiar names included Hooper the purser, and Nias and Reid, lieutenants.

Parry's instructions ordered him to go through Hudson Strait to Repulse Bay and then to examine every bend and inlet of the coast that might provide 'a practicable passage westward, in which direction it is the principal object of your voyage to endevour to find your way from the Atlantic into the Pacific Ocean.' Should he find a Passage he was not to stop to explore the land, but to push west as rapidly as possible. If he failed to find a channel in the north of Hudson Bay, it was left to his discretion how to proceed. The objects of the expedition were: first, to find a Passage between the oceans; second, to establish the boundary of the American continent; and third, to make scientific observations and collect specimens. A lookout was to be kept for Captain John Franklin, who had been commissioned at the same time to explore the northern shore of the continent. Any assistance he could render that explorer was to be provided, and should the Franklin party wish to be taken on board and brought home, he was to accommodate them. Flagstaffs that Franklin might see were to be erected on the most prominent points along the coast.

On 8 May, *Fury, Hecla,* and *Nautilus* weighed anchor from the Little Nore for an uneventful crossing. When the ships reached ice off Hudson Strait, the stores were transferred from *Nautilus,* and they parted company 1 July. Lyon, seeing the ice for the first time, wrote:

> The pack edge was in a straight line, and presented the appearance of a low rugged wall. The morning was gloomy, and the wind which set on to the ice kept it in continual motion: snow fell occasionally, and a slight coating of ice formed on the rigging. Over the pack I observed, for the first time, the luminous appearance called the blink, which, although very white, was not of course to be compared with the body by which it was caused. Flocks of divers and gulls swam with unconcern amongst the rolling masses by which they were surrounded, and occasionally rising to avoid a coming wave, resumed their search for food.

Nineteen days were needed to sail sixty miles past Resolution Island, and passage through the Strait was painfully slow.

At the entrance to Foxe Channel, Parry decided it would save time to go north of Southampton Island through Middleton's Frozen Strait rather than around south of the island and up Roes Welcome to Repulse Bay. It was a good gamble. Conditions were favorable, and sailing through Frozen Strait he soon discovered that there was no channel westward out of Repulse Bay. Thus the discoveries of Middleton, which Parry had trusted, were confirmed, and Arthur Dobbs's assertions that Frozen Strait did not exist and that there was probably a passage out of Repulse Bay, proven wrong.

After this auspicious start, the expedition bogged down in extremely severe weather. Following his instructions to explore every inlet, Parry, during the remainder of the season, got only a little farther north to Winter Island, short of the Arctic Circle. There the winter of 1821–2 was spent in circumstances similar to the previous one at Winter Harbour. The summer of 1822 he worked up the coast of Melville Peninsula to a strait which the Eskimos had told him about.

> The morning of the 26th [August] was fine, and favoured by a light breeze, we ran with great anxiety for the mouth of the new strait. Soon after noon we succeeded in passing the narrow entrance, which extended about four miles east and west, and was formed by two projecting head-lands. That on the left was high, but of gradual ascent, perfectly smooth, and composed entirely of beautifully variegated sandstone. The width of the opening was from three to one mile, and through this a most powerful tide of current was rushing from the westward.[6]

For sixty-five days they struggled to get through the new strait. They succeeded in making only forty miles west from Igloolik, an island near the strait's mouth. Unable to push his ships further, Parry sent out foot parties who found a connection with a sea to the west.

The winter of 1822–3 was spent frozen in off Igloolik Island at the entrance of Fury and Hecla Strait, as Parry named the new channel. Parry had planned to send *Hecla* home the following summer and continue exploring in *Fury,* but on 1 August the ships were still frozen in solid. A total of 319 days had been spent in winter quarters, all but nine frozen in the same floe. A movement of the floe eventually aided in freeing the ships. Parry decided to sail home, where he arrived in October and reported to the Admiralty.

The expedition of 1821–3 was considered a success even though it had made no such spectacular progress toward the west as the previous voyage. Middleton's discoveries were confirmed, the east coast of Melville Peninsula surveyed, and Fury and Hecla Strait discovered. This channel apparently opened into a sea that might be navigated to Cape Turnagain, which Franklin reached in his coastal journey east. Parry gave his opinion that Prince Regent Inlet and Fury and Hecla Strait joined and further argued that Prince Regent Inlet, which most probably led to the open sea Franklin had seen, should be approached through Lancaster Sound. Although Fury and Hecla Strait was farther south, ice conditions were less severe in the north. An enormous amount of meteorological and other scientific data was gathered. Captain Lyon lived for periods of several days at a time with the Eskimos and became fond of them. His excellent studies of the life and customs of the Melville Peninsula Eskimos were an important by-product of the expedition.

When Parry set off in 1819 Captain John Franklin was leading an overland party to explore and survey the shore of North America from the mouth of the Coppermine River to the eastern extremity of the continent.[7] The other members of this naval expedition were: George Back, second in command and Franklin's old shipmate in *Trent;* Robert Hood, a midshipman; Dr. John Richardson, a naval surgeon and naturalist; and John Hepburn, sailor. This was Franklin's first great land expedition and the first of several land parties sent out to co-operate with those going by sea. Advice was obtained from the officers of the Hudson's Bay and North-West Companies, and Franklin interviewed Sir Alexander Mackenzie, the only man living who had led a similar expedition. Franklin's group embarked for Hudson Bay 23 May on *Prince of Wales,* a Hudson's Bay Company ship, and arrived at York Factory in mid-August. They began the long journey up the Hayes River 9 September.

Following the path blazed by Samuel Hearne, from Cumberland House, Carlton House, and the North-West Company's post of Fort Providence on Great Slave Lake, Franklin reached the mouth of the Coppermine 18 July 1821. He corrected Hearne's latitude and longitude for the mouth of the river. Pushing eastward along the unexplored coast, the party surveyed over 550 miles of shoreline. At Point Turnagain on the Kent Peninsula, Franklin turned back after determining that the coast once more trended to the east. He had originally planned to return by the Coppermine but supplies were short and he thought that game might be more plentiful and the journey shorter by an unexplored river — named for Hood who was killed by one of the half-breed guides. This was an unfortunate error in judgment, for the party very nearly starved to death and the expedition took three years, not returning to England until the summer of 1822.

Franklin's report combined with Parry's inspired the Admiralty to send an expedition out immediately to explore the coast between Repulse Bay and Point Turnagain. The Eskimos had told Parry that a short distance overland from Repulse Bay was a great sea. It was then possible to surmise the general shape of Melville Peninsula, whose neck was assumed to run almost due west to Franklin's Point Turnagain. The existence of the Boothia Peninsula was not even suspected.

Lieutenant George F. Lyon, Parry's second in command, was chosen to lead the expedition. His instructions were to go to

Repulse Bay, winter his ship, and in the spring of 1825 take a party overland across the neck of the Melville Peninsula. Arriving at the sea, he was to follow the coastline to Franklin's Point Turnagain. For some reason, presumably because she was already strengthened for Arctic service, the slow, cranky H.M.S. *Griper* was assigned to Lyon. She had not improved with age; a poor sailing ship at best, she was further slowed by her load for an extra season. She was towed down from Deptford 10 June 1824 and after various delays dropped the pilot on the twenty-sixth off Shields. *Griper,* poorly designed for ice conditions being unusually sharp forward and very deep, pitched unmercifully. The surveying ship *Snap,* carrying part of the supplies, accompanied her on the slow ocean crossing to Hudson Strait.

The ice in the Strait and northern Hudson Bay was excessively heavy that year. Lyon chose to go south of Southampton Island and reach Repulse Bay through Roes Welcome Strait, rather than by Frozen Strait as Parry had done. From his narrative it appears that the ice gave him no choice. In Roes Welcome the ship met one savage storm after another. They lost the deck load of stores from *Snap* overboard. They also lost the hay for two ponies purchased in the Shetlands for the overland trek, and had to shoot the ponies. All the ship's anchors were lost. Finally, they ascertained that a head current was running down Roes Welcome faster than *Griper* could sail under ideal conditions. *Griper* could not claw off a lee shore as almost any other vessel could have. The season was far advanced. Viewing all of these circumstances, Lyon decided, 13 September, to turn back. At first thinking to run into Fort York or Fort Churchill, he found this impossible with no anchors and no pilot who knew those shoal waters. To return to England was the only sensible course. *Griper* put into Portsmouth Harbor in a heavy squall, 10 November.[8]

Parry's opinion that the Northwest Passage might be found through Prince Regent Inlet, combined with John Franklin's

account of open sea north of the American mainland, inspired
the Lords of the Admiralty to send them out again in 1825. The
reliable old *Hecla,* once more his flagship, with *Fury* as consort
under veteran Lieutenant Henry Parkyns Hoppner, was refitted. The transport *William Harris* was assigned to accompany them into Davis Strait. All arrangements, preparations,
and suppplies were similar to the previous voyage.[9] The instructions are also similar, except that Parry was to use his judgment
whether to conduct the search through Prince Regent Inlet or
Barrow Strait, and that two other expeditions were sent out
simultaneously. Captain John Franklin's second party was to
send out two groups from the mouth of the Mackenzie River —
one to survey eastward to the Coppermine and the other to go
westward to Icy Cape, where they would attempt to join a ship
to be sent through Bering Strait. This last expedition was under
the command of their old shipmate and fellow explorer, Captain Frederick William Beechey.

Hecla and *Fury* dropped down from Deptford 8 May and
stood to sea on the nineteenth. Thick weather was encountered
in Davis Strait and, after transferring stores, the transport left
them 3 July. Stopping for a short visit with the Danes, Parry
plunged into the middle pack to cross Baffin Bay. There he
stayed in the ice all summer, not being able to reach Lancaster
Sound until nearly mid-September. Already young ice was beginning to make. After struggling with it against head winds
for about a fortnight, he eventually decided to enter Prince Regent Inlet and to winter in Port Bowen on its eastern side. On
20 July 1825, the ships were again able to put to sea. Crossing
over to the westerly side of the inlet and taking a look at ice-
free Barrow Strait, he turned south. Ten days later *Fury* was
forced aground by ice. They managed to get her off, but she ran
aground again 5 August and leaked badly. She was then un-
loaded as Parry intended to make repairs. Damaged still more
extensively by ice, the ship, as was soon obvious, could not be

saved. As an expedition so crippled could accomplish nothing, Parry decided to return to England. He landed at Peterhead 12 October and reported at the Admiralty four days later. Although he still believed a Northwest Passage would eventually be found, this was his last attempt. He did, however, lead an expedition across the ice from Spitsbergen toward the Pole. He then rested on his laurels, was knighted, and eventually retired as a Rear Admiral. He died in Ems, Germany, 8 July 1855.

Franklin's second expedition did not embark until 16 February 1825. It was an experienced group, including as before the able Dr. John Richardson, naturalist as well as physician, Lieutenant George Back as second in command, and E. N. Kendall, the Admiralty Mate who had been with Lyon. Franklin's orders were to send out in the spring of 1826 two parties from the mouth of the Mackenzie. One, under Dr. Richardson accompanied by Mr. Kendall, was to explore the coast to the east as far as the Coppermine River. Franklin with Back was to go west along the coast, to round Icy Cape, and meet Beechey in H.M.S. *Blossom* at Kotzebue Inlet. If detained by ice, land, or unforeseen contingencies, he was under no circumstances, unless he could stay safely with Eskimos, to winter on the coast but to return to his base.

Franklin had no intention of leaving any chance that the hardships and difficulties due to inexperience, poor planning, and the unreliability of local people would be endured again. Consequently he made his preparations with elaborate care. Three lightweight boats, stronger and more suitable for salt-water work than canoes, were especially built at Woolwich Yard under the watchful eye of Franklin's old commander, Captain David Buchan. They were sent to York Factory on a Hudson's Bay Company ship together with supplies, carpenters, and men to set up depots along the expedition route. Additional stores were sent on three big north canoes, in March 1824, by way of New York to the Hudson's Bay Company at Athabasca Lake. In the spring of 1825 an amply stocked base was set up at Great Bear Lake to receive the expedition.

Landing in New York 15 March 1825, Franklin and his party enjoyed the hospitality of the city for eight days. Beginning their journey on the Hudson River boat *Olive Branch*, they traveled mostly by water across the lakes and rivers of central North America to their destination. Franklin selected the site of an old North-West Company post on Great Bear Lake for his winter quarters. Leaving Back in charge of construction, and sending Richardson to explore the northern shore of Great Bear Lake for a rendezvous point, Franklin made a preliminary run down the Mackenzie River to the sea. At Fort Franklin, as the base was called, a fourth boat, similar to those built at Woolwich, was constructed. Winter began to break up by mid-March and by 1 June preparations for leaving the fort were nearly completed. The ice went out of Bear Lake River 21 June and the explorers followed it. Franklin with Back, thirteen men, two Canadian *voyageurs,* and an Indian were in the two twenty-six foot boats named *Lion* and *Reliance,* while Richardson and Kendall with nine men and an Indian took the two twenty-four footers christened *Dolphin* and *Union.* New sky-blue, waterproof uniforms and a drink of rum were issued to each man, and after religious services the boats shoved off.

Franklin and Richardson separated at the estuary 3 July. Richardson moved steadily eastward along the coast, successively discovering (and naming) Liverpool Bay, Cape Bathurst, Franklin Bay, Cape Parry, Darnley Bay, and Cape Lyon. Sighting part of Victoria Island to the northward, he named it Wollaston Land, and the channel between it and the mainland he called Dolphin and Union Strait. Arriving at Coronation Gulf he was in familiar territory. He ascended the Coppermine and crossed over to the selected rendezvous on Dease Arm of Great Bear Lake, 18 August. The party from the fort arrived on the twenty-fourth and Richardson was back at Fort Franklin, 1 September, having explored 800 miles of coastline between the two river mouths.

Westerly, Franklin ran into more difficulty. The Eskimos were more hostile, the ice heavier, the weather tempestuous. His slow progress netted some 374 miles to 148° 42′ W., at a point he named Return Cape. From here he could see another headland which he named Beechey Point. It was a shallow, ice-bound coast unrelieved by harbors. Turning back in mid-August, he retraced his steps along the Arctic shore and up the river where the party again wintered at Fort Franklin. Late in February they started their return journey. Franklin arrived in Liverpool 26 September 1827, and Captain Back landed at Portsmouth two weeks later.[10]

While Franklin was performing his tasks, Captain Frederick Beechey was rounding Cape Horn and approaching Bering Strait by a leisurely cruise through the Pacific islands. Beechey had sailed from Spithead in the sloop-of-war *Blossom,* 19 May 1825, with orders to wait for Franklin and Parry at Bering Strait, but not later than 10 July 1826. If they did not show up he was to winter at a convenient, more southerly place and return to Bering Strait by 1 August 1827. Beechey passed through Bering Strait and entered Kotzebue Sound on 22 July. He continued on and took *Blossom* to Icy Cape from where he dispatched his mate, Mr. Elson, in his tender, a small schooner carried on deck. Elson pushed on another four days and arrived at Point Barrow on 23 August.[11] Thus Beechey's party and Franklin's approached within 160 miles of each other. Most of the northern mainland coast of North America was now delineated. The gap between Beechey and Franklin and the long, important stretch from Point Turnagain to Fury and Hecla Strait were the only unknown parts. Franklin, Richardson, and Beechey had explored over 1200 miles of coastline.

Franklin now believed a Passage voyage was perfectly feasible, but the Admiralty, discouraged by the loss of *Fury* and the failure of Parry's polar expedition, was not interested in further exploration. The next important expedition was a privately financed enterprise.

22

Boothia Felix

For ten years John Ross must wait, discredited, while the younger man Parry was supported most generously by the Admiralty on expedition after expedition. Feeling the criticism that he had received was unjustified, and encouraged by his many influential friends, Ross was eager to prove his competence in commanding another and more successful expedition. Therefore, he studied the accounts of all the expeditions as they appeared and bided his time. Upon Parry's retirement from exploration for the Passage, Ross submitted to the Admiralty a plan to explore for a Passage through Prince Regent Inlet from the point where Parry had stopped to Franklin's Point Turnagain. He recommended the use of a steam vessel. A steamship drew less water, an advantage in ice and along uncharted shores, and was not dependent on a fair, fresh breeze to force her way through loose ice.

The Admiralty not only rejected the proposal but implied it would reject all similar schemes. Barrow, to whom Ross was now an anathema, would, if he could, certainly have foiled any plans of that officer's. Ross thereupon sought private backing and approached his old friend Felix Booth, head of the Booth Distilleries. The wealthy man was sympathetic but oversensitive, for he declined because he did not wish to be criticized for seeking the £20,000 reward. Ross, his determination unshaken, approached the Admiralty again in 1828 and received the same negative answer. For some three months another London merchant considered — and then turned down — Ross's proposal that he put up the money in return for the salvage of the abandoned stores from *Fury* which lay perfectly preserved on an Arctic beach. When shortly afterward the Government repealed the act which offered the rewards, Booth had no further scruples and liberally financed the expedition.[1]

Ross's first job was to buy a vessel with auxiliary steam power. Like Scoresby, he believed that Parry's ships were too large for efficient exploration. They had required large crews and consequently enormous amounts of stores and fuel, and perhaps more important the eighteen feet of water they drew prevented them from approaching shelving shores and investigating small channels. Ross therefore purchased the small side-wheeler *Victory,* once a packet between Liverpool and the Isle of Man. Ross increased her capacity from 85 to 150 tons by raising her sides five and one-half feet, and engaged the engineering firm of Braithwaite and Erickson to make and install patent high-pressure engines. The smokestack was eliminated by keeping the fires going with a bellows to provide the draft, and the paddle wheels were so constructed that in a minute they could be lifted clear of the water to avoid ice.

The ship was provisioned and fueled for a thousand days. Ross intended to supplement his stores by fishing and from the *Fury* cache. The whaler *John* was chartered to transport stores as far as Prince Regent Inlet and to bring back part of the *Fury* stores for salvage. The Admiralty, most co-operative as long as it did not have to put up any money, provided the sixteen-ton decked vessel *Krusenstern* and lent two of the boats used by John Franklin. It also allowed leaves of absence to two experienced men, and lent instruments and books that had been used on former expeditions. As soon as plans were announced many experienced men, including Captains Henry Hoppner and George Back, volunteered.* Ross had already made his choice, however, and selected his nephew James Clark Ross, veteran of five Arctic expeditions, as his second in command. Another old shipmate William Thom, purser on *Isabella* in 1818, was engaged for the same position on *Victory*. There were besides a surgeon, three mates, a carpenter, two engineers, and fourteen others — in all twenty-four men.

Ross and his companions left Woolwich 23 May 1829. They hove up their paddles, set sails, and discharged the pilot. Almost as soon as they put to sea the machinery began to give trouble. The boilers leaked, using up precious fresh water; the engine room was so hot that the men could hardly work there. They stopped the engine and proceeded under sail. The vessel herself required constant use of two pumps. The engine was again used briefly in the Irish Sea, and then broke down and took two days for repairs. Even when the power worked properly

---

* Besides the applications from experienced Naval men, Ross received the usual assortment of gratuitous applications and letters from numerous crackpots, cranks, and eager adolescents that are always heard from when planning an expedition. Among them was one from a thirty-eight-year-old Gosport cook who wrote that a person appeared to him in a dream and said, 'Go with Captain Ross, he will be crowned with *success*.' Ross needed a cook and as the man had credentials from H.M.S. *Victory,* he wrote him to apply in person. On the appointed day the cook did not appear. In his place Ross received a letter: [2]

April 9, 1829

Sir,

I have just found out that my husband has made an engagement with you to join your expedition, through a dream, *without consulting me;* I must beg to tell you, sir, that he shall not go — I will not let him have his clothes. He must be mad ever to think of leaving a comfortable home, to be frozen in with ice, or torn to pieces with bears; therefore, I am determined he shall not leave Gosport, so I hope you will not expect him.

Yours, Sir, &c., and so forth,
Mary L.

it was inadequate; the ship could make only three miles an hour. Nursing the engine along, one of the stokers got his arm so badly mutilated that Ross had to amputate it. Nine miles off Port Logan, 8 June, the teeth on a flywheel let go. There was a crash, boiler joints gave way, the water put out the fire and flowed from the furnace door, and the engine stopped.

Another day had dawned before they tied up in Port Logan. Mr. Thom with the chartered *John* was in nearby Loch Ryan with trouble on his hands. The ship was in slovenly condition and her officers and crew refused to sail unless a written agreement guaranteed them the same amount of money they would receive if they brought home a full cargo of whale oil. Repeated attempts to persuade them to sail ended in a mutiny of thirty-eight men, leaving only eleven including the master to work the ship. All thought of taking the whaler was abandoned. Ross writes that afterwards these men reaped a weird sort of justice for their disgraceful conduct:

> It was but in the following year, that the *John,* under the same master and officers, and with the same crew, barring one or two exceptions, sailed to Baffin's bay on a whaling expedition. From causes which have never come to light, a mutiny took place on board, attended by the death of the master, Coombe, but under circumstances which have not yet been rightly explained, as far as I can understand. The mate, with a boat's crew, were expelled at the same time; and having never since been heard of, are supposed to have perished in the ice. The ship, then put under the command of the Spikesoneer, was afterwards lost on the western coast, when most of the crew were drowned; the remainder being saved by a whaler which was accidentally passing.

After transferring as much of the stores from *John* as possible and shipping three new volunteers, Ross got to sea, 13 June, with *Krusenstern* in tow. Three days later *Victory* lost her foretopmast in a gale and Ross entertained thoughts of putting into Lough Swilly for repairs, but when a fresh breeze came up he decided to continue the voyage. During the ocean crossing the engine and boilers were put into the best possible repair for emergency use. Cape Farewell was sighted 2 July. Ross worked up the Greenland coast to Holsteinsborg, where he purchased stores from the wrecked whaler *Rockwood* (formerly the sloop-of-war *Rattler*) and obtained her mizzenmast as a new foremast for *Victory*. Disko Island was passed 28 July. Ross crossed Baffin Bay, which was free of ice, and saw towering Cape Byam Martin burst out of the clouds on 6 August. This was the second of two mild summers.

Entering Lancaster Sound, Ross reached the spot where he had turned back on his first voyage. Reviewing that moment and recalling again all of the subsequent controversy that had raged around his decision, he wrote:

> I can here, on the very spot itself, where every recollection seems but that of yesterday, reassert with the most perfect confidence, that no officer then expressed any belief that there was a passage through this opening, or even suggested a hint to that effect. So far from this, I was led to infer, by the general remarks on board my own ship, and by the expressions of those who considered that they had more especially a right to be consulted, that I had according to their opinions, already proceeded, not merely far enough, but too far.[3]

Through Lancaster Sound and into Prince Regent Inlet little ice was seen. They tried to use the engine but gave it up. If it had been possible for a machine to run on curses that engine would have, for its cussedness and the antecedents of its builders strained the vocabularies of the explorers. In spite of the engine good time was made under sail through the open channels. By 12 August the place where *Fury* was wrecked was sighted; tent poles were still standing but the ship had vanished. On the beach were stores in abundance; *Victory* was stocked with canned goods, flour, cocoa, sugar, and such canvas, spars, and gear as was needed. 'Yet all that we could possibly stow away seemed scarcely to diminish the piles of canisters, of which we embarked whatever we could . . . all that we took being in excellent condition.' Bringing their provisions up to a supply adequate for two years and three months, Ross again headed south.

Passing Cape Garry, the southernmost point reached by Parry, he also passed without recognizing it the entrance of Bellot Strait, which marks the northernmost point of continental North America. He then landed, thirty miles south of Cape Garry, taking possession of the land and naming it Boothia Felix. The unusual mildness for that season continued and enabled Ross to keep on exploring during September. The gradually increasing ice and cold eventually made it obvious he must prepare for the coming winter. By this time he reckoned that he was not more than 280 miles from Point Turnagain. The worthless engine was left ashore to make more room.

On 8 October they were in Felix Harbor, Lord Mayor Bay, near the narrow neck of the Boothia Peninsula. Writing on various aspects of life in the Arctic while preparing for the winter, Ross makes the interesting remark that

> It would be very desirable indeed if the men could acquire the taste for Greenland food; since all experience has shown that the large use of oil and fat meats is the true secret of life in these frozen countries, and that the natives cannot subsist without it; becoming diseased, and dying under a more meagre diet.

a point proved and emphasized by Vilhjalmur Stefansson in recent years.

The roofing of the ship was completed 26 October and she was insulated by treading down two and a half feet of snow on the upper deck, which turned to a solid mass of ice, and then covering it with sand. The ship's sides were banked with snow to meet the housing. Ross rigged an ingenious heating system which eliminated the debilitating moisture, with the result that the men spent a warm, dry, healthful winter.

Shortly after the New Year 1830, Eskimos arrived at their winter village nearby. Throughout the long winter night they proved good neighbors. Their knowledge of the surrounding country was good, and they drew maps, which turned out to be quite accurate, showing that Prince Regent Inlet terminated in a bay. The Eskimos also told Ross of the passage to the north through Bellot Strait, which severs Somerset Island from Boothia. Since he had not seen it Ross assumed they were talking about Barrow Strait.

With Eskimo guides James C. Ross made a series of important land explorations during April, May, and June. He found that Boothia Felix was a peninsula connected to the mainland by a narrow isthmus dotted with lakes. He ascertained that there was a considerable difference in the elevation of the sea on the eastern and western sides of the isthmus. In further exploration he crossed over what is now James Ross Strait to Matty Island, skirted its northern shore, and crossed again to King William Island, which he thought was an extension of Boothia and therefore part of the mainland. He followed the coast of King William Island to its most northerly extremity, which he named Cape Felix. Seeing the frozen ocean before him and the shore trending southwesterly, he followed it to Victory Point and could see another point, Cape Franklin, in the distance beyond. From here he speculated that, as the coast was running southwesterly, it must continue to Point Turnagain.

The summer passed and it was not until 17 September that they were able to get under sail. But, when ice blocked the way out of Lord Mayor Bay, they knew they were in for another winter. In April the land explorations began once more. J. C. Ross (the nephew) now decided to try to locate the North Magnetic Pole, which they knew from the behavior of their instruments must be near them. Slogging up the western shore of Boothia he reached, 1 June 1831, a point where his dipping needle registered 89° 59′, within one minute of the vertical, and where all his horizontal needles were inert. This spot, close enough for all practical purposes, was in 70° 5′ 17″ latitude by 96° 46′ 4″ W. longitude and was the first recorded location of that constantly changing point.

The summer of 1831 produced little change in their icy prison. *Victory* was not clear until late August and could then be moved only a few miles. After two winters of isolation and monotony the prospect of another was almost intolerable. Ross wrote:

> We were weary for want of occupation, for want of variety, for want of the means of mental exertion, for want of thought, and (why should I not say it?) for want of society. Today was as yesterday, and as was to-day, so would be to-morrow: while if there was no variety, as no hope of better, is it wonderful that even the visits of barbarians were welcome, or can any thing more strongly show the nature of our pleasures, than the confession that these were delightful; even as the society of London might be amid the business of London?

Prepared for winter by mid-October, 'a lane of clear water was again seen to the northward, but this had now become a matter of indifference.' Scurvy made its first dreaded appearance during this third winter, but the disease was brought under control by Ross's sensible use of fresh meat — in sharp contrast to their fellow naval officer explorers he and his nephew were constantly hunting, fishing, and buying fresh supplies from the Eskimos.

In April 1832, Ross decided to abandon his ship and attempt to move his supplies and boats northward on sledges to Fury Beach, and sail out to Baffin Bay in time to be picked up by a homeward bound whaler. He divided his crew into working parties and supplies were moved from the ship. *Victory* was abandoned 29 May. Pulling the supplies and boats on sledges was tortuous and exhausting labor. The boats were ultimately abandoned, for hauling them was beyond the men's strength. Fury Beach was reached 1 July and here they built themselves a dwelling called Somerset House. Luckily three of *Fury*'s boats were found intact and the carpenter set to work strengthening them. Leaving the beach exactly one month later, they fought gales and ice all the way to Barrow Strait which was reached in late September, only to find the pack there solid; they could not get out. It was agreed there was no hope of reaching open water before the last of the whalers was gone. Ross abandoned his great collection of minerals (which were picked up by Captain Humphreys of *Isabella* two years later), having concluded that their only chance for survival was to return to Fury Beach where supplies and shelter were sufficient to carry them through. After experiencing another severe journey they were forced by ice to leave their boats a few miles north of Fury Beach, where they could be found next year, and continue on foot to Somerset House, where they arrived 7 October 1832. No sooner had they arrived than a severe cold and a driving tempest kept them under cover for days. When the storm cleared, they prepared the house for winter by building a snow wall around it four feet thick, and by strengthening the roof and covering it with snow. Two stoves were set up and with the remaining *Fury* provisions they were once more snug.

Ross reflects upon the curious series of circumstances, each considered a disaster at the time, without any one of which they could not have survived this fourth winter.

First, I may enumerate the loss of the *Fury*, by which accident the stores and provisions were left: next, the mutiny of the *John*'s crew, for if that ship had come with us, we intended to have cleared Fury beach: thirdly, the engine boilers, without which, we might have got so far that we could not have returned: fourthly, the *Fury*'s boats, after having been carried off in the storms of the winter; having been cast on shore near the

same place, without any material damage: and lastly, the construction of a habitation in summer, to which we were now
mercifully permitted to return.

Scurvy carried off the carpenter during the winter and others
developed symptoms of the disease. Laboriously moving supplies they arrived, 24 May, at the place where the boats were
left and dug them out of the snow. Having transported to the
boats everything needed for a voyage, they returned to Somerset
House 1 June and waited for the ice to begin moving. In July
they moved to the boats, carrying three sick men the entire way.
Here they camped for weeks until a lane of water appeared
leading northward. Launching the three boats they embarked
15 August. Two days later they had worked eastward nearly
to Cape York and by the twenty-fifth crossed Navy Board Inlet.
At four that morning a sail was sighted in the distance. Unluck-
ily a breeze sprang up and the ship moved off to the southeast.
At ten o'clock another sail was seen. She too started to sail off
but the wind dropped and as they came up on her she lowered
a boat to meet them. As the mate of the ship came alongside,
Ross inquired the name of the vessel and received the answer,
'the *Isabella* of Hull, once commanded by Captain Ross.' On
telling the astonished mate that he was that very man, the mate
assured Ross that he had been dead for two years.

> I easily convinced him, however [says Ross], that what ought
> to have been true, according to his estimate, was a somewhat
> premature conclusion; as the bear-like form of the whole set
> of us might have shown him, had he taken time to consider,
> that we were certainly not whaling gentlemen, and that we car-
> ried tolerable evidence of our being 'true men, and no imposters,'
> on our backs, and in our starved and unshaven countenances.

Isabella was now commanded by Captain John Humphreys,
who welcomed the explorers aboard and made them comfortable for 'never was seen a more miserable-looking set of

wretches; while, that we were but a repulsive-looking people none of us could doubt.' Ross continues:

> Unshaven since I know not when, dirty, dressed in the rags of wild beasts instead of the tatters of civilization, and starved to the very bones, our gaunt and grim looks, when contrasted with those of the well-dressed and well-fed men around us, made us all feel, I believe for the first time, what we really were, as well as what we seemed to others.

And thus, by one of those ironic pranks of fate, Ross returned from his second voyage on board the same ship that had brought him home from his first.

News of the explorers' rescue preceded them. Long given up for lost, when they reached Hull they were greeted as if they had risen from the dead. After enjoying the freedom of the town they embarked for London, where Ross reported to the Admiralty on 19 October and the next day was presented to William IV. Although the Admiralty was under no obligation to do so, it assumed the payment of the men — double time up until *Victory* was abandoned and regular pay from then until they arrived home. Excepting one man who was not recommended, all that wished were given naval positions and promotions. J. C. Ross was soon promoted to Captain. John Ross himself was at last given credit for his notable achievements and he was voted £5000, which more than reimbursed him for his expenses. In 1834 John Ross was knighted, and in 1851 he was made a Rear Admiral. Only John Barrow now refused to give Ross any credit; in his book published thirteen years after Ross's return his sarcastic remarks on the expedition are most unworthy.[4] Actually the results of the expedition were notable. The Rosses had discovered King William Island, the peninsula of Boothia Felix, the Gulf of Boothia, and the North Magnetic Pole. They had made creditable surveys of hundreds of miles of previously unknown coast and proved that Prince Regent

Inlet was a dead end. They brought back the greatest continuous series of scientific observations compiled until present times, recognized a diet for Arctic living that enabled them to survive four successive winters — a record not equalled until the twentieth century. Ross's feat of maintaining discipline, his men's health, and extricating them with the loss of only three lives was magnificent.

By the third winter Ross's protracted absence had become a subject of general discussion, speculation, and public concern. Traders had heard no reports from Indians or Eskimos; whalers had seen no one. The silence surrounding the expedition was unbroken. Captain George Back, veteran Arctic explorer and companion of Sir John Franklin on his two overland and coastal journeys, heard a rumor in Italy that Ross's expedition had perished. Finding no basis for it, he hastened back to England to volunteer to lead a search party. He found that a similar offer made to the Government by his friend and former companion, Dr. John Richardson, had not been accepted. He then learned that following Richardson's plan George Ross, brother of Captain John and father of J. C. Ross, was seeking a qualified officer to lead a party overland to search for his relatives.

As soon as George Ross had signed up Back, he petitioned the King to sanction an expedition to rescue or at least to ascertain the fate of his brother and son. Not only was the petition granted, but the Treasury provided £2000 toward expenses, on condition that Captain Back was to lead the expedition. The Hudson's Bay Company offered to furnish all supplies and canoes free of charge, and the remaining necessary funds were raised by private contributions. The Hudson's Bay Company gave Back a Company commission, and the Admiralty issued an official instruction that gave him strong authority for obtaining assistance in Canada. Accompanied by Richard King, who was engaged as doctor and naturalist, Back left England

17 February 1833. His orders were to set up a base at Great Slave Lake and to descend little-known Great Fish River to the Arctic Ocean, and then to follow the coast to the wreck of *Fury* where it was correctly supposed Ross might be camped. If after two seasons he failed to find any sign of the Ross party he was to endeavor to survey the coast from the mouth of the Great Fish River to Point Turnagain.

He reached Great Slave Lake during the summer and while his men established Fort Reliance as a winter base he successfully located the Great Fish River. While wintering at Fort Reliance, Back received a letter from England by special Hudson's Bay Company messenger* informing him of Ross's safe arrival in England but, since all was ready for a trip, he decided to follow the Great Fish River to its mouth and proceed with the coastal exploring. The Great Fish is a burly, turbulent, twisting stream with innumerable falls and rapids, a stream which at times loses itself in large lakes. Back successfully mapped the river (now named for him) and Montreal Island at its mouth in 1834, but he was prevented by boggy ground from following the coast to Point Turnagain. There was open water to the eastward and Richard King strongly criticized him for not exploring in that direction. Back, lacking imagination on this occasion, considered that his orders forbade him to do so.[5]

Shortly after Back's return the Royal Geographical Society proposed that he command an expedition to fill in the mostly unknown coastline between Fury and Hecla Strait and Point Turnagain. The plans for this attempt were similar to those given Captain George Lyon in 1824. Back, in command of H.M.S. *Terror,* was ordered, in May 1835, to proceed either to the Wager River or to Repulse Bay. He was to cross what is now

* When Ross arrived in England an official letter to Back was written in London, 22 October 1833. The message traveled with remarkable speed for the times. When the letter arrived in Canada it was sent by special Hudson's Bay Company courier through the wilderness to Back who received it 25 April 1834.

known as the Rae Isthmus of the Melville Peninsula and, turning north, follow its shore to the western end of Fury and Hecla Strait. A second objective was to explore, from wherever he reached the coast on Prince Regent Inlet, westerly to the mouth of the Back River and beyond that to Franklin's Point Turnagain. Back firmly believed, in spite of the Ross reports, that Boothia was an island. If there was sufficient time he was also to link his surveys with those of Captain Ross. Although the plan was ambitious for one season, every attempt was to be made to return to England in the fall.

The sturdy bomb vessel was strengthened and outfitted in the usual manner. After a tedious passage of Hudson Strait in August, Back headed north of Southampton Island for Frozen Strait — the same course Parry had taken in 1821. He was not so fortunate in his season, for it was one of extraordinary severity. On 28 August he was beset in Foxe Channel with Winter Island in sight from the crow's nest. The last day of the month, wedged in masses of ice, a driving snowstorm notified him that an early winter had set in.

Captain Back never reached Repulse Bay to undertake the planned land journey. Not only could no headway be made through the ice, but *Terror* was firmly frozen in. The pressure kept increasing, placing an enormous strain on the ship. The Greenland pilots were astonished that any vessel could survive under such pressure. The ship's reinforcing was good, but nevertheless she was badly damaged. Her sternpost was broken and deadwood planking torn loose. Wrenched, twisted, seams open, and timbers cracked, she was bulled about by the Arctic for ten months. During that time she was lifted entirely out of water and rested on an ice floe where she stayed for four months, going wherever it drifted. On one occasion Back prepared to abandon ship as there were indications she might be released from the ice and grave doubt that the vessel would float.

The men had all they could do to stay alive and keep the

ship in repair. Back, from the Rosses' experience, had learned the value of fresh game as a preventive for scurvy. On one happy occasion, 'thirty loons, which being first skinned, and allowed to steep for two days in salt and water, were then dressed like jugged hare and with red wine sauce and currant jelly, were esteemed by us as nearly equal in flavour.' High in his floating prison aboard *Terror*, Back wrote:

> It is not a little remarkable to reflect on the various ineffectual attempts that have been made by different commanders in modern days, to fill up the small blank on the northern charts, between the bottom or south part of Regent's Inlet and Point Turnagain. Parry's and Franklin's achievements are too well known to require observation or eulogium from me; yet the former could not penetrate through Fury and Hecla Strait, and the latter found it impracticable . . . to proceed beyond Point Turnagain. Of Sir John Ross's eventful expedition all have heard. My own, in search of him, is also before the public. Captain Lyon, in trying to reach Repulse Bay by the Welcome, was baffled by a succession of bad weather and heavy gales; and now again, I, acting upon the united experience of most of the distinguished names just mentioned, under circumstances considered favourable, after getting nearly within sight of my port, am stopped by drift ice, at what is generally the very best period for navigating the Polar Seas — am frozen fast, in October 1836, at the entrance of Frozen Strait — and now, June 16th, am carried into Hudson's Strait, on some of the very same ice that originally begirt the ship, without having had it once in my power either to advance or retreat. In short, from north, south, east, and west, the attempt has been made, and in all equally without effect; and yet, with a tolerably open season, the whole affair is within the accomplishment of six months.[6]

The alarming damage to the sternpost created a serious problem:

> . . . there were reasons for apprehending an insuperable difficulty in shipping the rudder; and, indeed, if, as was conjectured,

the split stern-post projected three or four feet at right angles to
the keel, to say nothing of the doubling forced up, it seemed
evident, that even if the old rudder could by any management
be fixed in its place, it would serve only for an additional purchase to weaken the already broken parts thereabouts. To provide against a contingency so serious as well as probable, it
was requisite to devise a rudder of an entirely different construction, yet so contrived as to lose little of its power, and such
a one was ingeniously hit upon by Lieutenant Smyth. It was
effected by the simple operation of transposing the wood, forming the lower part or heel of the rudder, to that forming the
upper part, thus giving to it when finished an oblong form,
not much unlike that used by a Thames barge rigged with
sails, and at the same time the desirable property that it could
be hung on the strongest part of the stern-post.

To prevent the sternpost from falling off, and to secure the
deadwood planking, the chain of the stream anchor was passed
under its heel, through two ringbolts three feet from but level
with the eleven foot mark, and secured firmly on the deck.
When the ship was eventually released from the ice 'the bolts
wept.' Both pumps were going constantly.

As they passed Resolution Island and got out into the heavy
swells of the Atlantic, the ship was working so that it was necessary to further frap her together by passing anchor chains under
her bottom, heaving them tight by the capstan, and fastening
them to ring bolts in the deck. The heavy swell started the bolts
and the constant pitching, rolling, and straining of the ship
loosened the entire stern frame, but the weather luckily remained
favorable. Lower and lower she settled in the water, each hour
more heavy and sodden, more waterlogged.

On we struggled, crazy and waterlogged . . . and on Sept.
3d, crowding every stitch of canvas, we descried a sail in the
distance, the first we had yet seen. Under ordinary circumstances a signal would have been made to attract her attention,
but time was too precious with us now that we were pressing

forward for our lives; and about two o'clock in the afternoon, within half an hour of our calculation, the joyful sound of land was announced from the look-out man at the masthead.

As he raised the Irish coast it became obvious the ship was not going to float much longer. Running into Lough Swilly and anchoring briefly, he ran *Terror* ashore on a sandy beach. Back stayed by his ship while a party of shipwrights sent over from Chatham repaired her sufficiently for him to put to sea again in late October and bring her first to Devonport and then to Chatham where she was taken into drydock.

The problem of filling the gaps in the Arctic coastline of the continent was completed not by expensive Government expeditions, but by the Hudson's Bay Company's personnel. It will be remembered that that venerable Company had been strongly criticized and investigated in the mid-eighteenth century for its evident lack of interest in exploring for a Northwest Passage. As its charter was coming up for renewal, and it perhaps feared that the criticism might be repeated, it redeemed its reputation. Also, the Company was now apparently interested in mapping the wilderness. Without its assistance Franklin, Richardson, and Back would have been unable to explore the rivers and the sections of the coast now known. The results were even better when the Company used its own experienced woodsmen. For example, in 1836, the year of Back's experience with the ice of Foxe Channel, the Hudson's Bay Company sent out two of its officers — Chief Factor Peter Warren Dease, who had assisted Sir John Franklin, and Thomas Simpson, a young Scot — with instructions to set up advanced winter quarters, to descend the Mackenzie, and to trace the coast westward to Point Barrow where Captain Beechey's boat had put back. They were then to return and follow the coast from Franklin's Point Turnagain eastward to Back's Great Fish River.

The first part of this plan was accomplished in the summer

of 1837. Descending the Mackenzie in two boats called *Castor* and *Pollux,* Dease and Simpson reached Return Reef, where Franklin had been forced to turn back, by the end of July. They then continued, under the usual climatic difficulties of that region, until, about one in the morning of 4 August, Simpson, who had gone on, leaving Dease with the boats, saw 'with indescribable emotions, *Point Barrow,* stretching out to northward.'

The party returned to winter quarters on Great Bear Lake and the following summer descended the Coppermine and followed the coast beyond Point Turnagain. Simpson, in a foot journey beyond the boats, sighted and named Victoria Island across Dease Strait. Returning to Fort Confidence on Great Bear they spent another winter. Again in 1839, descending the Coppermine where the ice had much retreated from the previous year, Simpson sailed past Point Turnagain. Favored by good weather, he entered on 10 August the channel now called Simpson Strait, which separated King William Island from the mainland and, continuing on, found the cache left by Back on Montreal Island in the estuary of his river. Another great stretch of coast was charted.[7]

Simpson, whose extraordinary energy was mainly responsible for the successful accomplishments, hoped to be authorized to conduct one final expedition the following year to complete the last section of unknown coast from Back River to Fury and Hecla Strait. Like Back, he believed there was a strait separating Boothia from the mainland. Impatient for an answer to his proposal to the Company, he walked 1910 miles in sixty-one days in mid-winter to the Red River settlement, where he arrived 2 February 1840. No letter arrived and on 6 June Simpson left Red River intending to go to England by way of the United States to plead his cause. Dashing on ahead of his main party, accompanied by four halfbreeds, his records show that by 11 June they had made forty-seven miles as the crow flies. No one knows what happened from then until the afternoon of 13 or 14

June, when he shot two of his companions. The other two fled back to the main party and returned with them the next morning. Simpson was dead or had been killed by that time.*

Simpson's tragic death halted the Company coast survey, but in 1846 and 1847, while Franklin was on his last expedition, John Rae, another able Company man, filled in the last gap of shoreline. Living off the land, he crossed over Rae Isthmus from Repulse Bay to Committee Bay in the southern extremity of Prince Regent Inlet and surveyed from Lord Mayor Bay at Boothia peninsula — whose islands were named by Ross in a manner reminiscent of Luke Foxe: the 'Sons of the Clergy of the Church of Scotland' — to within ten miles of Fury and Hecla Strait.[9]

Thus the entire northern coast of the North American continent, from Point Barrow to Fury and Hecla Strait, with the exception of the Boothia peninsula, was discovered and surveyed by parties traveling with sledges and in small boats or canoes, and not by the far more experienced and elaborate naval expeditions.

---

* No one knows what happened.[8] Did he kill his companions in self-defense and was then killed in turn by their friends? Or did he, as his companions maintained, go crazy, breaking at last under the strain of his superhuman exertions, kill them in a frenzy, and then commit suicide?

23

The Passage Discovered

Five degrees of latitude separated the two known passages. Through Lancaster Sound and Barrow Strait from the east, Parry had carried the northernmost one beyond 110° W., to Melville Island. Through Bering Strait from the west, Beechey, Franklin, Richardson, Dease, and Simpson found a passage along the mainland as far as Back River — this more southerly waterway running parallel for about fifteen degrees with that to the north. Parry thought he had found the eastern end of the southernmost passage by his discovery of Fury and Hecla Strait, but the ice conditions in that region made it impractical for navigation. Ross showed Prince Regent Inlet a dead end. Both Back and Simpson doubted this and believed the coast continued easterly beyond Back River through a strait separating Boothia from the mainland. Rae proved Ross correct, but not before the last and most elaborate of the British expeditions seeking the Northwest Passage had left. It remained to establish a navigable connection between the northern and southern parallel waterways. Authorities were generally agreed that the eastern entrance must be through Lancaster Sound westerly along Barrow Strait, and the western exit through Bering Strait. From Barrow Strait due west through Melville Sound and McClure Strait lay the most direct passage — and the most impractical, as the ice forced into the funnel of McClure Strait from the Arctic Ocean was immensely thick. Most authorities reasoned that ships might instead proceed southwestward beyond Cape Walker and so from the south of Banks Island enter the channel known to run along the continent. As neither Parry nor the explorers on the mainland realized the vast extent of Banks Island and Victoria Island, it was hoped that in this region would lie open sea or, at worst, small islands separated by navigable channels. Parry had seen only frozen sea south of Cape Walker, the northernmost point on Russell Island off the shore of Prince of Wales Island. Owing to the ice conditions, Fury and Hecla Strait was ruled out as the entrance to the Northwest Passage.

With such solid speculations current, popular interest in further exploration was great. In 1844 Sir John Barrow, backed by Sir Edward Parry, Sir John Franklin, Sir James Clark Ross, and other experienced and eminent men, urged the Admiralty to undertake another expedition. Barrow also appealed to the national honor to forestall some other country from making the discovery. The Royal Society added its strong approval, pointing out that magnetic observations in hitherto unexplored regions would be important even if a Passage were not discovered.[1] A leading authority on terrestrial magnetism, Colonel Edward Sabine, submitted a written report supporting this view.

Faced with the insistence of distinguished authority and popular clamor the Prime Minister, Sir Robert Peel, gave his consent for another Government expedition. Haddington, First Lord of the Admiralty, had some misgivings about the potential usefulness of the Northwest Passage and others had doubts about the expedition. That blunt old Scot, Sir John Ross, flatly stated the ships would never return. Back's companion and severe

critic, Dr. Richard King, did not hesitate to send Sir John Barrow a contrary opinion.

> Had you advocated in favour of the Polar Land Journeys with
> a tithe of the zeal you have the Polar Sea Expeditions the North-
> West Passage would have long since ceased to be a problem,
> and, instead of a Baronetcy you would deserve a Peerage, for
> the country would have been saved at least two hundred thou-
> sand pounds. . . . If you are really in earnest upon this sub-
> ject, you have but one course to pursue; search for the truth,
> and value it when you find it. Another fruitless Polar Sea Ex-
> pedition, and fruitless it will assuredly be, if not well digested,
> will be a lasting blot in the annals of our voyages of discovery.[2]

King had much more to say on the subject in the same tone.
Barrow, furious that any one should have the temerity to write
him in this insolent manner, dismissed King's objections as
those of a crank, and the Admiralty's decision allowed Sir John
Barrow, who had served as Second Secretary of the Admiralty
since 1804, to retire happy.

Barrow had intended that Captain James Fitzjames, a thirty-
three-year-old officer who had served with distinction in the
Far East, should command the expedition. The Admiralty, for-
getting that Parry had made his greatest voyage at twenty-
eight, turned him down as too young and offered the post to
Sir James Ross who, at forty-five, refused because he was too
old. Then Sir John Franklin, fifty-nine years old, volunteered
and, after some good-natured discussion about his age, was accepted.*

---

* Why did Sir John Franklin volunteer for this arduous service at this time
and at his age? To the fact that he was a brave and adventurous officer his
career attests. As a young man he accompanied Matthew Flinders on his
voyage charting the Australian coast. He served at the battles of Copenhagen
and Trafalgar, and was wounded at the battle of New Orleans. We have
already followed his career as a lieutenant in command of *Trent* under David
Buchan in 1818, and in command of two overland and boat expeditions to
and along the Arctic Ocean. At this time he had recently been recalled after

The bombs *Erebus* and *Terror,* which had served Sir James Ross during his four years of Antarctic exploration, were put in condition and, at Parry's suggestion, locomotive engines turning screws were installed as auxiliary power. The slightly larger, 370-ton *Erebus* was chosen as flagship, and *Terror* was placed under Captain Francis R. M. Crozier as second in command. Crozier had commanded the same ship on Ross's Antarctic expedition and had served on Parry's last three voyages. Commander Fitzjames, third in the chain of command and making his first Arctic voyage, was Franklin's executive officer. Five other officers had previous Arctic experience, and the seamen were chosen with similar care. Supplies for three years were provided.

Franklin's instructions were to proceed through Lancaster Sound and Barrow Strait and, after passing Cape Walker, to sail southward and westward in as direct a course toward Bering Strait as the ice and land masses would allow. If he found his way blocked at Cape Walker he was authorized to proceed north through Wellington Channel and endeavor to get around the north of Parry Islands into the open ocean and on to his destination, Bering Strait. James Ross and Franklin himself both thought there actually might be a better chance of success this way than southward and westward. It should here be noted that Parry, returning from his first voyage along the southern side of Barrow Strait, suspected there might be a channel opening to the south before reaching Cape Walker. The state of the ice had prevented him from investigating it, but he had noted

---

completing seven years as Governor of Tasmania, the last part marred by minor intrigues and petty quarrels. He easily could have rested on his laurels, but the completion of the survey of the northern coast of America and the discovery of the Northwest Passage were matters close to his heart. The Admiralty felt he was too old for the job, but it was not easy to refuse so experienced and distinguished an officer, and Sir Edward Parry's opinion was that Franklin would be most disappointed if he did not go. He was appointed to the command and preparations for the voyage went speedily ahead.

good, bold water with a strong rippling on the surface. Actually it was the entrance of the channel we know as Peel Sound. In short, Franklin was given considerable latitude to choose his route based on conditions and his own experience.

On 19 May 1845 the two barks, accompanied by the supply ship *Baretto Junior,* sailed from the Thames — the most hopeful expedition ever to leave England. Franklin made a good passage to Baffin Bay and in early July, at the Whalefish Islands near Disko, transferred stores from *Baretto Junior* and sent her home. On 26 July 1845, Captain Dannett of the whaler *Prince of Wales* saw *Erebus* and *Terror* moored to an iceberg off Melville Bay in latitude 74° 48′, longitude 66° 13′, waiting to cross over to Lancaster Sound. Ten of Franklin's officers visited the whaler in good spirits, expecting to complete their assignment in good season. No further word of the expedition was ever heard.

With the passing of the first winter and the second, the lack of news from the expedition caused little anxiety. After all, the Rosses had spent four winters in the Arctic and had come out with the loss of only three men. But by autumn of 1847 the Admiralty began to be concerned. Dr. Richard King's offer to lead a land expedition to the western shore of Boothia, a sound idea from an irritating man, was rejected. However, plans were made for three relief expeditions. The survey ship *Plover* under Lieutenant W. J. S. Pullen left England the first of the year to join *Herald* under Captain Henry Kellett at Panama and proceed to Bering Strait. Unfortunately she was so long getting out there (not reaching the Hawaiian Islands until 22 August) that Pullen spent the winter on the Kamchatka coast. The two ships met at their appointed rendezvous in Bering Strait on 15 July 1849. In the meantime Sir John Richardson and Dr. John Rae had descended the Mackenzie River and searched the coastline from there to the Coppermine and Coronation Gulf. They knew that no ships had gone through that season (summer of 1848), and the Eskimos told them none had passed through the previous summer. The main searching party set out 12 June 1848 under Sir James Ross in the ships *Enterprise* (530 tons) and *Investigator* (480 tons). His first and second lieutenants were Robert McClure and Francis Leopold McClintock. Ross, after entering Lancaster Sound, was forced to winter his ships at Prince Leopold Islands off the northeastern shore of Somerset Island near the entrance of Prince Regent Inlet. During the winter, reasoning that the missing explorers would be trapping foxes as food, animals that roamed widely, they caught and released numerous foxes fitted with collars to which were fastened copper capsules telling Franklin where he could find relief. With the coming of spring, sledging parties searched the coasts. Ross traveled 150 miles down the western shore of Somerset Island along Peel Sound to a promontory where he could see another point fifty miles beyond, and failed to find a sign of the Franklin party. Another group visited Fury Beach with the same result. Ross intended to search farther westward in the summer of 1849, but his ships were beset and swept out into Baffin Bay by the ice. He arrived back in England 5 November. The transport *North Star* sent to renew his supplies for another winter put them ashore at Navy Board Inlet. The observations on sledging techniques made by McClintock and their consequent improvement proved the principal accomplishment of the expedition.

Altogether in the course of a decade forty expeditions were sent out to search for the lost explorers. Almost $4,000,000 was spent and five ships abandoned. At first it was hoped the explorers would be found alive; as time went on it became a certainty that at best only their remains and records could be found. It is extraordinary that just about every part of the Canadian Arctic was searched except King William Island, the west coast of Boothia, and the mouth of Back River — the very region where the survivors were struggling to stay alive and where their ships were frozen in. And yet this was the region where

James Ross saw the sea and the coast trending toward Point Turnagain, the region of the magnetic pole which Franklin had intended to investigate further, the region Franklin would have gone in following his orders. That he had been forced somewhat east might have been surmised from the location of the southern parts of Victoria Island seen by Richardson, Simpson, and Dease. Probably one red herring was the clause in the instructions allowing Franklin to go north through Wellington Channel if his way was blocked south and west. James Ross, during his sledging trip from *Enterprise* in 1848, had found a channel (Peel Sound) which Franklin could have taken and was certainly what Franklin was looking for — a link between Barrow Strait and the channel along the northern coast of America. Peel Sound ran directly toward the region James Ross had already explored, and Franklin had stated that if he reached the western end of Simpson Strait he should be able to make the rest of the voyage with no great difficulty.

When James Ross's unsuccessful expedition returned, the Admiralty decided on an extensive undertaking, offering a reward of £20,000 for the rescue of any of the men and another of 10,000 for the first person to discover their fate. Captain Sherard Osborn of *Pioneer* wrote the Admiralty that he believed the missing ships would be found off the east coast of Victoria Island and that the crews had retreated toward Repulse Bay and Back River. His common sense was ignored and the massive search continued westward and northward.

The ships *Enterprise,* under Captain Richard Collinson, and *Investigator,* under Captain Robert McClure, were again dispatched, this time to Bering Strait with orders to search toward Melville Island. Six vessels, the barks *Resolute* and *Assistance,* the steamers *Pioneer* and *Intrepid,* and the brigs *Lady Franklin* and *Sophia,* were to go by Lancaster Sound under the command of Captain Henry Austin. This fleet was accompanied by two privately financed vessels: *Felix* under Sir John Ross now over seventy years old, and *Prince Albert* sent out by Lady Franklin. Besides these, the brigantines *Advance* and *Rescue* of the United States Grinnell expedition under Lieutenant E. J. DeHaven arrived at Lancaster Sound late in the 1850 season. But the remains of Franklin's winter camp and the graves of three of his men on Beechey Island were all that were found. The American vessels and *Prince Albert* departed but the others wintered. Again sledging parties, guided largely by McClintock who was captain of *Intrepid,* were sent out and a great deal of new territory explored westerly and northerly. All were back in England in September 1851, where inquiries were held into squabbles between the various commanders.[3]

It is the western contingent that concerns our quest of the Northwest Passage. The two ships under Collinson headed by way of the Strait of Magellan for the Hawaiian Islands where they planned a rendezvous, the faster *Enterprise* sailing on ahead. Collinson reached Honolulu 24 June 1850, waited five days, and then, fearful of missing the season if he delayed too long, sailed for Bering Strait. McClure in *Investigator* arrived at Honolulu on 1 July, the day after *Enterprise* sailed. Collinson set his course for Bering Strait out around the Aleutian Islands, while McClure, stopping only two days at Honolulu, took the more direct route through the Islands and gained three weeks on *Enterprise*. McClure crossed the Arctic Circle 29 July and learned from the depot ship *Plover* that *Enterprise* had not been seen. Continuing north to Cape Lisburne, he fell in with his senior officer Captain Henry Kellett in *Herald*. Because Kellett did not believe that Collinson had passed, he thought McClure should not proceed until *Enterprise* arrived. McClure persuaded him otherwise and resumed his voyage eastward along the shore.

After running *Investigator* aground near Return Reef and getting off, McClure continued past Cape Bathurst. Sighting land to the northeast he headed in that direction, taking possession of and naming Nelson Head. He discovered Prince of Wales Strait between Banks and Victoria islands and, as the channel headed directly for Melville Island, sailed into it. By 16 September ice had carried *Investigator* within thirty miles of Melville Sound. Exploring the rest of the strait by sledge, he reached the northeastern point of Banks Island. From a six-hundred foot hill he saw Prince of Wales Strait join Melville Sound and looked across toward Melville Island even as Parry had looked in the opposite direction thirty years before.

McClure knew that he had discovered the Northwest Passage, and 'never from the lips of man burst a more fervent *Thank God!* than now from those of that little company.' [4] He left a record of his discovery which Vilhjalmur Stefansson recovered in 1916. The Passage was there, but he could not get his ship through the remaining twenty-five miles. The northern part of Prince of Wales Strait remained icebound the next summer. He therefore decided to sail west around Banks Island. In leaving the Strait 17 August he missed *Enterprise* who sailed in ten days later. On the same day he passed Nelson Head and its southern extremity; by the twentieth he had completed his run up the western coast and was beset in the ice off the northwest shore of the island. A month later he was free again but for a few days only. On 24 September after a night run he found himself in Mercy Bay and prepared to winter.

In April 1852 McClure sledged to Winter Harbour on Melville Island and, arriving on the twenty-eighth, found that McClintock had been there the summer before. Leaving a message of his proceedings since his departure from Kellett and telling his present whereabouts, he returned to his ship. *Investigator* did not get free in 1852, and he passed a very difficult winter on short rations with scurvy making inroads on his crew.

Collinson, who had reached Bering Strait two weeks after McClure in 1850, had been stopped by the ice after rounding Point Barrow; he had gone to Honolulu and Hong Kong during the winter. Returning in 1851, he followed almost exactly the course McClure had taken. He sailed up Prince of Wales Strait as McClure had done, and met the same ice blocking his way. He also found, 29 August, a cache of food and a message left by McClure, thereby learning that the *Investigator* had wintered safely. Collinson came even closer than McClure to getting his ship all the way through Prince of Wales Strait, but near its mouth he too was forced back. Retreating from the Strait with the intention of rounding Banks Island by the west, Collinson, on 6 September, discovered a message left by McClure dated 18 August saying that he was doing the same thing. Again Collinson was a little late. Just as the ice had closed in against the Alaskan coast after McClure got through the previous year, so it did on the western shore of Banks Island. The winter 1851–2 was spent in Walker Bay, the south entrance of Prince of Wales Strait. A sledge party under Lieutenant M. T. Parker was sent the remaining length of the strait and crossed to Melville Island. Short of Winter Harbour three-week-old tracks of McClure's party seen 16 May were mistaken for those of Eskimos, so the unarmed party decided to return.

The following year Collinson worked the big *Enterprise* eastward through Dolphin and Union Strait, Coronation Gulf, and Dease Strait to Cambridge Bay on Victoria Island, where he again went into winter quarters for 1852–3. Sending out the usual sledging parties he surveyed the eastern coast of Victoria Island beyond Collinson Peninsula. If he had sent his sledges across Victoria Strait to King William Island — and it was only forty-five miles distant at one point — they would have found the remains of the Franklin party. In July 1853 a piece of door casing marked with a broad cross was picked up, and was thought to be from the Franklin ship. That summer Collinson managed to return westerly to Camden Bay short of Point Barrow on the northern Alaskan coast, where he was again shut in and forced to spend the winter of 1853–4, his third in the

Arctic. The next spring he got out and returned via Hong Kong to England, where he arrived in 1855.[5]

While Collinson and McClure were searching for Franklin from the west the quest also continued from the east. In the summer of 1852 the Admiralty dispatched to Barrow Strait Sir Edward Belcher with *Resolute, Assistance, Intrepid,* and *Pioneer,* the ships that had returned the previous year. Belcher in *Assistance,* with *Pioneer* under Captain Sherard Osborn, explored up Wellington Channel, making some interesting discoveries to the north. Captain Henry Kellett, back from his duty in Bering Strait, took *Resolute,* and *Intrepid* under McClintock, to Melville Island. Reaching Winter Harbour 5 September they did not find McClure's message and retreated a few miles to Dealy Island where they wintered. Visiting Winter Harbour again later in the month a sledge party under Lieutenant Mecham of *Resolute* found McClure's message. In the spring Lieutenant Bedford Pim found *Investigator* in Mercy Bay. On 6 April 1853, while selecting a spot for digging a grave for a man who had died the day before, McClure describing the meeting writes:

> . . . we perceived a figure walking rapidly towards us from the rough ice at the entrance of the bay. From his pace and gestures we both naturally supposed at first that he was some one of our party pursued by a bear, but as we approached him doubts arose as to who it could be. He was certainly unlike any of our men; but recollecting that it was possible some one might be trying a new travelling dress, preparatory to the departure of our sledges, and certain that no one else was near, we continued to advance. When within about two hundred yards of us, this strange figure threw up his arms, and made gesticulations resembling those used by Esquimaux, besides shouting, at the top of his voice, words which, from the wind and the intense excitement of the moment, sounded like a wild screech; and this brought us both fairly to a stand-still. The

stranger came quietly on, and we saw that his face was as black as ebony, and really at the moment we might be pardoned for wondering whether he was a denizen of this or the other world, and had he but given us a glimpse of a tail or a cloven hoof, we should assuredly have taken to our legs: as it was, we gallantly stood our ground, and had the skies fallen upon us, we could hardly have been more astonished than when the dark-faced stranger called out, —

'I'm Lieutenant Pim, late of the *Herald,* and now in the *Resolute.* Captain Kellett is in her at Dealy Island!'

Pim arrived just in time for McClure was about to send his weakened men off in two parties to attempt to find their way out by sledges, one east and the other south to the Mackenzie River. He planned to keep his thirty strongest men to try to get his ship out. McClure changed his plans and immediately set off with a sledge party for Captain Kellett's ships, where he arrived 19 April. On 2 May a party of some of the weakest men from *Investigator* reached *Resolute.* Kellett at first consented to McClure's plan to remain with thirty men through another winter, but a medical survey showed few men were in sufficient health. When only four volunteered, Kellett ordered *Investigator* abandoned and the men brought to *Resolute* and *Intrepid.*

During the spring and early summer Captain McClintock and Lieutenants Mecham and Hamilton made sledge journeys covering thousands of miles. The searching expeditions had perfected this mode of travel. One sledge came all the way from *Assistance* and *Pioneer* in Wellington Channel to Dealy Island to inform Captain Kellett of the position of Belcher's ships. Lieutenant Cresswell of *Investigator* took dispatches for the Admiralty to Beechey Island with the news of the rescue of the men of *Investigator.* With the territory to the northwest of their position thoroughly searched and no signs of Franklin, Captain Kellett decided to take his ships to the rendezvous with Belcher

at Beechey Island. Getting clear, 18 August, they remained so
only twenty-four hours and were then stopped by the pack
coming down Byam Martin Channel. Stalled off the eastern
end of Melville Island, they made good use of their time by collecting about 10,000 pounds of game, mostly musk oxen, badly
needed to supplement their fast dwindling meat supplies.

Attempting desperately to force through the pack, both ships
were beset, 9 September, and at the mercy of the ice. The ice
pushed them easterly between Bathurst and Prince of Wales
islands, where they remained for the winter. With the exception of Lieutenant Gurney Cresswell and one or two others who
had returned to England on *Phoenix,* the others from *Investigator* were then forced to endure another Arctic winter. Once
more extensive sledging began and Lieutenant Mecham, 12
June, returned from a trip down Prince of Wales Inlet where
he had found Captain Collinson's message dated 27 August 1852
informing them that he would try to get east.

While Kellett was wintering in Barrow Strait, Sir Edward
Belcher with his two ships was wintering north of Wellington
Channel. In the summer of 1854 Belcher sent a letter to Kellett
telling him to abandon his ships and meet him with his men
at Beechey Island not later than 26 August. Kellett was amazed
and sent McClintock to point out to Sir Edward that if they
could not get clear they were perfectly prepared to spend another winter and confident they could save the ships. Furthermore, it was expected that at least some volunteers would be left
to attempt to locate Collinson whose *Enterprise* it was feared
might be in the same predicament as McClure's *Investigator.*
Belcher sent McClintock back with an order to abandon.
Belcher himself did the same with his ships, and on 26 August,
leaving Collinson to shift for himself, all ships were deserted.
The officers and crews of H.M.S. *Assistance, Resolute, Pioneer,
Intrepid,* and *Investigator* were jammed aboard *North Star* at
Beechey Island. Just as the overcrowded transport was making

sail, the supply ships *Phoenix* and *Talbot* hove in sight. The men were divided among the three vessels and arrived in England 28 September 1854.[6]

The only one of the ships ever recovered was *Resolute*. She was carried by the ice 1100 miles into Baffin Bay and south to Davis Strait, where she was found by Captain James Buddington of the American whaler *George Henry* in September 1855. Captain Buddington salvaged the ship and took her to New London. At the suggestion of Henry Grinnell, the philanthropist who had financed one of the American expeditions that searched for Franklin, she was purchased by the United States Government for $40,000, refitted, and returned to England, where she was presented to Queen Victoria in December 1856.[7]

Curiously enough there is substantial evidence that the two ships of Franklin, after their abandonment, followed much the some course as *Resolute*. Stories received from the Eskimos indicated that one of the Franklin ships had been driven ashore and wrecked while the other sank. However, the brig *Renovation* in a passage from Limerick to Quebec in April 1851 sighted two vessels on an ice floe off Newfoundland. In appearance they resembled the Franklin ships, and there were no other vessels they could have been. Admiral Noel Wright in an ingenious piece of detective work believes the ships were *Erebus* and *Terror,* and that the ship the Eskimos saw off King William Island was McClure's *Investigator* which had drifted down McClintock Channel to a place near that where Franklin's vessels were abandoned.[8]

The return of the expedition without its ships created a public uproar. Both McClure and Belcher were court-martialed. But whereas McClure was commended and eventually knighted for discovering the Northwest Passage, Belcher, although acquitted, had his sword returned in silence and was widely and severely criticized for not making a greater effort to save his ships.

The month after the return of Belcher's expedition with Mc-Clure, the Admiralty received a letter from Dr. John Rae, who had been continuing his exploration for the Hudson's Bay Company from Repulse Bay. He said he had met Eskimos who told him of the death by starvation of white men to the westward. From the natives he had also obtained spoons, forks, and other relics that proved these men must have been members of Sir John Franklin's expedition. Rae reported that there were evidences of cannibalism. On the basis of this information he claimed and received, over the strenuous objections of Lady Jane Franklin, the £10,000 offered for the discovery of Franklin's fate.

Lady Franklin was now determined to learn as much of the story as possible. After unsuccessfully imploring the Admiralty to send a party to search for the remains, she fitted out her own expedition. Its objective was to rescue any possible survivors, recover the expedition records, and confirm her claim that Sir John Franklin was the discoverer of the Northwest Passage. The schooner rigged, screw-steam yacht *Fox* was purchased and furnished with supplies and equipment, and the Admiralty gave Captain McClintock leave to command her. John Rae, whom Lady Franklin disliked, had applied for the job but she wrote: 'Dr. Rae has cut off his odious beard, but looks still very hairy & disagreeable.'

Fox sailed the first of July and all went well until she was frozen in the ice in Melville Bay. McClintock could not get free and remained in the ice all winter and was carried south into Davis Strait as far as Cumberland Sound. Getting free in late April 1858, he once more started north. At Godhavn he picked up a memorial tablet to Franklin and his men, made in New York under the direction of Henry Grinnell and at the request of Lady Franklin. Since the 1855 American expedition had been unable to reach Beechey Island, McClintock took the tablet there and set it in place. Then, finding his way blocked at

Peel Sound, he sailed down Prince Regent Inlet to Bellot Strait. This channel, which cuts off Somerset Island from the Boothia peninsula, was discovered by Captain Kennedy on *Prince Albert* in 1851. McClintock tried unsuccessfully to get *Fox* through the narrow channel but was forced to winter in a harbor at its eastern end. From there he and his officers explored by sledge the southwestern shore of Prince of Wales Island, establishing the existence of the channel named for McClintock, both shores of Franklin Strait, the western shore of Boothia, and encircling King William Island.

On this Island, in May 1859, the remains and relics of the Franklin party were found, and Lieutenant Hobson found the often reproduced paper carrying the messages from Gore and Fitzjames.

Apparently unable to penetrate south beyond Cape Walker, Franklin had returned to his alternative, Wellington Channel. Sailing about a hundred miles north up Wellington Channel to 77°, he circumnavigated Cornwallis Island and, turning back, wintered at Beechey Island. Three men died during the winter. After the ships were free in the summer of 1848, he evidently found Peel Sound clear and made his way through that waterway and its wider extension, now called Franklin Strait. Believing, as the Rosses had reported, that King William Island was a peninsula of Boothia, he endeavored to force his way west of that Island through the heavy pack that presses down McClintock Channel. There, off Cape Felix at the entrance to Victoria Strait in latitude 70° 05′, longitude 98° 23′, his ships remained for the second winter. In the spring, sledging parties were sent out to explore the land. This information is contained in Lieutenant Graham Gore's note dated 28 May 1847 with the postscript, 'All well.'

Nearly a year later Commander Fitzjames found Gore's note at Cape Felix in a cairn built by James Clark Ross, and all was not well. Around the margin Fitzjames wrote that the ships,

beset since 12 September 1846, were deserted 22 April 1848. Sir
John Franklin died 11 June 1847, and total deaths had mounted
to nine officers, including Gore, and fifteen men. The survivors,
105 souls under the command of Captain F. R. M. Crozier, had
landed in latitude 69° 37′ 42″, longitude 98° 41′, on King William Island, 'and start on to-morrow 26th for Back's Fish River.'
Scurvy-riddled and starving, one group reduced to cannibalism,
they dragged the heavy sledges, abandoning boats and equipment, until they could go on no longer.[9] They had found the
connecting link in the Northwest Passage, but 129 lives and
two ships had been lost. Why Crozier attempted to return by the
river that Back had descended with such great difficulty rather
than to head for Fury Beach no one will ever know. Ample
supplies for another winter were stored on the beach; Crozier
himself had helped to put them there. As the Rosses' experience
had shown, the chances of rescue by that direction were good.
Scholars and Arctic experts have been speculating about the
disaster ever since.[10]

McClintock returned to England with this news 20 September 1859.[11] It was now realized that Franklin had also discovered a Northwest Passage a dozen years before. He had come
within ninety miles of linking the discovery of Parry with those
of himself and Simpson. Thus James Ross's two lieutenants of
the first searching expedition connected the final links: Mc-
Clure by being the first man to lead his men through a Northwest Passage on three different ships and by sledge, and Mc-
Clintock by discovering the whereabouts of Franklin and by
learning that Sir John and his men had proved their objective
before they had perished. No doubt remained that the Northwest Passage existed. It had yet to be navigated.

24

The Passage Traversed

Exactly three hundred and sixty years (1497–1857) had passed from the time John Cabot made his first voyage until Leopold McClintock confirmed reports that a navigable Passage linked the Atlantic with the Pacific. Governments — the British most notably — as well as royalty and private individuals had expended huge sums of money and untold effort to organize expeditions. Men perished. Stout ships were lost. By one of the strange ironies of history, it was not a powerful ship, abundantly outfitted, manned by a crew of the greatest contemporary maritime power, that succeeded, but rather a tiny herring sloop and seven obscure adventurers.

Roald Amundsen, born in Borge, Norway, 16 July 1872, as a boy was fascinated by the Franklin tragedy. His admiration for the great Norwegian Arctic explorer Fridtjof Nansen led him, while still a youth, to train himself for a similar life. He hiked over mountains, camped out in the cold Norwegian winters, and when he was twenty-two shipped as an ordinary seaman on an Arctic sealing voyage. Loving the Far North, he began even then to formulate his plans to conquer the Northwest Passage and locate the ever-shifting North Magnetic Pole. On his return he consulted officials of the Meteorological Institute in Christiana (now Oslo) and, receiving encouragement, went to Hamburg to study terrestrial magnetism at the German Marine Observatory under Dr. G. von Neumayer, the most eminent authority on the subject of his day. From 1897–9 he served on the Belgian Antarctic Expedition ship *Belgica,* studying magnetism in the vicinity of the South Magnetic Pole. When he considered himself prepared and his plans sufficiently matured, he submitted them, with some trepidation, to his hero. Nansen not only gave his approval and provided expert advice but also assisted Amundsen to make his final preparations and raise money.[1]

In 1901 Amundsen selected and bought the forty-seven-ton *Gjöa* built in 1872 on the Hardanger. A veteran of the Norwegian herring fishery, *Gjöa* had proved herself a sound, able craft. As a result of a practice cruise to the north, Amundsen had her altered and strengthened the following year; three-inch oak sheathing, iron strapping on the stern, and extra frames, beams, and knees were added and an excellent thirteen horsepower kerosene-burning motor with extra fuel tanks installed.[2] The following spring at Christiana she was stowed with provisions and supplies for five years, and by May was ready for her departure. The effort of getting supplies and equipment strained Amundsen's financial resources to the limit.

Amundsen selected Lieutenant Godfred Hansen, a Dane who had voyaged to Iceland, as his second in command. He also signed on a cook and four other young men with skills and experience in northern navigation, engineering, astronomy, and meteorology. Six sled dogs completed the crew.

On a dark, rainy night, 16 June 1903, to escape a persistent creditor, Amundsen cast off and was towed to sea.[3] He made an uneventful passage to Greenland, arriving at Godhavn, Disko Island, 25 July, where he loaded extra supplies that had been shipped on ahead. Leaving Godhavn the last day of the month he successfully crossed Melville Bay and reached Dalrymple Rock, where two Scottish whalers had deposited more stores for him. Friendly Eskimos helped with the task of putting the load on board as did members of a Danish expedition which was working in the neighborhood. On 17 August the voyage was resumed. They entered Lancaster Sound on 20 August and anchored at Beechey Island two days later. They spent four days making magnetic observations, and found the Franklin tablet, a small one to the memory of Bellot, and a pillar in memory of those who had died on Belcher's expedition.

Departing from Beechey Island, 24 August, *Gjöa* made her way unimpeded across Barrow Strait, down Peel Sound, past the end of Bellot Strait, through Franklin Strait. Her progress along the coast of Boothia and into James Ross Strait was uneventful. Then disaster nearly overwhelmed her: a fire broke out in the engine room in the midst of tanks holding 2200 gallons of fuel, but was promptly put out by their two fire extinguishers. In the shoals between Boothia and Matty Island, *Gjöa,* which when loaded drew over ten feet of water, grounded and was nearly lost. By discarding the deck cargo and hoisting the sails in the strong breeze, Amundsen literally sailed her off; she scraped and bumped against the rocks, until at last she slid over the reef. Then in an exposed anchorage they rode out a gale for five terrible days and nights before they could continue on through Rae Strait. At the entrance of Simpson Strait, *Gjöa* was brought to anchor in a neat and sheltered little harbor on King William Island which Amundsen christened Gjöahavn (now Gjöa Haven). Although there had been no difficulty whatever with ice and Simpson Strait stretched open to the westward, Amundsen decided to take advantage of the good harbor and make it his winter quarters, instead of completing the Northwest Passage that season. Located about ninety nautical miles from the North Magnetic Pole, the harbor would admirably serve his principal objective: to ascertain the Pole's position and to make extensive observations of it.

By 17 September they had discharged supplies. They constructed a storehouse, a building for the magnetic instruments, an observatory, and a hut for Peter Ristvedt and Gustav Wiik, who were to make meteorological and magnetic observations. Two men went off to secure fresh meat for the winter and returned in a few days with twenty caribou, the first of many game bags. *Gjöa* was fitted up for winter living by moving the galley below deck and covering the entire vessel with a sail cloth. By 29 September all preparations for wintering were completed. *Gjöa* was soon frozen in, and a snow house, free of any distracting metal, was built for the absolute magnetic observations.

Amundsen and his party spent two winters at Gjöa Haven, during which they remained perfectly healthy. There, where over a hundred of Franklin's men had died of starvation, they found fish and game in abundance; Amundsen referred to the land as an Arctic paradise. They maintained close contact with a colony of Eskimos settled nearby, and employed some of them as guides, huntsmen, and laborers. They surveyed the region and carried on constant magnetic and astronomical observations. After several abortive attempts in exceedingly low temperatures, Amundsen made a sledge journey to Boothia and the vicinity of the Magnetic Pole.

The ice never opened up in 1904, but the spring of 1905 promised a better season for continuing the Passage: the ice around *Gjöa* was only six feet thick instead of twelve. The men were further heartened when on 20 May an Eskimo, to whom they had entrusted letters the previous year, arrived with mail and news from Major Moodie of the North-West Mounted Police, the captain of the police vessel *Arctic* wintering in northern Hudson Bay, and Captain Comer of the American whaler *Era,* wintering in the same place. The self-registering magnetic instruments, that had worked without interruption for nineteen months, were stopped 1 June and the observations terminated. The milder weather enabled the first engineer Lieutenant Hansen and Peter Ristvedt to make an eighty-four day survey by sledge across Victoria Strait and up the eastern coast of Victoria Island. They also investigated the Royal Geographical Society Islands and others in Victoria Strait.

At last, 13 August, the ice opened and the small expedition left Gjöa Haven. A bright Eskimo youth was taken along as an extra hand. Two days later Amundsen was through Simpson Strait and working along an ice pack in Queen Maud Gulf, where new islands were discovered and named for his countryman Nordenskiöld. Victoria Strait was crossed and, on 17 August, they reached Cambridge Bay, where Captain Collinson had wintered with *Enterprise*. *Gjöa* had now sailed 'through the hitherto unsolved link in the North West Passage.' Amundsen pays just tribute to Collinson, who had been rather critically received after his return to England.

> Sir Richard Collinson appears to me to have been one of the most capable and enterprising sailors the world has ever produced. He guided his great, heavy vessel into waters that hardly afforded sufficient room for the tiny 'Gjöa.' But, better still, he brought her safely home. His recompense for the heroism shown was, however, but scant. His second in command, Sir Robert McClure, who had had to abandon his vessel the 'Investigator' in Mercy Bay, on the north-east coast of Bank's Land, and who was helped home by others, received all the honour, and one-half of the promised reward went to him and his men as discoverers of the North West Passage.

The waters of Dease Strait, Coronation Gulf, and Dolphin and Union Strait successively passed under *Gjöa*'s keel. The 26 August, Nelson Head on Banks Island was sighted; Amundsen had expected to sight Cape Parry on the mainland and was surprised to find himself on the north side of the Gulf now named for him. Strong currents and the distracted compass had thrown him off. The next morning, Amundsen was awakened by Lieutenant Hansen's rushing into his cabin and singing out, 'Vessel in sight, sir!' He knew then that the Northwest Passage was his.

Amundsen and three of his men rowed across to the black schooner, *Charles Hanson* of San Francisco, riding low in the water. Pulling themselves on board, they fell into a deck crowded with Eskimo women in red dresses and Negroes in variegated clothing. It was an unusual spectacle for the Norwegians. The master, Captain James McKenna, a stout, white-whiskered man, came up and, recognizing his distinguished visitor, asked: 'Is this the first vessel you have met?' When Amundsen admitted it was, they shook hands and McKenna said: 'I am exceedingly pleased to be the first one to welcome you on getting through the North West Passage.' After leaving the Arctic trader, Amundsen fell in with ice as he approached Cape Bathurst. He successfully worked his way through it, rounded the cape, and set his course for Herschel Island. Several whalers were seen on the way, but Amundsen was now impatient and did not speak them. Later the whaling barks *Alexander* and *Bowhead* of San Francisco were sighted and their offered assistance was declined with thanks.

So far they had experienced little difficulty with the ice, but now it shut in and they were forced to moor to the pack near Cape Sabine where only a narrow channel remained along shore. They sailed *Gjöa* to King Point, where she was made fast to the ice outside the wreck of the San Francisco whaler *Bonanza*. Amundsen had hoped to reach Herschel Island where there was a good harbor, but the ice made and lasted for the next ten months. The explorers' third winter in the Arctic was different from the others in its more lively social life. Between *Bonanza* caretakers, halfbreeds, parties of Eskimos coming and going, a traveling missionary, the crews of eleven whalers —

five shut in at Herschel Island and six to the east — there was a considerable population. Buildings were constructed as before, including a house where five of the explorers lived; Amundsen, Lieutenant Hansen, and their young Eskimo hand Manni were to live on the housed-in *Gjöa*.

In late September, Amundsen sledged the thirty-five miles to Herschel Island and visited the whalers and the missionary there. This small island, discovered and named by Franklin, although he missed its excellent harbor, had been since 1889 the most important anchorage for American whalers. There Amundsen received a year-old letter from home and another from the Norwegian consul in San Francisco. All of the whaling Captains knew of the *Gjöa* expedition and had instructions from their owners to assist Amundsen in any way possible. Finding that a post was to leave Herschel for Fort Yukon, Alaska, in late October, Amundsen obtained permission to go along. Whereupon he returned to King Point to complete final arrangements for the winter. On 24 October the mail party left Herschel, the temperature registered four below zero. Traveling by sledge and toboggan, they arrived at Eagle City, Alaska, in about five weeks. Amundsen dispatched a cable home. After two months at Eagle City with the Army officers stationed there, he set out for the north on 3 February and by 12 March was back on board *Gjöa* with letters and newspapers. Amundsen's shipmates were relieved and overjoyed to welcome him back. For those at King Point it had been a cold, stormy winter. In late March Gustav Wiik, the genial magnetic observer and second engineer, died after an illness of a few days.

Spring with its migrating animals and birds turned into summer with its swarms of blackflies. The ice softened, the pack stirred, and open water appeared in places. *Gjöa* was prepared for her last lap. When on the evening of 10 July three whalers came through the open water outside the ice, one reaching the channel where *Gjöa* lay, Amundsen knew it was time to go.

With a passenger from the whaler *Alexander,* they left King Point, dipping their colors to their dead comrade. On 13 July they reached Herschel Island, where they remained nearly a month, during which time Manni was drowned. At last, 9 August, they got under way and headed west into the open coastal channel. Continuing in this narrow channel, usually through thick fog, and skirting ice, Amundsen worked his way to Point Barrow, where he was delayed by storms and driving ice. The propeller hit ice and, with its shaft bent, the engine broke down. After a struggle Point Barrow was rounded. On the western side were five ships — among them *Duchess of Bedford,* with the Anglo-American Polar expedition of Einar Mikkelsen, and the U.S. Revenue cutter *Thetis,* with a packet of letters for the Norwegians. Pressing huriedly on, they saw the last of the ice after passing Cape Belcher.

On 30 August, Cape Prince of Wales, the eastern entrance of Bering Strait, was rounded. The Diomedes were glimpsed to the westward. The six surviving Norwegians gathered on deck to celebrate. As darkness fell, 13 August 1906, they were greeted by a tumultuous welcome at Nome, Alaska. *Gjöa* had linked the waters of the Atlantic and the Pacific by the Northwest Passage. The quest inspired by the speculations of fifteenth-century geographers had ended, over 400 years later, at Nome.

Notes

In order to keep notes to a minimum, they have been provided only for the more significant quotations and for particularly disputable points. The major sources for each chapter are indicated also; complete title and and details of publication will be found in the bibliography, as will other important references. Complete bibliographical information is given for minor works and articles to be found in periodicals.

1. Conquerors of the Ice

1. For the complete published story of the Polar Voyage see Anderson (with Clay Blair, Jr.), *Nautilus 90 North*. Also, William G. Lalor, Jr., 'Submarine Through the North Pole,' *The National Geographic Magazine*, Jan. 1959, Vol. CXV, No. 1, pp. 1–20. Much information on the operations of nuclear submarines under the ice is classified.

2. James F. Calvert, 'Up Through the Ice of the North Pole,' *The National Geographic Magazine*, July 1959, Vol. CXVI, No. 1, pp. 1–41.

3. William R. Anderson, 'The Arctic as a Sea Route of the Future,' *The National Geographic Magazine*, Jan. 1959, Vol. CXV, No. 1, pp. 21–4.

4. T. A. Irvine, *The Ice Was All Between*, Toronto, 1959. Also, Thomas C. Pullen, 'We Found a New Northwest Passage,' *The Saturday Evening Post*, 10 May 1958, pp. 23ff.

5. For the voyages of *St. Roch* see Larsen, *The North-West Passage . . .* 1940. Also for first voyage, G. J. Tranter, *Plowing the Arctic*, Toronto and New York, 1945.

6. *Sailing Directions for Northern Canada*, 2nd ed. Washington, 1951, Hydrographic Office Publication No. 77, Ch. 6.

2. Cabots Out of Bristol

1. The reader who wishes to pursue all of the geographical and political ramifications of the fifteenth and sixteenth centuries, which are the setting for the early voyages to America, is referred to: Taylor, *Tudor Geography*

1485–1583; Late Tudor and Early Stuart Geography 1583–1650, and William-son, *The Voyages of the Cabots* . . . These books will show the way to a vast literature on the subject.

2. *The Encyclopaedia Britannica*, 11th ed., v, p. 922. Hakluyt, *The Principal Navigations*, VII, p. 145, gives 3 Feb. (1497?) as record on rolls.

3. Historians have never agreed on what part, if any, Sebastian played in his father's voyages. The best evidence indicates that he was too young to have taken any active part. Anyone who wishes to read the evidence and follow the arguments concerning the various theories about the lives, move-ments, and discoveries of the Cabots will find them in the following books which also lead to other sources on the subject. I have generally followed Williamson.

Harrisse, *John Cabot the Discoverer of North America and Sebastian his Son;* Bigger, *Voyages of the Cabots and the Corte-Reals;* Williamson, op. cit.

4. A. Davies, 'The Last Voyage of John Cabot and the Rock at Grates Cove,' *Nature*, 26 Nov. 1955, Vol. 176, No. 4491, pp. 996–9.

5. These conclusions on Sebastian Cabot's little-known and disputed voyage are based on Williamson's evidence and speculations, op. cit. pp. 70–84, 225–43. Davies, op. cit., does not believe that Sebastian made a voyage in 1509, but that the evidence connected with it by Williamson refers to the John Cabot voyage of 1498.

3. The Unknown Coast

1. Williamson, op. cit., has done an excellent piece of historical detective work on those entangled Bristol and Portuguese voyages. See also Bigger, *Voyages of the Cabots and the Corte-Reals.*

2. Williamson, op. cit. p. 207.

3. Hakluyt, op. cit. VII, p. 155.

4. Winsor, *Narrative and Critical History of America*, IV, is the source of this information as of the material on Verrazano's life and that of Cartier.

4. The Timid, the Lost, and the Hungry

1. A. W. Reed, 'John Rastell's Voyage in the Year 1517,' *The Mariners' Mirror*, 1923, IX, pp. 137–47.

2. Hakluyt, op. cit. VIII, pp. 1–2.

3. Purchas, *Hakluytus Posthumus or Purchas His Pilgrimes*, XIV, pp. 303–5.

4. Williamson, op. cit. pp. 102–11.

5. E. G. R. Taylor, 'Master Hore's Voyage of 1536,' *The Geographical Journal*, 1931, LXXVII, pp. 469–70.

5. Hunt a Dragon, Bag a Bear

1. Nordenskiöld, *Voyage of the Vega Round Asia and Europe*, pp. 39–41. Taylor, *Tudor Geography*, op. cit. 90–91.
2. Hakluyt, op. cit. II, pp. 322–3.
3. Ibid. p. 336.
4. Taylor (ed.), *The Original Writings & Correspondence of the Two Richard Hakluyts*, I, pp. 147–58.

6. The Great Dutchman

1. Beynen, in his introduction to *The Three Voyages of William Barents* . . . by De Veer, pp. vi–xvi, gives an extensive account of Brunel and his activities.
2. The most complete account of the three Dutch voyages is *The True and Perfect Description of Three Voyages* . . . by De Veer, translated from the Dutch in 1598, published in 1609. It has been reprinted twice by the Hakluyt Society: first as *A True Description of Three Voyages,* edited and with an introduction by Charles T. Beke; second under the title cited above.
3. De Veer, op. cit. p. 25.
4. Nordenskiöld, op. cit. p. 184.
5. De Veer, op. cit. pp. 62–4.
6. Ibid. pp. 75–6.
7. Ibid. p. 171.

7. All That Glitters

1. Quinn, *The Voyages . . . of Sir Humphrey Gilbert*, p. 7.
2. Ibid. p. 9.
3. Stefansson, *The Three Voyages of Martin Frobisher* . . . p. ci. This is the best edition of George Best's book and contains an invaluable Introduction and Appendices. This work also includes all other contemporary accounts of Frobisher's voyages. Best was also edited and published with other related documents by R. Collinson, *The Three Voyages of Martin Frobisher.*
4. Waters, *The Art of Navigation* . . . pp. 145–6, makes valuable professional observations on the instruments carried on this expedition.
5. Stefansson, op. cit. facing p. cxiv, reproduces the Zeno chart superimposed on a modern chart of the North Atlantic; by indicating the actual and supposed routes sailed by Frobisher, he clearly shows how the confusion came about.
6. Those who wish to delve further into this extremely interesting prob-

lem should read: first, R. Major, *The Voyages of . . . Nicolo & Antonio Zeno . . . ;* and second, Lucas, *The Annals of the Voyages of the Brothers Nicolo and Antonio Zeno.*

W. H. Hobbs, 'Zeno and the Cartography of Greenland,' *Imago Mundi,* VI, pp. 15–19, shows that the shape of southern Greenland is given more accurately on the Zeno chart than on any contemporary or even some later ones.

7. Taylor, *Tudor Geography,* op. cit. p. 108; Stefansson, op. cit. pp. ciii–iv.

8. Stefansson, op. cit. pp. cviii–ix, 49, believes that the behavior of the Eskimos indicates they had met Europeans before, possibly fishermen or members of the Rut expedition.

9. Ibid. 'Michael Lok's Account of the First Voyage' is the source for this and the succeeding quotations concerning the voyage.

10. Ibid. p. cxi.

11. Collinson, op. cit., prints the State papers relating to the voyages and the business dealings of the Cathay Company. Stefansson, op. cit., in the Appendices of his work gives much additional valuable information, including modern opinion on 'The Frobisher Mineral.'

12. McFee's *The Life of Sir Martin Frobisher* contains a spirited account of his later life and adventures.

13. The best and fullest account of the reports and cartographical history of this island is by Miller Cristy, 'On "Busse Island,"' in Gosch, *Danish Arctic Expeditions 1605 to 1620,* Appendix B, pp. 164–202.

14. Hall, *Arctic Researches and Life Among the Esquimaux,* contains a fascinating account of the author's detective work in tracing the Frobisher locations from the time he first heard the stories from the Eskimos to the finding of the relics.

15. Stefansson made every attempt to find the Frobisher relics without success, op. cit. II, pp. 240–47.

8. Mariner and Scholar

1. The fullest account of Hakluyt is Parks, *Richard Hakluyt and the English Voyages.* There is also an excellent introduction to his life in *The Original Writings . . . of the Two Richard Hakluyts,* op. cit.

2. The *Discourse* was edited by Leonard Woods and Charles Deane and published for the first time in the Maine Historical Society, 2 *Collections,* II, Cambridge, Mass., 1877. It has been printed again with notes in *The Original Writings . . .* op. cit. pp. 211–326.

3. Hakluyt, op. cit. VIII, p. 112.

4. Taylor, *Tudor Geography,* op. cit. I, pp. 137–9. Quinn op. cit. pp. 95–100; II, pp. 483–9.

5. Taylor, ibid. p. 138. Quinn, ibid. pp. 97–8.

6. Markham, *The Voyages and Works of John Davis,* is the source of this information, as of the report quoted in subsequent pages.

7. Ibid. Dedication, *The Seamans Secrets;* see also pp. 233–4.

9. *Frustration*

1. Rundall, *Narrative of Voyages Towards the North-West* . . . p. 62.

2. Purchas, op. cit. XIV, p. 308.

3. The information on Captain James Hall's voyages for the Danish government is taken from Gosch, op. cit. I.

4. See Chapter 12, p. 139.

5. *The Journal of the Voyage of John Knight to seek the North-West Passage, 1606,* is printed in *The Voyages of Sir James Lancaster* . . . ed. by C. R. Markham.

6. Christy, *The Voyages of Captain Luke Foxe of Hull and Captain Thomas James of Bristol in Search of a Northwest Passage in 1631–32,* I, p. 85.

10. *Mutiny*

1. The most complete edition of the journals of Hudson's voyages is in Asher, *Henry Hudson the Navigator.*

2. Ibid. p. 44.

3. Ibid. p. 28.

4. Ibid. p. 191.

11. *In Hudson's Wake*

1. Christy, op. cit. II, Appendix D, reprints the entire charter which contains a complete list of the names of the incorporators.

2. Foxe, *North-West Fox,* pp. 117–36.

3. Markham, *The Voyages of William Baffin, 1612–1622,* pp. xxx–xxxi; in 'The Fourth Recorded Voyage of William Baffin 1615,' the Baffin map is reproduced in color, pp. 103–37.

4. Ibid. pp. 122–3 and notes.

5. Ibid. p. 137.

6. For a detailed technical account of Baffin's observations and achievements in navigation, see Waters, *The Art of Navigation* . . . pp. 276–84.

12. Beyond Hope Sanderson

1. Gosch, op. cit. I, pp. xxxii–iii.
2. Markham, *William Baffin,* op. cit.
3. See Chapter 9, p. 110.
4. S. F. Haven, ed., *Transactions and Collections of the American Antiquarian Society,* IV, 1860, pp. 285–314.
5. Markham, *William Baffin,* p. xlv.

13. Three Came Back

1. This account of Munk's life is condensed from Gosch, op. cit. introduction.
2. This book, entitled *Navigatio Septentrionalis,* is translated and reprinted
by Gosch, ibid. The succeeding quotations from Munk may be found in
Vol. II, pp. 1–184.
3. Ibid. p. 135.
4. Ibid. p. 146–84. This map is described in great detail.
5. Rundall, op. cit. pp. 150–51.
6. Gosch, op. cit. pp. lxxxvi–xciv. Christy, 'Captain William Hawkeridge
and his Voyage in Search of a North-West Passage in 1625,' *The Mariners'
Mirror,* XIII, No. 1, Jan. 1927, pp. 51–78.
7. Christy, ibid. p. 55.

14. 'North-West Fox'

1. The Hakluyt Society's reprint, edited by Christy, op. cit. has notes showing its differences from Foxe's and the Master's original journals, copies of
which are in the British Museum. The following quotations, unless otherwise
identified, are from Foxe's 'My Preparations to the Voyage,' in Christy, II.
2. Ibid. I, p. lxi.
3. Purchas, op. cit. XIV, pp. 422–6.
4. Christy, op. cit. I, p. lxviii.
5. Ibid. I, p. cvi.

15. 'The Strange and Dangerous Voyage'

1. *The Strange and Dangerous Voyage of Captain Thomas James* was first
published in 1633. For convenience, all quotations from James's account may
be found in the Hakluyt Society reprint, ed. by Christy, op. cit.

16. Fiction and Fact

1. Nunn, *Origin of the Strait of Anian Concept,* describes in detail the geographical confusion of this problem.
2. Purchas, op. cit. XIV, pp. 415–21.
3. Dobbs, *An Account* . . . pp. 123–30.
4. Jefferys, *The Great Probability of a Northwest Passage* . . .
5. For a detailed summary of the cartographical aspects of this problem, see Henry R. Wagner, 'Apocryphal Voyages to the Northwest Coast of America,' *Proceedings of the American Antiquarian Society,* New Series, Vol. 41, Part 1, 1931, pp. 179–234. This is an excellent account of the most important fictitious voyages.
6. John Seller, *Atlas Maritimus* . . . p. 11. The Shepherd story and Gillam report are gone into in some detail by Lucas, *The Annals* . . . op. cit. pp. 127–30. Also, in Seller's *English Pilot* (*c.* 1673) there is an elaborate and detailed map of the island based on the entirely false account of one Captain Thomas Shepherd of the ship *Golden Lion.* He claimed to have made a survey during his visit to the island in 1671; he named most of its geographical features for the patentees of the new Hudson's Bay Company. In support of Shepherd's story it was also stated that 'This Island has several times been seen by Captain Gillam, in his Passages to and from the North West.' A later work of Seller less precisely describes the position of the fictitious island:

> South-westward from Iseland, about 140 leagues, lyeth an Island called Buss; in the latitude of 57 degrees 35 minutes, not yet fully discovered, but only as it hath been accidentally seen by some, who upon other Discoveries have occasionally passed those Seas, as Captain Gillam in his first voyage to the North-West Passage had soundings near unto it.

7. There are several histories of the Hudson's Bay Company, all of which relate the story of its founding, but Rich's *The History of the Hudson's Bay Company* is the most recent and reliable. Dobbs, op. cit., prints in an Appendix *His Majesty's Royal Charter to the Governor and Company of Hudson's Bay,* pp. 171–87.
8. Hearne, *A Journey from Prince of Wale's Fort* . . . pp. xxvi–xxvii.
9. Rich, op. cit. p. 447.
10. Hearne, op. cit. pp. xxx, xxxi–xxxii.

17. The Wild Irishman

1. For a full account of Dobbs's background, life, and activities, see Clarke, *Arthur Dobbs Esquire 1689–1765.*
2. The principal sources for information on Middleton's voyage and the

circumstances leading up to it are: Dobbs, *An Account of the Countries adjoining to Hudson's Bay* . . . ; Coats, *The Geography of Hudson's Bay* . . . with an Appendix containing extracts from the log of Captain Middleton; Rich, *James Isham's Observations* . . . ; Rich, *The History of the Hudson's Bay Company,* op. cit. I.

3. Dobbs, op. cit. p. 103.

4. Middleton, *A Vindication of the Conduct of Captain Middleton* (1743); Dobbs, *Remarks upon Captain Middleton's Defense* (1744); Middleton, *A Reply to the Remarks of Arthur Dobbs* (1744); Middleton, *Forgery Detected* (1745); Dobbs, *A Reply to Captain Middleton's Answer* (1745); Middleton, *A Reply to Mr. Dobbs Answer to a Pamphlet Entitled Forgery Detected* (1745).

5. Dobbs, *An Account* . . . op. cit. This and the following quotations may be found in this work.

6. Coats, op. cit. pp. 2–3.

7. Ellis, *A Voyage to Hudson's Bay* . . .

8. Clerk of the California, *An Account of a Voyage* . . . In the second volume of this book the pages run to 328; then, through an obvious error, they begin again with 313 and run through 320; the pages of index that follow are not numbered.

9. Ibid.

10. Rich, op. cit. p. 199.

11. Ibid. p. 238.

12. Rich, op. cit. p. 581.

13. Bryce, *The Remarkable History of the Hudson's Bay Company,* pp. 61–77.

18. The American 'Argo'

1. Forster, *History of the Voyages and Discoveries Made in the North,* p. 454.

2. Jefferys, op. cit. Although 'By Thomas Jefferys' appears on the title page, this evidently refers only to the three maps in the book. Jefferys was a geographer and printer and almost certainly did not write the book.

3. Barrow, op. cit. pp. 287–8.

4. Nourse, *Narrative of the Second Arctic Expedition* . . . pp. xxxix–xliii; also his *American Explorations in the Ice Zones,* Boston, 1884, pp. 25–9.

5. Eavenson, *Two Early Works on Arctic Exploration by an Anonymous Author.* He made a detailed study of comparable parts of the texts of the two works and reached this conclusion. A condensed version of this article was published in *Notes and Queries* (London), 6 Nov. 1943.

Bertha Solis-Cohen, 'An American Search for the Northwest Passage,' *The Beaver,* Sept. 1943, pp. 24–7. Miss Solis-Cohen has also published two Bibliographical Notes on the problem in the *Biographical Society of America Papers,* Vol. 37, 1943, and Vol. 39, 1945.

I am greatly indebted to my colleague M. V. Brewington for the use of his notes on the *Argo* voyages.

6. Rich, op. cit. p. 277. Letter, 26 Dec. 1746.

7. Ibid. pp. 287–8. Letters, 24 & 25, Feb. 1747.

8. Ibid. p. 297.

9. Ibid. p. 238 and *passim.*

10. Original document in the Historical Society of Pennsylvania. Printed by Solis-Cohen, op. cit. pp. 24–5.

11. Cadwalader Colden Papers, IV, 373. Printed by Nourse, op. cit. p. xxxix, and quoted in part by Eavenson, op. cit. p. 4. Rich, op. cit. pp. 265–7, quotes both the commission and the letter.

12. Eavenson, op. cit. p. 5.

13. Herma Briffault, in unpublished biographical sketches of Theodore Swaine Drage and Charles Swaine written for the *Encyclopedia Arctica* (which has never been published), believes that the two men were relatives, possibly cousins — a sensible conclusion for which there is unfortunately no proof.

A. D. Chidsey, Jr., in *Charles Swaine,* a paper read before The Northampton County [Pa.] Historical and Genealogical Society, 25 June 1942, makes no mention of Drage. Copies of these manuscripts by Briffault and Chidsey are in the Stefansson Collection, Baker Library, Dartmouth College.

I have relied largely on the Briffault and Chidsey manuscripts for the summary of dates and events.

14. A. H. Smyth, *The Life and Writings of Benjamin Franklin,* letter of Franklin to Strahan, July 1744.

15. Letter, Franklin to James Logan, 20 Nov. 1748, *Logan Papers;* and Logan to Franklin, 9 Nov. 1748, *James Logan Miscellaneous Letter Book 1748–50,* Historical Society of Pennsylvania.

16. *Ship Register of Philadelphia,* No. 18, shows *Argo* registered 27 Feb. 1753, Historical Society of Pennsylvania.

17. Mss. document signed by Charles Swaine in Historical Society of Pennsylvania.

18. *Journal of the Commissioners for Trade and Plantations,* Vol. 60, folio 149–52, p. 299. Letters, 18 Nov. 1752, William Allen to Thomas Penn, *Penn Private Papers,* IV, 93; and 11 Jan. 1753, Thomas Penn to William Allen, *Penn Letter Book,* 1750–54, p. 202.

19. Letter, William Allen to Thomas Penn, 7 July 1753, *Penn Official Correspondence,* VI, 79. Historical Society of Pennsylvania.

20. *Pennsylvania Gazette,* 15 Nov. 1753, No. 1299. The same article with the omission of the last sentence was reprinted in *The Gentleman's Magazine* (London), XXIV, Jan. 1754, p. 46.

21. Jefferys, op. cit. pp. 15–16.

22. *Pennsylvania Gazette,* 29 Nov. 1753, No. 1301.

23. *Pennsylvania Gazette*, 2 May 1754, No. 1323; and 24 Oct. 1754, No. 1348.
Maryland Gazette (Annapolis), 23 May 1754 and 21 Oct. 1754.
24. Jefferys, op. cit. p. xii.
25. Letter, Robert Levers to 'William Parson, Oct. 1754, Historical Society of Pennsylvania.
26. *Pennsylvania Gazette*, 24 Oct. 1754, No. 1348; and 14 Nov. 1754, No. 1351.
27. *Maryland Gazette*, 28 Nov. 1754.
28. Smyth, op. cit. III, p. 268.
29. *Notes and Queries*, 4th, IV, 406, 13 Nov. 1869.

19. Old Hopes Revived

1. Coxe, *Account of the Russian Discoveries Between Asia and America;* Golder, *Bering's Voyages* prints the logs and journals. See also Waxell, *The American Expedition,* for a popular edition of one of the journals.
2. Hearne, op. cit.
3. Mackenzie, *Voyages From Montreal . . . Through the Continent of North America . . .*
4. Phipps, *A Voyage Towards the North Pole . . .* p. 10.
5. Barrington's assembled papers were first published in 1775. They were reissued under the title, *The Possibility of Approaching the North Pole . . . by Colonel Beaufoy.*
6. Barrow, op. cit. pp. 324–5.
7. Pickersgill's journal was never published but he wrote a small history of Northwest Passage voyages which was published under a pseudonym after his death, called *A Concise Account of Voyages for the Discovery of a North-West Passage,* By a Sea Officer.
8. Cook and King, *A Voyage to the Pacific Ocean . . . in the Years 1776, 1777, 1778, 1779, 1780,* Introduction.
9. Ibid. This quotation and the three following it are taken from Vol. II.
10. Ibid. III.
11. For a good, brief account of these voyages, see Introduction of Jane, *A Spanish Voyage to Vancouver and the North West Coast of America . . .* and for the voyages themselves, see Wagner, *Spanish Explorations in the Strait of Juan de Fuca.*
12. Meares, *Voyages Made in the Years 1788 and 1789, from China to the North West Coast of America . . .* pp. xli–lxvi.
13. Vancouver, *A Voyage of Discovery to the North Pacific Ocean, and Round the World . . . in the Years 1790 . . . 1794, and 1795.*

20. *The Twin Attack*

1. Beaufoy, op. cit.
2. Barrow, op. cit.
3. Scoresby, Jr., *An Account of the Arctic Regions* . . . p. 24.
4. Crouse, *The Search for the Northwest Passage,* pp. 26–35, has an extended discussion of the Barrow-Scoresby arguments.
5. Ross, *A Voyage of Discovery* . . .
6. Beechey, *A Voyage of Discovery Towards the North Pole* . . .
7. Parry, *Journal of a Voyage of Discovery, to the Arctic Regions* . . .
8. Ross, op. cit. p. 183.
9. Parry, op. cit. p. 72–3.
10. Sabine, *Remarks on the Account of the Late Voyage of Discovery to Baffin's Bay.*
11. *The Quarterly Review,* XXV, April & July 1821, p. 251.

21. *Opening the Door*

1. There are three published accounts by men on this voyage: (a) Parry, *Journal of a Voyage for the Discovery of a North-West Passage from the Atlantic to the Pacific: Performed in the Years 1819–20* . . . (b) Fisher, *A Journal of a Voyage of Discovery to the Arctic Regions . . . in the Years 1819 & 1820;* (c) *Letters Written During the Late Voyage of Discovery in the Western Arctic Sea,* By an Officer of the Expedition.
2. Fisher, op. cit.
3. These papers were later printed in a single volume with an introductory note by Edward Sabine: *The North Georgia Gazette, and Winter Chronicle,* London, 1821.
4. Parry, op. cit.
5. References for this voyage are: Parry, *Journal of a Second Voyage* . . . *in the Years 1821–22–23* . . . and also Lyon, *The Private Journal of Captain G. F. Lyon* . . .
6. Ibid.
7. Franklin, *Narrative of a Journey to the Shores of the Polar Sea, in the Years 1819, 20, 21, and 22.*
8. Lyon, *A Brief Narrative of an Unsuccessful Attempt to Reach Repulse Bay.*
9. Parry, *Journal of a Third Voyage* . . . *in the Years 1824–25* . . .
10. Franklin, *Narrative of a Second Expedition to the Shores of the Polar Sea, in the Years 1825, 1826 and 1827* . . .
11. Beechey, *Narrative of a Voyage to the Pacific and Beering Strait . . . in the Years 1825, 26, 27, 28.*

22. Boothia Felix

1. Ross, *Narrative of a Second Voyage in Search of a North-West Passage* . . .

2. Ibid. Appendix.

3. Ibid. p. 90.

4. Barrow, *Voyages of Discovery* . . . *from the Year 1818 to the Present Time*, pp. 508–25.

5. Back, *Narrative of the Arctic Land Expedition* . . . *in the Years 1833, 1834, and 1835;* and King, *Narrative of a Journey to the Shores of the Arctic Ocean, in 1833, 1834, and 1835* . . .

6. Back, *Narrative of an Expedition* . . . *in the Years 1836–7.*

7. Simpson, *Narrative of the Discoveries on the North Coast of America* . . . *During the Years 1836–39.*

8. For an excellent summary of the evidence for both the suicide and murder theories, see Stefansson, *Unsolved Mysteries of the Arctic*, pp. 130–91.

9. Rae, *Narrative of an Expedition to the Shores of the Arctic Sea in 1846 and 1847.*

23. The Passage Discovered

1. Cyriax, *Sir John Franklin's Last Arctic Expedition*, pp. 17–25, prints the texts of Barrow's proposal to the Admiralty, the Royal Society's resolution, and Sir John Franklin's letter.

2. King, *The Franklin Expedition from First to Last*, pp. 171–80.

3. Accounts of the activities of the various searching ships and commanders can be found in the general works on the subject already cited, especially in those by Crouse and J. Mirsky, and in Sir Clement R. Markham, *The Lands of Silence.*

4. Osborn (ed.), *The Discovery of the North-West Passage by H.M.S. 'Investigator,' Capt. R. McClure, 1850, 1851, 1852, 1853, 1854.*

5. Collinson, *Journal of H.M.S. Enterprise, on the Expedition in Search of Sir John Franklin's Ships by Behring Strait, 1850–55.*

6. For varying accounts of this rather disgraceful climax to the expedition, see Osborn, op. cit.; Belcher, *The Last of the Arctic Voyages;* and McDougall, *The Eventful Voyage of H. M. Discovery Ship 'Resolute' to the Arctic Regions* . . .

7. McDougall, ibid. See also Sidney Withington, *Two Dramatic Episodes of New England Whaling*, Mystic, Conn., 1958.

8. Wright, op. cit. pp. 216–39. See also Rupert T. Gould, *Oddities: A Book of Unexplained Facts*, New York, 1928, pp. 79–124.

9. The tragic story of the Franklin expedition has been told many times.

The latest is Wright's fascinating book, *Quest for Franklin*. Others include Brown, *The North-West Passage, and the Plans for the Search for Sir John Franklin;* A. H. Markham, *The Life of Sir John Franklin, and the North-West Passage;* Osborn, *The Career, Last Voyage, and Fate of Captain Sir John Franklin;* and Cyriax, op. cit. These works will lead the interested reader to other important literature on the subject.

10. Stefansson, op. cit. pp. 36–129, is one of the most revealing articles on the subject. See also Wright, op. cit.

11. McClintock, *The Voyage of the 'Fox' in the Arctic Seas* . . . For a detailed account of all of Lady Franklin's efforts, see Frances J. Woodward, *Portrait of Jane: A Life of Lady Franklin,* London, 1951. Also Markham, *Life of Admiral Sir Leopold McClintock.*

24. The Passage Traversed

1. Amundsen, *My Life as an Explorer.*

2. The best account of *Gjöa* is William A. Baker's *'The Gjöa,' The American Neptune,* Salem, Mass., 1952, XII, No. 1, pp. 7–21. *Gjöa,* now restored, is on exhibition at Golden Gate Park, San Francisco.

3. The principal source for this chapter is Amundsen, *The Northwest Passage.*

Selected
Bibliography*

Amundsen, R., *My Life as an Explorer*, New York, 1927.

Amundsen, R., *The Northwest Passage*, 2 vols., New York, 1908.

Anderson, W. R., *Nautilus 90 North*, New York and Cleveland, 1959.

Armstrong, A., *A Personal Narrative of the Discovery of the North-West Passage*, London, 1857.

Asher, G. M., *Henry Hudson the Navigator*, Hakluyt Society, London, 1, 27, 1860.

Babcock, W. H., *Legendary Islands of the Atlantic*, American Geographical Society, Research Series No. 8, New York, 1922.

Back, G., *Narrative of an Expedition in H.M.S. Terror, Undertaken with a View to Geographical Discovery on the Arctic Shores in the Years 1836-7*, London, 1838.

——, *Narrative of the Arctic Land Expedition to the Mouth of the Great Fish River and Along the Shores of the Arctic Ocean in the Years 1833, 1834, and 1835*, Philadelphia, 1836.

Barlow, R., *A Brief Summe of Geographie* (edited by E. G. R. Taylor), Hakluyt Society, London, 2, 69, 1932.

Barrington, D. See Beaufoy.

Barrow, J., *A Chronological History of Voyages into the Arctic Regions; undertaken chiefly for the purpose of Discovering a North-East, North-West, or Polar Passage between the Atlantic and Pacific*, London, 1881.

——, *Voyages of Discovery and Research within the Arctic Regions from the Year 1818 to the Present Time*, London, 1846.

Beaufoy, Col., *The Possibility of Approaching the North Pole Asserted by the Hon. D. Barrington. A New Edition with an Appendix, containing Papers on the Same Subject, and on a Northwest Passage, by Colonel Beaufoy*, New York, 1818.

Beazley, C. R., *John and Sebastian Cabot*, London, 1898.

* Series number and volume number of Hakluyt Society publications are indicated before date of publication. The Hakluyt Society editions contain valuable introductions with biographical data about the principals and illuminating notes. They are of course more readily available to the interested reader than are the original journals.

Beechey, F. W., *Narrative of a Voyage to the Pacific and Beering Strait, to Co-operate with the Polar Expeditions: Performed in His Majesty's Ship Blossom in the Years 1825, 26, 27, 28,* London, 1831.

———, *A Voyage of Discovery Towards the North Pole, Performed in His Majesty's Ships Dorothea and Trent, Under the Command of Captain David Buchan, R.N; 1818,* London, 1843.

Beke, C. T., *Three Voyages by the North-East,* Hakluyt Society, London, 1, 13, 1853.

Belcher, E., *The Last of the Arctic Voyages,* 2 vols., London, 1855.

Bigger, H. P., *The Precursors of Jacques Cartier, 1497–1534,* Ottawa, 1911.

———, *Voyages of the Cabots and the Corte-Reals,* Paris, 1903.

Braithwaite, J., *Supplement to Captain John Ross's Narrative of a Second Voyage,* London, 1835.

Brown, J., *The North-West Passage, and the Plans for the Search for Sir John Franklin,* 2nd ed., London, 1860.

Bryce, G., *The Remarkable History of the Hudson's Bay Company,* London, 1902.

Burnett, A. C. See Tiele, P. A.

Burney, J., *A Chronological History of North-Eastern Voyages of Discovery,* London, 1819.

Burpee, L. J., *The Search for the Western Sea,* New York, 1908.

Burrage, H. S., 'Early English and French Voyages,' *American Historical Association,* 1906.

Christy, M., *The Voyages of Captain Luke Foxe of Hull and Captain Thomas James of Bristol in Search of a Northwest Passage in 1631–32,* Hakluyt Society, London, 1, 88 & 89, 2 vols., 1894.

Clark, W. B., *Captain Dauntless' The Story of Nicholas Biddle of the Continental Navy,* Louisiana State University Press, 1949.

Clarke, D., *Arthur Dobbs Esquire 1689–1765,* London, 1958.

Clerk of the California, *An Account of a Voyage for the Discovery of a North-West Passage by Hudson's Streights, to the Western and Southern Ocean of America,* London, Vol. I, 1748, Vol. II, 1749.

Coats, W., *The Geography of Hudson's Bay: Being the Remarks of Captain W. Coats in many Voyages to that Locality, between the Years 1727 and 1751,* ed. by J. Barrow, Hakluyt Society, London, 1, 12, 1852.

Collinson, R., *Journal of H.M.S. Enterprise, on the Expedition in Search of Sir John Franklin's Ships by Behring Strait, 1850–55,* London, 1889.

———, *The Three Voyages of Martin Frobisher,* Hakluyt Society, London, 1, 38, 1867.

Conway, W. M., *Early Dutch and English Voyages to Spitzbergen,* Hakluyt Society, London, 2, 11, 1904.

Cook, J. and King, J., *A Voyage to the Pacific Ocean Undertaken by the Command of His Majesty, for Making Discoveries in the Northern Hemisphere, Performed under the Direction of Captains Cook, Clerke, and*

Gore, in *His Majesty's Ships the Resolution and Discovery; in the Years 1776, 1777, 1778, 1779, 1780*, 3 vols., London, 1784.

Coxe, W., *Account of the Russian Discoveries Between Asia and America*, London, 1787.

Crouse, N. M., *In Quest of the Western Ocean*, London, 1928.

———, *The Search for the Northwest Passage*, New York, 1934.

Cyriax, R. J., *Sir John Franklin's Last Arctic Expedition*, London, 1939.

Dobbs, A., *An Account of the Countries adjoining to Hudson's Bay*, London, 1744.

———, *Remarks upon Captain Middleton's Defense*, London, 1744.

———, *A Reply to Captain Middleton's Answer*, London, 1745.

Eavenson, H. N., *Two Early Works on Arctic Exploration by an Anonymous Author*, privately issued, 1945–6.

Ellis, Henry, *A Voyage to Hudson's Bay, by the Dobbs Galley and California, In the years 1746 and 1747, For Discovering a North West Passage*, London, 1748.

Fisher, A., *A Journal of a Voyage of Discovery to the Arctic Regions in His Majesty's Ships Hecla and Griper. 1819–1820*, London, 1821.

Forster, J. R., *History of the Voyages and Discoveries made in the North*, Dublin, 1786.

Foxe, L., *North-West Fox, or Fox from the North-West Passage*, London, 1635.

Franklin, J., *Narrative of a Journey to the Shores of the Polar Sea, in the Years 1819, 20, 21, and 22*, London, 1823.

———, *Narrative of a Second Expedition to the Shores of the Polar Sea, in the Years 1825, 1826 and 1827, Including an Account of the Progress of a Detachment to the Eastward by John Richardson*, London, 1828.

Golder, F. A., *Bering's Voyages*, American Geographical Society, Research Series Nos. 1 & 2, New York, 1922, 1925.

Gosch, C. C. A., *Danish Arctic Expeditions 1605 to 1620*, Hakluyt Society, London, 1, 96 & 97, 1897.

Greely, A. W., *Handbook of Polar Discoveries*, Boston, 1906.

Hakluyt, R., *Divers Voyages Touching the Discovery of America*, edited by J. W. Jones, Hakluyt Society, London, 1, 7, 1850.

———, *The Principal Navigations Voyages Traffiques and Discoveries of the English Nation*, 12 vols., Glasgow, 1903–5.

Hall, C. F., *Arctic Researches and Life Among the Esquimaux*, New York, 1865.

Harrisse, H., *John Cabot the Discoverer of North-America and Sebastian his Son*, London, 1896.

———, *The Discovery of North America by John Cabot*, 3rd ed., London, 1897.

Hearne, S., *A Journey from Prince of Wales's Fort in Hudson's Bay, to the Northern Ocean*, London, 1795.

Hoare, J. *Arctic Exploration,* London, 1906.

Hobbs, W. H., 'Zeno and the Cartography of Greenland,' *Imago Mundi,* VI, 1949.

Huish, R., *A Narrative of the Voyages and Travels of Captain Beechey, R.N. to the Pacific and Behring's Straits and Travels of Captain Back to the Great Fish River and Arctic Seas,* London, 1839.

——, *The Last Voyage of Capt. Sir John Ross, R.N. Knt., To The Arctic Regions,* London, 1836.

James, T., *The Strange and Dangerous Voyage of Captaine Thomas James, in his intended Discovery of the Northwest Passage into the South Sea. Wherein the Miseries Indured Both Going, Wintering, Returning; and the Rarities observed, both Philosophicall and Mathematicall, are related in this Journal of it,* London, 1633.

Jane, C., *A Spanish Voyage to Vancouver and the North-West Coast of America, Being the Voyage made in the Year 1792 By the Schooners Sutil and Mexicana to Explore the Strait of Fuca,* London, 1930.

Jefferys, T., *The Great Probability of a North West Passage: Deduced from Observations on the Letter of Admiral De Fonte, Who sailed from the Callao of Lima on the Discovery of a Communication Between The South Sea and the Atlantic Ocean; And to intercept some Navigators from Boston in New England, whom he met with, Then in Search of a North West Passage. Proving the Authenticity of the Admiral's Letter.* With Three Explanatory Maps, London, 1768.

Jegerbiol, M., 'Eubalaena Glacialis (Bonnat.),' *Mamalia Zoology of the Faroes,* LXV, Copenhagen, 1940, Vol. III, part II.

Kennedy, W., *A Short Narrative of the Second Voyage of the Prince Albert, in Search of Sir John Franklin,* London, 1853.

King, R., *Narrative of a Journey to the Shores of the Arctic Ocean in 1833, 1834, and 1835; Under the Command of Capt. Back, R.N.,* London, 1836.

—— *The Franklin Expedition from First to Last,* London, 1855.

Larsen, H., *The North-West Passage 1940–1942 and 1944,* Vancouver, 1954.

Lucas, F. W., *The Annals of the Voyages of the Brothers Nicolo and Antonio Zeno,* London, 1898.

Lyon, G. F., *A Brief Narrative of an Unsuccessful Attempt to Reach Repulse Bay, Through Sir Thomas Rowe's 'Welcome,' in His Majesty's Ship Griper, in the Year MDCCCXXIV,* London, 1825.

—— *The Private Journal of Captain G. F. Lyon, of H.M.S. Hecla, During the Recent Voyage of Discovery Under Captain Parry,* London, 1824.

McClintock, L., *The Voyage of the 'Fox' in the Arctic Seas. A Narrative of the Discovery of the Fate of Sir John Franklin and His Companions,* London, 1859.

McClure, R. See Osborn, S.

McDougall, G. F., *The Eventful Voyage of H. M. Discovery Ship 'Resolute' to the Arctic Regions in Search of Sir John Franklin and the Missing*

Crews of H. M. Discovery Ships 'Erebus' and 'Terror,' 1852, 1853, 1854, London, 1857.

McFee, W., *The Life of Sir Martin Frobisher,* New York, 1928.

McIlraith, J., *Life of Sir John Richardson,* London, 1868.

MacKay, D., *The Honorable Company,* London, 1937.

M'Keevor, T., *A Voyage to Hudson's Bay, during the summer of 1812,* London, 1819.

Mackenzie, A., *Voyages from Montreal on the River St. Laurence Through the Continent of North America, to the Frozen and Pacific Oceans; in the Years 1789 and 1793,* London, 1801.

Major, R. H., *The Voyages of the Venetian Brothers Nicolo & Antonio Zeno to the Northern Seas, in the XIVth Century,* Hakluyt Society, London, 1, 50, 1873.

Markham, A. H., *Life of Sir John Franklin and the North-West Passage,* London, 1891.

———— *Northward Ho!,* London, 1879.

———— *The Voyages and Works of John Davis,* Hakluyt Society, London, 1, 59, 1880.

Markham, C. R., *The Journal of Christopher Columbus and Documents Relating to the Voyages of John Cabot and Gaspar Corte Real,* Hakluyt Society, London, 1, 86, 1893.

———— *The Lands of Silence,* Cambridge, 1921.

———— *Life of Admiral Sir Leopold McClintock,* London, 1909.

———— *A Life of John Davis, the Navigator, 1550–1605, Discoverer of Davis Straits,* London, 1889.

———— *The Threshold of the Unknown,* 4th ed., London, 1876.

———— *The Voyages of Sir James Lancaster, Kt., to the East Indies,* Hakluyt Society, London, 1, 56, 1877.

———— *The Voyages of William Baffin, 1612–1622,* Hakluyt Society, London, 1, 63, 1881.

Meares, J., *Voyages Made in the Years 1788 and 1789, from China to the North West Coast of America, to which are Prefixed, an Introductory Narrative of A Voyage performed in 1786, from Bengal, in the Ship Nootka; Observations on the Probable Existence of a North-West Passage,* London, 1790.

Mecking, L. See Nordenskjöld, O.

Middleton, C., *Forgery Detected,* London, 1745.

———— *A Reply to Mr. Dobbs Answer to a Pamphlet Entitled Forgery Detected,* London, 1745.

———— *A Reply to the Remarks of Arthur Dobbs,* London, 1744.

———— *A Vindication of the Conduct of Captain Middleton,* London, 1743.

Mirsky, J., *To the Arctic,* London and New York, 1949.

Morison, S. E., *Admiral of the Ocean Sea: A Life of Christopher Columbus,* 2 vols., Boston, 1942.

Müller, S., *The Arctic North-West Passage*, Amsterdam, 1878.

Neatby, L. H., *In Quest of the North-West Passage*, Toronto, 1958.

Nordenskiöld, A. E., *The Voyage of the Vega Round Asia and Europe*, New York, 1882.

Nordenskjöld, O. and Mecking, L., *The Geography of the Polar Regions*. American Geographical Society, Special Publication No. 8. New York, 1928.

Nourse, J. E., *Narrative of the Second Arctic Expedition made by Charles F. Hall*, Washington, 1879.

Nunn, G. E., *Origin of the Strait of Anian Concept*, privately printed, Philadelphia, 1929.

An Officer of the Expedition, *Letters Written During the Late Voyage of Discovery in the Western Arctic Sea*, London, 1821.

O'Reilly, B., *Greenland, the Adjacent Seas, and the North-West Passage to the Pacific Ocean*, London, 1818.

Osborn, S., *The Career, Last Voyage, and Fate of Captain Sir John Franklin*, London, 1860.

—— (ed.), *The Discovery of the North-West Passage by H.M.S. 'Investigator,' Capt. R. McClure, 1850, 1851, 1852, 1853, 1854*, London, 1857.

Parks, G. B., *Richard Hakluyt and the English Voyages*, American Geographical Society, Special Publication No. 10, New York, 1928.

Parliamentary Papers, also known as Arctic Blue Books, published by Parliament after each expedition, contain narratives, reports, letters, and notes dealing with the British Arctic explorations of the mid-nineteenth century, especially with Sir John Franklin and the expeditions searching for him.

Parry, W. E., *Journal of a Second Voyage for the Discovery of a North-West Passage from the Atlantic to the Pacific; Performed in the Years 1821–22–23 in His Majesty's Ships Fury and Hecla*, London, 1824.

—— *Journal of a Third Voyage for the Discovery of a North-West Passage from the Atlantic to the Pacific; Performed in the Years 1824–25, in His Majesty's Ships Hecla and Fury*, London, 1826.

—— *Journal of a Voyage for the Discovery of a North-West Passage from the Atlantic to the Pacific; Performed in the Years 1819–20, in His Majesty's Ships Hecla and Griper*, London, 1821.

—— *Journal of a Voyage of Discovery, to the Arctic Regions; Performed between the 4th of April and the 18th of November, 1818, in His Majesty's Ship Alexander*, London, n.d.

Phipps, C. J., *A Voyage Towards the North Pole Undertaken by His Majesty's Command 1773*, London, 1774.

Powys, L., *Henry Hudson*, London, 1927.

Purchas, S., *Hakluytus Posthumus, or Purchas his Pilgrimes*, 20 vols., Glasgow, 1905–6.

Quinn, D. B., *The Voyages and Colonizing Enterprises of Sir Humphrey Gilbert*, Hakluyt Society, London, 2, 83 & 84, 1840.

Rae, J., *Narrative of an Expedition to the Shores of the Arctic Sea in 1846 and 1847*, London, 1850.

Rich, E. E., *The History of the Hudson's Bay Company 1670–1870*, Vol. I, Hudson's Bay Record Society XXI, London, 1958.

——— (ed.), *James Isham's Observations on Hudsons Bay, 1743 and Notes and Observations on a Book Entitled* A Voyage to Hudsons Bay in the Dobbs Galley, 1749, Champlain Society, Hudson's Bay Company Series XII, Toronto, 1949.

Richardson, J., *Arctic Searching Expedition: A Journal of a Boat Voyage Through Rupert's Land and the Arctic Sea, in Search of the Discovery Ships Under Command of Sir John Franklin*, London, 1851.

——— *The Polar Region*, Edinburgh, 1861.

Robson, J., *An Account of Six Years Residence in Hudson's Bay*, London, 1752.

Ross, J., *An Explanation of Captain Sabine's Remarks on the Late Voyage of Discovery to Baffin's Bay*, London, 1819.

——— *Explanation and Answer to Mr. Braithwaite's Supplement to Captain Sir John Ross's Narrative*, London, 1835.

——— *Narrative of a Second Voyage in Search of a North-West Passage and of a Residence in the Arctic Regions During the Years 1829, 1830, 1831, 1832, 1833*, 2 vols., London, 1835.

——— *Observations on a Work Entitled Voyages of Discovery*, London, 1846.

——— *A Voyage of Discovery, made under the orders of the Admiralty, in His Majesty's Ships Isabella and Alexander for the Purpose of Exploring Baffin's Bay, and Inquiring into the Probability of a North-West Passage*, London, 1819.

Rundall, T., *Narrative of Voyages Towards the North-West, in search of a Passage to Cathay and India 1496 to 1631*, Hakluyt Society, London, 1, 5, 1849.

Sabine, E., *Remarks on the Account of the Late Voyage of Discovery to Baffin's Bay*, London, 1819.

Scoresby, W. Jr., *An Account of the Arctic Regions, with a History and Description of the Northern Whale-Fishery*, 2 vols., Edinburgh, 1820.

——— *Journal of a Voyage to the Northern Whale-Fishery*, Edinburgh, 1823.

——— 'On the Greenland or Polar Ice,' *Memoirs of the Wernerian Natural History Society*, Vol. II, 1815.

Scoresby-Jackson, R. E., *Life of William Scoresby*, London, 1861.

A Sea Officer, *A Concise Account of Voyages for the Discovery of a North-West Passage*, London, 1782.

Seller, J., *Atlas Maritimus or Sea Atlas*, London, 1675.

Simpson, T., *Narrative of the Discoveries on the North Coast of America, Effected by the Officers of the Hudson's Bay Company During the Years 1836–39*, London, 1843.

Skelton, R. A., *Explorers' Maps*, London, 1958.

Smith, D. M., *Arctic Expeditions from British and Foreign Shores from the Earliest to the Expedition of 1875*, Edinburgh, 1877.

Stefansson, V., *Northwest to Fortune*, New York, 1958.

Stefansson, V., *The Three Voyages of Martin Frobisher In Search of a passage to Cathay and India by the North-West, A.D. 1576–8. From the original 1578 text of George Best*, 2 vols., London, 1938.
——— *Ultima Thule*, New York, 1943.
——— *Unsolved Mysteries of the Arctic*, New York, 1956.
Taylor, E. G. R., *A Brief Summe of Geographie by Roger Barlow*, Hakluyt Society, London, 2, 69, 1932.
——— *Late Tudor and Early Stuart Geography 1583–1650*, London, 1934.
——— (ed.), *The Original Writings & Correspondence of the Two Richard Hakluyts*, Hakluyt Society, London, 2, 76 & 77, 1935.
——— *Tudor Geography 1485–1583*, London, 1930.
Tiele, P. A. and A. C. Burnett, *The Voyage of John Huyghen van Linshoten to the East Indies*, Hakluyt Society, London, 1, 70 & 71, 1885.
Traill, H. D., *The Life of Sir John Franklin*, London, 1896.
Vancouver, G., *A Voyage of Discovery to the North Pacific Ocean, and Round the World in which the Coast of North-West America has been Carefully Examined and Accurately Surveyed, Undertaken by His Majesty's Command, Principally with a view to Ascertain the Existence of any Navigable Communication Between the North Pacific and North Atlantic Oceans; and Performed in the Years 1790, 1791, 1792, 1793, 1794, and 1795, in the Discovery Sloop of War, and Armed Tender Chatham, under the Command of Captain George Vancouver*, 3 vols., London, 1798.
De Veer, G., *The Three Voyages of William Barents to the Arctic Regions*, ed. by K. Beynen, Hakluyt Society, London, 1, 54, 1876.
——— *A True Description of Three Voyages by the Northeast towards Cathay and China*, ed. by C. T. Beke, Hakluyt Society, London, 1, 13, 1853.
Wagner, H. R., *Spanish Voyages to the Northwest Coast of America*, California Historical Society, 1929.
Waters, D. W., *The Art of Navigation in England in Elizabethan and Early Stuart Times*, New Haven, 1958.
Waxell, S., *The American Expedition*, London, 1952.
Weare, G. E., *Cabot's Discovery of North America*, London, 1897.
White, A., *A Collection of Documents on Spitzbergen & Greenland*, Hakluyt Society, London, 1, 18, 1855.
Williamson, J. A., *Maritime Enterprise 1483–1558*, Oxford, 1913.
——— *The Voyages of the Cabots and the English Discovery of North America under Henry VII and Henry VIII*, London, 1929.
Winsor, J., *Narrative and Critical History of America*, 8 vols., Boston and New York, 1889.
Wright, I. A., *Spanish Documents Concerning English Voyages to the Caribbean 1527–1568*, Hakluyt Society, London, 2, 62, 1929.
Wright, N., *Quest for Franklin*, London, 1959.
Yule, H., *Cathay and the Way Thither*, Hakluyt Society, London, 2, 33, 37, 38 & 41, 1913–1916.

Index

Agnello, John Baptista
    74, 79
Alfred, King
    35
Amundsen, Roald
    3, 311–18
Anderson, William R.
    4–6
Anian, Strait of (fictitious)
    181–4, 222, 224
Anikiew, Grigory
    45
Anikiew, Jakor
    45
Aubert, Thomas
    23
Austin, Henry
    300

Back, George
    240, 267, 271–2, 277, 286–91
Baffin Bay, discovery of
    142
Baffin, William
    134–44, 236
Banks, Sir Joseph
    237–9
Barents, William
    47–61
Barker, Andrew
    138–40
Barlow, Roger
    32–3

Barrington, Daines
    142, 225, 227, 235–6
Barrow, Sir John
    142, 211, 235–7, 239, 251, 285, 295
Bear Island, discovery of
    54
Beechey, Frederick William
    240, 242, 255, 261, 270–71, 273
Belcher, Sir Edward
    304–8
Bering Strait, discovery of
    222
Bering, Vitus
    221–2, 231
Berley, George
    188
Best, George
    76, 81, 85
Biddle, Nicholas
    226
Booth, Felix
    276
Borough, Stephen
    36, 40–41, 66
Borough, William
    36, 66
Briggs, Henry
    129, 157–8, 160
Bristol Society of Merchants, *see* Merchant Adventurers of Bristol
Brooke, Sir John
    158
Brunel, Olivier
    44–6, 111–13

Bruton, William
   93
Buchan, David
   240–45, 271
Buddington, James
   307
Burghley, Lord
   63, 65, 90
Bush, Henrich
   221
Bushnan, John
   255, 264
Buss Island (fictitious)
   81, 187, 228
Buts, Thomas
   33
Button, Thomas
   129–34, 158, 162
Bylot, Robert
   120, 122–5, 127–30, 134–7, 141

Cabot, John
   15–18, 20–22
Cabot, Sebastian
   18–19, 25, 28–30, 36, 40–41
Calvert, James F.
   5
Cape Breton Island, discovery of
   17
Carlsen, Elling
   60
Cartier, Jacques
   25–7
Cartwright, John
   106
Cathay Company
   75, 80, 88
Cavendish, Sir Thomas
   101–2
Cecil, William, see Burghley, Lord
Chancellor, Richard
   36–41

China trade, origin of American and English
   233
Chouart, Médard,
   see Groseilliers, Sieur des
Clerk of the *California,*
   see Drage, Theodore Swaine
Clerke, Charles
   232
Collinson, Richard
   300–304, 306, 315
Colman, John
   119
Columbus, Christopher
   13–16
Cook, James
   227–34
Coppermine River, mouth of
   223–4
Corte Real, Gaspar
   20–22
Corte Real, Miguel
   21
Croker's Mountains (fictitious)
   249, 252, 257
Crow, Robert
   192
Crozier, Francis R. M.
   264, 297, 310
Cunningham, John
   107–9

Danby, Earl of
   166
Danish East India Company
   146
Davis, John
   85, 89–104, 137–8
Dease, Peter Warren
   291–2
Dee, John
   41, 66, 89–90

de Fonte, Bartholomew
182–4, 197
de Fuca, Juan
182–4
Deshnev, Semyon Ivanovich
221
De Veer, Gerrit
49, 51, 56, 58–60
Digges, Sir Dudley
120, 129–30, 134, 154, 159, 235
Dobbs, Arthur
183, 191–200, 207–10, 235, 266
Douglas, Bishop John
229, 233
Drage, Theodore Swaine
183, 211–14; Clerk of the *California*, 200, 207, 210–14; Swaine, Charles, 211–20
Dudley, Robert,
see Leicester, Earl of
Dutch East India Company
116–18

East India Company
102–3, 111, 125, 129, 154–5
Eden, Richard
66
Edwards, John
264
Eliot, Hugh
32
Ellis, Henry
200–210

Fabyan, Robert
22
Fenton, Edward
76, 82
Fernandez, Francisco
22

Fernandez, João
20–22
Fisher, Alexander
255, 261, 264
Fisher, George
240, 264
Fitzjames, James
296, 309
Fotherby, Robert
140
Foxe, Luke
113, 130, 156–69, 175–7
Franklin, Benjamin
213, 215, 217, 220
Franklin, John
240, 265, 267–74, 286, 295–300, 308–10
Frisland, island of (fictitious)
69–70, 85
Frobisher, Martin
30, 65–86
Frobisher Strait, discovery of
71, 76; Meta Incognita, 80; Molyneux Globe location, 100

Gardiner, Charles L. W.
61
Gascoigne, George
67
Gatonbe, John
139
Gerritz, Hessel
126, 133
Gibbons, William
129–30, 134
Gilbert, Adrian
89–91
Gilbert, Humphrey
62–4, 67, 88–9
Gilbert, Sir John
64–5
Gillam, Zachariah
186–7

Gjöa Haven, Amundsen winters at
    313–15
Gomez, Estevan
    24–5
Gonsalvez, João
    22
Gore, Graham
    309
Gore, James
    233
Greene, Henry
    121, 123–4
Griffyn, Owen
    70–71
Grinnell, Henry
    307
Groseilliers, Sieur des
    184–6
Gunderson, M.
    61

Hakluyt, Richard, the elder, of the
Middle Temple
    33, 42, 66
Hakluyt, Rev. Richard, the historian
    30, 33, 87–8, 96, 129
Hall, Charles Francis
    86
Hall, Christopher
    66, 69–72, 75–8, 81–2
Hall, James
    107–11, 138–9
Hancock, John
    190
Hawkeridge, William
    130, 153–5
Hearne, Samuel
    189, 222–4, 229, 233, 268
Heemskerck, Jacob van
    51, 53, 58–61
Henry VII
    14–18, 22

Henry VIII
    19, 28–30, 34
Hondius, Jadocus
    118
Hood, Robert
    267
Hoppner, Henry Parkyns
    240, 255, 270, 277
Hore, Richard
    33–4
Hudson Bay, discovery of
    121
Hudson, Henry
    114–29
Hudson, John
    114
Hudson, Richard
    125
Hudson's Bay Company
    181, 186–203, 210, 222–4, **268,**
    286, 291, 308
Huntriss, William
    138–40

Ice Haven, Barents at, first arctic
wintering
    56–9
Isham, James
    201–3, 212–13

Jackman, Charles
    41–3, 76, 81
James, Thomas
    125, 160, 162, 165–77
Janes, John
    91–2, 98
Jan Mayen, discovery of
    115
Jefferys, Thomas
    183, 211

Jenkinson, Anthony
63
Jones, Francis
134
Juet, Robert
118, 120–21, 123–4

Kaufmann, Gerard
68–9
Kellett, Henry
298, 301, 304–6
Kelly, Edward
90
Kelsey, Henry
190
King, James
232
King, John
120, 122–3
King, Richard
286–7, 296, 298
Knight, James
188–90
Knight, John
107, 110–13, 156–7

Labrador, origin of name
20
La France, Joseph
197
Lake, Sir Bibye
192–3
Lancaster, Sir James
102, 129, 139
Lancaster Sound, discovery of
142, 249, 252, 257
Larsen, Henry A.
7–8, 10–11
Latimer, Henry
32

Leicester, Earl of
65, 88
Liddon, Matthew
254
Lindenow, Godske
107
Linschoten, Jan Huygen van
47, 50
Lok, Michael
66, 74–5, 83, 182, 235
London Merchant Companies
29
Lutwidge, Skiffington
225
Lyon, George Francis
264–5, 267–9, 287
Lyons, Israel
225

McClintock, Francis Leopold
299, 301–2, 305–6, 308–11
McClure, Robert
299–308, 310
Mackenzie, Alexander
224, 268
Mackenzie River, mouth of
224
Malaspina, Alejandro
184
Maldonado, Lorenzo Ferrer
183–4
Martin, Sir Thomas Byam
259, 264
Mears, John
233
Mecham, Lieutenant
304–5
Mercator, *see* Kaufmann, Gerard
Merchant Adventurers, Association of, *see* Muscovy Company
Merchant Adventurers of Bristol
163

Merchant Adventurers of London
154
Merchant Venturers of Bristol,
Company of
165
Meteren, Emmanuel van
116, 119
Middleton, Christopher
193–9, 201, 206, 266
Molyneux, Emery
100
Moor, William
194, 200–206, 210, 212
Morgan, Henry
97
Moucheron, Balthasar de
46
Munk, Jens
144–53
Muscovy Company
36, 38–40, 64, 67, 111, 114, 129,
134, 140

Napper, James
190, 192
Nay, Cornelius
46, 51–3
Nelson, Horatio
226
Newfoundland, discovery of
17; establishment of cod fishery,
27
Nordenskiöld, A. E.
61
North Magnetic Pole, discovery of
281–2, 285
North Pole, first crossing
5
Northwest Company
(of London, 1612)
129–30, 141

North-West Company (of Montreal)
224, 268
North-West Company
(of Philadelphia)
216, 219–20
Nourse, J. E.
212
Novaya Zemlya,
English discovery of
41

Ogle, Samuel
211–12, 216
Ortelius, Abraham
69
Osborn, Sherard
300, 304
Othere
35

Parliamentary reward
199, 215, 227, 239, 259
Parry, William Edward
240, 248, 250, 253–71, 295
Peckham, Sir George
88
Pet, Arthur
36, 41–3
Petiver, James
182
Pett, Phineas
130, 133, 154
Phipps, Constantine John
225–7
Pickersgill, Richard
228
Plancius, Peter
117, 120, 126
Pope, Richard
95
Pricket, Abacuck
120, 122–5, 129–30, 133

Pringle, John
220
Pullen, Thomas C.
7
Pullen, W. J. S.
298
Purchas, Samuel
30

Queen Elizabeth's Foreland, *see*
Resolution Island

Radisson, Pierre Esprit
184-6
Rae, John
293, 298, 308
Raleigh, Sir Walter
88, 90-91
Rastell, John
28-9
Rayvn, John
29
Resolution Island
71, 76
Richardson, Carsten
109, 111
Richardson, John
267, 271-3, 286, 298
Rijp, Jan Corneliszoon
51, 53-5, 60
Robertson, O. C. S.
7
Roe, Sir Thomas
130, 159, 166
Ross, James Clark
240, 247, 255, 258, 264, 277, 281,
295-6, 299-300
Ross, Sir John
143, 240-41, 245-53, 275-89, 295
Royal Society
237, 239, 295; Council of, 225,
227

Russian trade with England first
established
38
Rut, John
30-32

Sabine, Edward
240, 252, 255, 261
Sacheuse, John
240, 248
Sanderson, William
91, 99-100, 235
Sandwich, Earl of
225
Scoresby, William Jr.
237-9
Scroggs, John
189
Settle, Dionyse
76
Shutz, Jonas
79
Simpson, Thomas, 291-3
Skene, A. M.
240, 247, 255
Smith, Francis
200-206, 212-13
Smith, John
117, 119
Smith, Sir Thomas
101, 120, 125, 129, 130, 134, 139,
142, 154
Smith, William
79
South Sea Company
191
Spert, Thomas
28
Spitsbergen, discovery of
55
Staffe, Philip
120, 123

Stefansson, Vilhjalmur
  280, 302
Strogonoff, commercial house of
  45
Swaine, Charles,
see Drage, Theodore Swaine

Tapp, John
  157
Tetgales, Brant
  47, 51
Thorne, Robert
  32, 114
Tordesillas, Treaty of, 1494,
  13
Trinity House, Masters of
  125, 159

Urdaneta, Friar Andro
  67

Vancouver, George
  234
Vaughan, David
  188
Verrazano, Giovanni da
  23-4, 117

Wager, Sir Charles
  191, 195
Walsingham, Sir Francis
  65, 74, 88-91, 94, 101
Warwick, Earl and Countess of
  65
Weymouth, George
  103-7, 117, 120

Whale fishery, establishment of
English and Dutch
  115
Wilkins, Sir Hubert
  3, 5
Willis, Richard
  66
Willoughby, Sir Hugh
  36-9
Wilson, Edward
  120, 125, 129
Wilson, William
  122-4
Winter Harbour, Parry at
  260-62
Wolstenholm, John
  120, 129, 134-5, 143, 154, 159,
  164, 166
Wolstenholm, Sir John
  235
Wright, Edward
  68, 129
Wydhouse, Thomas
  120, 122-3

York, Sir John
  65
Yorke, Gilbert
  76, 81
Young, Walter
  229

Zeno, Antonio
  69
Zeno map
  68-9, 76, 84-5, 100
Zeno, Nicolo
  68-9

ARCTIC AMERICA

1. Wellington Channel
2. Beechey Island
3. Cape Walker
4. Peel Sound
5. Bellot Strait
6. Franklin Strait
7. Victoria Strait
8. Ross Strait
9. Rae Strait
10. Simpson Strait
11. Dease Strait
12. Dolphin & Union Strait
13. Walker Bay
14. Prince of Wales Strait
15. Prince Regent Inlet

Wrangel Island

RUSSIA

CHUKCHEE SEA

Point Barrow

Bering Strait

Kotzebue Sound

Beechey Pt.
Return Cape

BEAUFORT SEA

Herschel I.

Cape Bathurst

Franklin Bay

Amundsen Gulf

Darnley Bay

Norton Sound

A L A S K A

Yukon River

Fairbanks

ARCTIC CIRCLE

NORTH

Fort Franklin

Mackenzie River

MAC

Anchorage

YUKON

C A

Bristol Bay

Gulf of Alaska

Kodiak Island

BRITISH

COLUMBIA

PACIFIC OCEAN

Prince Patrick Island

Mercy B.
Bank
Island

Nelson Head

13